The Challenge of Hegemony

The Challenge of Hegemony

Grand Strategy, Trade, and Domestic Politics

STEVEN E. LOBELL

The University of Michigan Press
Ann Arbor

First paperback edition 2005

Published in the United States of America by
The University of Michigan Press
Manufactured in the United States of America
♾ Printed on acid-free paper

2008 2007 2006 2005 5 4 3 2

A CIP catalog record for this book is available from the British Library.

Library of Congress Cataloging-in-Publication Data

Lobell, Steven E., 1964–
The challenge of hegemony : grand strategy, trade, and domestic politics / Steven E. Lobell.
p. cm.
Includes bibliographical references and index.
ISBN 0-472-11312-7 (Cloth : alk. paper)
1. International economic relations. 2. Commercial policy. 3. Great Britain—Foreign economic relations. I. Title.

HF1359 .L624 2003
306.3—dc21 2002153615

ISBN 0-472-03080-9 (pbk. : alk. paper)

FOR MY PARENTS, MY WIFE,
AND MY CHILDREN

Contents

Acknowledgments ix

1 Introduction 1

2 Second Image Reversed Plus a Second Image 19

3 Liberal Contenders and Britain's
Grand Strategy of Cooperation, 1889–1912 43

4 Imperial Contenders and Britain's
Grand Strategy of Restrained Punishment, 1932–1939 85

5 Imperial Contenders and Spain's
Grand Strategy of Punishment, 1621–1640 123

6 Great Power Tenure 153

Appendix 173

Notes 175

Bibliography 201

Index 235

Acknowledgments

I have been fortunate to have friends, teachers, and colleagues with able minds and generous hearts. My parents encouraged my early interest in Middle East politics, and a regional perspective is one of the kernels of this book. History courses at the University of Wisconsin-Madison left me with a clear understanding of the importance of economics in driving American diplomatic history. The other kernel for this book came from a graduate seminar paper for Arthur Stein on the "declining hegemon's dilemma" of how to restore the balance between the leader's capabilities and global commitments without eroding its economic capacity or undermining its military security. This book evolved through many long discussions with Art, and his insight for how to unpack and package an argument is uncanny. Key conversations with David Lake changed the nature of the project and the course of this book manuscript. I am grateful to both of them. Mark Brawley and John Owen IV, reviewers for the University of Michigan Press, provided engaging comments and encouraged the clarification and development of several points that honed the argument.

I have turned to many colleagues over the years for comment on parts of this manuscript. For their keen observations and criticisms I thank Michael Herb, Shale Horowitz, Neal Jesse, James Nolt, David Pervin, Galia Press-Barnathan, Norrin Ripsman, Katja Weber, Kristen Williams, and Paul Williams. I appreciate the encouragement from Michael Cox, Benjamin Frankel, Peter Gourevitch, Patrick James, Samir Khalaf, Benjamin Miller, T. V. Paul, Richard Rosecrance, Stephen Saideman, Lars Skålnes, Etel Solingen, and Steven Spiegel. Colleagues at the University of Northern Iowa were especially supportive, including Kenneth Basom, Matthias Kaelberer, Philip Mauceri, Tom Rice, and Dhirendra Vajpeyi. Ryan Fitzharris, Brent Steele, and Emily Taylor provided helpful research support. I also thank Jim Reische, Jeremy Shine, Erin Snoddy, and Kevin Rennells of the University of Michigan Press for their professionalism and editorial suggestions.

I have received financial support for this project from a number of institutions. For their support, I thank the University of Northern Iowa's Graduate College's Summer Fellowship and the Dean's Challenge Grant, the University of California's Institute on Global Conflict and Cooperation, the John D. and Catherine T. MacArthur Foundation, the Andrew W. Mellon Foundation Fellowship, and U.C.L.A.'s Dissertation Year Fellowship, Political Science Fellowship, Graham Fellowship, and the International Studies and Overseas Program Fellowship. A number of institutions allowed me to use their collections, including the Public Records Office (Kew), the Memorial Library at the University of Wisconsin-Madison, the London School of Economics, and Guildhall Library (London).

I dedicate this book to my parents, my wife, and my children. They have been a constant source of support. My father is truly a role model. His dedication to medicine and to his patients is a lesson for me. My wife and my children remind me of what is really important, and they keep my life in balance. I thank my sisters and close friends for their encouragement.

CHAPTER 1
Introduction

Why did Britain pursue a cooperative grand strategy prior to World War I, emphasizing freer trade, reducing defense spending, signing arms limitation agreements, and retreating from empire, but then, prior to World War II, punish contenders by adopting imperial preferences and closer ties to the empire, enacting colonial quotas, and increasing defense spending? The existing literature on grand strategy either black boxes the state, making the assumption of a unified nation, or focuses on the influence of domestic politics. Neglected in this literature is the effect of international politics on altering a hegemon's domestic constellation of interests and power, and the subsequent ramifications for the hegemon's grand strategy.[1] For Britain, between 1889 and 1932, the foreign commercial policy of the rising contenders shifted from a preponderance of liberal contenders before 1914 to a preponderance of imperial contenders in the 1930s. Within Britain, this shift in the commercial composition had the domestic effect of ratcheting-up the strength of the members of the economic nationalist coalition (while weakening the supporters of the entrenched free trade coalition). Empowered economic nationalists pushed London from a cooperative grand strategy to a strategy of punishment, while advancing their own faction's interests.

This book develops a *second image reversed plus a second image* argument or from the outside-in and then the inside-out argument.[2] What distinguishes this argument is that it focuses on how the nature of and changes in the hegemon's international environment will enable a domestic policy coalition to advance its preferred grand strategy. The first factor in this argument is the foreign commercial policy of the rising contenders. A declining hegemon will confront commercially liberal contenders, imperial contenders, or some mix of these states. The primary distinction is that a liberal foreign commercial policy entails an open door commercial order in any locale that the state comes to dominate, while an imperial commercial strategy translates into an exclusive or autarkic sphere, whether the current trading arrangement is open or closed door.

The second factor in this argument is the internal competition within the hegemon between the members of the free-trade coalition and the supporters of the economic nationalist coalition. Each broad and logrolled faction will lobby for the grand strategy that will advance its desired agenda, under certain conditions over the national interest. The free traders' policy preference calls for cooperating with liberal contenders (and in some instances imperial contenders) in order to reduce the costs of hegemony by means of freer trade, retreat from empire, fiscal orthodoxy (including reduced government allocation for defense spending), low-cost defense arrangements, and international arms limitation and disarmament agreements. Economic nationalists prefer punishing contenders (even liberal states where cooperation is possible) through tariff protection, greater military preparedness, offensive military operations, and closer economic and military links to the empire.

In integrating these variables, I argue that the declining hegemon's grand strategy is driven by the environment in which it finds itself; the commercial orientation of the contenders will affect the domestic balance of political power. The empowered coalition will use the political and economic gains to advance its preferred grand strategy.[3] If the hegemon faces mostly liberal contenders, this will strengthen members of the free-trade faction who will push for cooperation, which will have the domestic consequence of boosting efficient industry, the financial sector, consumers, and fiscal conservatives (while weakening the opposing economic nationalists). If the hegemon encounters mostly imperial contenders, this will enable constituents of the economic nationalist coalition who will lobby for punishment, which will have the internal result of bolstering inefficient and state industry, settler organizations and empire-oriented institutions, state bureaucrats, the military-industrial complex, and trading companies (while weakening the contending free traders). In capturing the distributional benefits from cooperation or punishment, the empowered coalition will apply pressure on the government to adopt a more accommodative or belligerent international posture.[4] Under certain circumstances, these external pressures will push the entrenched faction that is under threat of being rolled back to respond by advancing a grand strategy that will ratchet-up its own relative coalitional power—even though such actions will erode the hegemon's productive strength or undermine its military security. The consequence can shorten the leader's great power tenure. Any subsequent reversals in the foreign commercial policy of the rising states can again alter the domestic balance of power, the distributional gains and losses, and ultimately the hegemon's grand strategy. Thus, the domestic consequence of the contenders' foreign commercial policy adds to our existing understanding of the factors that guide the formation and the reformulation of grand strategy.

THE PUZZLE OF EXPLAINING GRAND STRATEGY

This book argues that the grand strategies of declining hegemons have exhibited an identifiable pattern. The specific puzzle is how a declining hegemon selects which states to punish, where to cooperate, and how to allocate its national resources between its productive capacity and military security. Addressed in the conclusion of this book is the policy question of why some states are more successful in managing their decline than others. The bulk of the literature on grand strategy ignores the influence of domestic politics on international relations, treating the state as a unitary and rational actor. Other scholars have tried to bring domestic politics back in to explain international relations. Neglected in this literature is the effect that international affairs has on domestic actors and interest groups.

Grand strategy incorporates several components.[5] First, grand strategy is not only military, but also fiscal and political in nature. Second, grand strategy does not cease at the end of a war or start at the beginning of a war but is about balancing ends and means in both peacetime and wartime (Kennedy 1991, 4). Finally, grand strategy involves long-term planning, over decades and perhaps centuries. The dilemma for a declining state is how to balance its capabilities and global commitments without eroding its economic staying power through prolonged resource extraction or endangering its national security interests by accommodating revisionist contenders.[6] As Walter Lippmann summarizes, "Foreign policy consists in bringing into balance, with a comfortable surplus in reserve, the nation's commitments and the nation's power" (1943, 9).

LONG CYCLE AND POWER TRANSITION THEORY

For long cycle and power transition theorists, a hegemon's decline (and its rise) is an undifferentiated event that occurs globally, rapidly, and simultaneously across its formal and/or informal empire.[7] Differential rates of growth allow a competitor to encroach on the hegemon's primacy. This is attributed to prolonged and sustained military spending by the hegemon to defend its extensive interests in the core and periphery that diverts resources from "wealth creating" domestic investment, erodes its productive strength, and ultimately undermines its ability to finance a modern military.[8] For Organski (1968) and Organski and Kugler (1980), the challenger comes from the ranks of the rapidly industrializing states that are powerful yet dissatisfied with the current system. For Modelski (1987) and Modelski and Thompson (1988), the challenger is a territorial state. The hegemon's response to this challenge is to punish everywhere. According to Dale Copeland (2000), the declining hegemon will initiate a preventive war because it fears worsening power differentials in the future.[9] A contender also fears that the hegemon will attack and push it down the power trajectory. Woosang Kim and James Morrow (1992) maintain that a risk-averse challenger will strike prior to the power transition while a risk-acceptant challenger will wait. As a result of a hegemonic war, the hegemon will lose global leadership to the rising contender in a single instance. Domestic and individual idiosyncrasies will have no effect on the hegemon's rate of decline, allocation of national resources, or response to the challenger.

One shortcoming in the long cycle and power transition literature is the assumption that the hegemon's descent is global, rapid, and uniform. These theorists also assume that there are only two major states in the international system, the hegemon and the contender. This framework oversimplifies the declining hegemon's dilemma. A hegemon is likely to confront several competitors that rise at uneven rates and challenge its leadership in disparate parts of its empire. The more geographically encompassing the hegemon's empire (formal and informal), the more contenders it is likely to confront. Consequently, the hegemon's loss of leadership over one locale rarely translates into a global loss of leadership as long cycle and power transition theorists suppose. The import of this differentiated view of world politics is that it is possible for the hegemon to moderate its rate of decline. By discriminating among protagonists, the hegemon can tailor its responses across locales. The dilemma for such a hegemon becomes whether it can respond without eroding its fiscal health through excessive military spending or undermining its national security by accommodating a revisionist challenger.

Second, hegemonic decline is not always associated with great power war. For long cycle and power transition theorists, a hegemon in its decline phase will punish the rising contender. Yet, a declining hegemon's war proneness can be affected by domestic politics. As discussed in the next chapter, the ruling coalition in the declining state (and the rising states too) will lobby the government for a grand strategy that will empower its members while rolling back the opposing faction's. In part, whether a conciliatory or belligerent grand strategy is advocated will depend on whether the dominant coalition consists of outward-looking free traders or inward-looking economic nationalists.

STRUCTURAL REALISM

For neorealists, relative power and geostrategic worth drive the hegemon's grand strategy. Because they assume that the hegemon is a unitary and rational actor, realists ignore the influence of domestic politics on international relations. Instead, operating in a frictionless environment, the hegemon will respond by increasing its rate of resource extraction for military spending or reducing its global commitments as necessary.[10] In the core, the hegemon will punish all contenders because the loss of a vital region could tip the global balance against the leader, at the same time strengthening an aspiring hegemon.[11] The hegemon will even punish an emerging ally (since today's ally might be tomorrow's enemy), by discouraging it from developing independent military capabilities (Posen and Ross 1996–97, 32–42; Mastanduno 1997). On the other hand, in the periphery the hegemon will disengage. The assumption is that even significant losses (by the hegemon) or gains (by the challenger) in the periphery will have little effect on the global balance of power. Thus, for such realists, cooperation among states, especially in vital locales, is rare.

How a hegemon manages its decline matters. The way such neorealists prioritize global commitments ignores the role of grand strategy in safeguarding a hegemon's economic strength. Grand strategy involves bringing into balance the declining state's military and economic capabilities with its overseas commitments. As many realists emphasize, insufficient military spending risks undermining the state's national security, leaving it weak and vulnerable to attack. Yet, in punishing potential allies, neorealists neglect the danger of undermining the leader's economic capacity for future military security due to prolonged and heightened levels of military spending and missed opportunities to lower the cost of hegemony without strengthening a rival (Brooks 1997).

DETERRENCE THEORY

Deterrence theory suggests that a declining hegemon will not distinguish among contenders, but will punish all challengers, in both the core and the periphery, in order to establish a reputation for predation.[12] Such a reputation will discourage potential contenders from mounting a challenge. According to deterrence theorists, the danger of a grand strategy of accommodation is that it will encourage potential contenders to challenge the leader for hegemony in disparate parts of its empire. As Harold Sprout and Margaret Sprout note, "It will be interesting to ask whether a government can relinquish territories, liquidate colonial responsibilities, withdraw from alliances, reduce obligations to allies, or otherwise retrench without starting chain reactions that accelerate the decline of its international potential" (1963, 661). There is a temporal component to this strategy. In the early stages, the deterrence strategy will be costly for the hegemon. Once the hegemon establishes a reputation for predation, it should not need to repeat the demonstration of resolve often. Thus, a "predation period" will lead to a "reputation period."

DOMESTIC POLITICS

Finally, there are two versions of arguments that emphasize the primacy of domestic influences on grand strategy (responding to neorealism's state-centric approach). While these scholars have tried to bring domestic politics back in to account for international relations, they largely ignore the influence of international forces on domestic actors and interest groups. The first version argues that domestic and individual idiosyncrasies will impair the hegemon's adjustment (from increasing extraction for defense or reducing commitments as necessary), resulting in self-defeating and nonrational foreign and domestic policies.[13] For instance, according to Aaron Friedberg (1988, 299–300), London prematurely surrendered its worldwide naval supremacy around the turn of the century because decision makers clung to ill-founded economic beliefs that Britain could not simultaneously increase government expenditure for defense and raise taxes without damaging the economy.[14] For Miles Kahler (1984), Britain was able to decolonize more easily than France because empire-oriented political parties, economic actors, and colonial and military administrators were less implanted. One implication is that there is an incentive for pressure groups with regional interests to become entrenched in the political process of a hegemon while the state is in its ascent phase in order to influence the hegemon's foreign policy in the retrenchment phase. Domestic political constraints can contribute to a condition of underextension too (Stein 1993a). Other domestic constraints include regime type (Lake 1992; Wallander 1992), state-society relations and the political cost of extracting societal resources (Barnett and Levy 1991; Lamborn 1991; Barnett 1992; D'Lugo and Rogowski 1993), and domestic institutions and entrenched images, such as embedded "strategic culture" and "myths" of national security (Friedberg 1988; Goldstein 1993; Kupchan 1994; Brawley 1999). Unfortunately, these arguments ignore the positive role of domestic constraints in restraining a hegemon from adopting suboptimal policies such as excessive peacetime defense expenditure.

A second approach seeks to revive domestic politics explanations for international relations. These scholars maintain that competition among logrolled coalitions, interest groups, and state institutions with opposing preferences will shape a state's economic and military foreign policy (Kehr 1977; Gaddis 1982; Milner 1988, 1997; Snyder 1991; Simmons 1994; Lawson 1996; Solingen 1998). These arguments build on a model of narrow interest groups that capture the state to advance their particularistic agenda (Hobson 1938; Lenin 1939). For Jack Snyder (1991), parochial interest groups with a stake in expanding the empire will pool their resources to muster societal support for their policies, resulting in greater expansion than any group desired. For Etel Solingen (1998), internationalist and statist-nationalist-confessionalist coalitions will compete to advance their preferred domestic, regional, and international agendas. Where the former coalitions dominate, cooperative regional orders will appear, and where the latter rule, zones of militarized disputes will arise. Historians such as William Appleman Williams (1972, 237–38) account for U.S. postwar foreign policy by examining a free-trade coalition whose members included farm leaders, labor, corporate executives, and the state. The unifying concern was that the United States could not maintain full production at home without free trade overseas. Michael Hogan (1987, 3–25) contends that after World War II, logrolling in the United States among members of an international block (public and private elites) prompted the U.S. government to propose the Marshall Plan for European reconstruction.

One shortcoming in this literature is its inability to account for changes in the domestic distribution of political power. These scholars neglect the reverberations that international politics will have on domestic political struggles; the extant international setting can enable or disable actors and interest groups, leading to shifts in foreign policy.[15] Thus, while domestic politics arguments open the black box of the state, they ignore the effect of the international environment on the outcome of this internal coalitional competition.

This book fills a gap that currently exists within the literature. Realism accentuates systemic pressures as determining but ignore the influence of domestic politics on a state's grand strategy. Domestic politics approaches grant domestic coalitions primacy but neglect the influence of international politics. In integrating this literature, I entangle domestic and international politics. I argue that the international environment and shifts in it will affect the constellation of political power within the declining hegemon. In going beyond a second image reversed argument, I contend that domestic winners will lobby the government to advance their preferred policy package. Thus, the declining hegemon's grand strategy is driven by the environment in which it finds itself.

AN ALTERNATIVE FRAMEWORK FOR UNDERSTANDING WORLD POLITICS

The framework used by long cycle, power transition theory, and hegemonic stability theory is ill-equipped to understand the dilemma that a hegemon faces in managing its decline. In this section I put forth a regionally differentiated framework of world politics.[16] This regional framework is based on the view that the international system is composed of multiple regions or spheres of influence.[17] A *hegemon* is thereby defined as a state that simultaneously dominates several regions of the globe and that as a unit comprises its informal and/or formal empire.[18] In this context, *hegemony* means the state creates and enforces the rules of the game over each region it dominates. Joshua Goldstein defines *hegemony* as being able "to dictate, or at least dominate, the rules and arrangements by which international relations, political and economic are conducted. . . . Economic hegemony implies the ability to center the world economy around itself. Political hegemony means being able to dominate the world militarily" (1988, 281). The import of this framework is that decline can be managed.

A regionally differentiated framework differs from the existing literature in several important aspects. First, the hegemon will confront different challengers across space due to the loss-of-strength gradient and the differentiated nature of power (discussed later). The more geographically extensive a hegemon's empire, the greater the number of potential contenders it can confront. Second, the hegemon will encounter different contenders over time due to differential rates of industrialization, with some states rising earlier and faster than others. In combining these characteristics, the hegemon will face competitors earlier in some regions than in others and these contenders will vary across locales.

The outcome of these characteristics of the international system challenge the assumptions of long cycle, power transition, and hegemonic stability theory. Specifically, a hegemon's loss of leadership over one locale rarely translates into a loss of global leadership to the emerging challenger. Even if a hegemon encounters the same challenger across regions, it will cede (or lose) leadership region by region or in territorial pieces, rather than transfer leadership over the entire international system to the contender in a single instance.

This differentiated framework of world politics more accurately captures how leadership is relinquished. For instance, long cycle and power transition theorists maintain that Britain transferred world leadership to a rising United States only after the end of World War II. But as early as the turn of the nineteenth century, Britain devolved leadership over the Americas to the United States and ceded governance over the Pacific to Japan. By doing so, Britain marshaled these freed-up resources against the remaining challengers. During and shortly after World War II, Britain ceded leadership over regions such as the Pacific and the Middle East to the United States (Abadi 1982; Devereux 1990). Thus, not only did Britain devolve leadership over different regions to the United States and at different junctures in time, but Britain also devolved regional hegemony to other contenders. Likewise, the advent of American hegemony was not global in nature and did not begin after World War II, but instead occurred first in the Americas around the turn of the century.

Similarly, some scholars argue that Japan has encroached on U.S. leadership over the Far East. As one article notes, "Japan, rather than the United States, is now the dominant economic player in Asia. Japan is the region's technology leader, its primary supplier of capital goods, its dominant exporter, and its largest foreign direct investor and foreign aid supplier" (Borrus et al. 1992, 23). However, even if the United States devolves leadership over the Pacific Rim to Japan, the United States has not transferred global leadership to Tokyo.[19] Once more, this does not preclude the United States from devolving hegemony to other contenders in different locales.

Two forces increase the likelihood that a declining hegemon will encounter different emerging competitors for regional hegemony and that these states will vary across regions. These forces are the loss-of-strength gradient and the differentiated nature of power.

LOSS-OF-STRENGTH GRADIENT

The loss-of-strength gradient describes how the effectiveness of military power declines in a linear fashion over space, reducing the ability of a state to project its power over long distances.[20] According to Kenneth Boulding (1963), this erosion occurs because long distances create organizational and command problems, damage military morale, encourage domestic dissension, and debilitate soldiers and their equipment. The 1904–5 Russo-Japanese War exemplifies the problem because Russia was unable to maintain long supply lines across Siberia (stretching several thousand miles), which contributed to Japan's victory.

The loss-of-strength gradient is important for this regionally differentiated framework because it reduces the likelihood that a single state can achieve a truly global position (i.e., simultaneously dominating all regions of the international system). By reducing the ability of a state to project its power over long distances, the loss-of-strength gradient allows states to emerge in regions beyond the effective reach of the hegemon. This characteristic of power increases the likelihood that a declining hegemon will confront different competitors across regions, especially on the fringes of its empire. The more extensive the hegemon's empire, the greater the number of contenders for regional leadership it is likely to confront.

Even today, in a world of intercontinental ballistic missiles and supersonic planes, distance continues to limit the ability of a superpower to project its power. Although the time it takes to move a large number of troops and equipment over distances has been shortened, logistical problems still exist, and modern technology has created new challenges. While long-range aircraft are capable of transporting troops and supplies quickly, they also require a long landing strip. Observing the U.S. operation in Somalia, Colin Powell, then chairman of the Joint Chiefs of Staff, noted: "Logistically, it is enormously challenging. When you say to somebody, 'Take 28,000 troops and send them 7,500 miles or so away, and by the way, there's no potable water there, and there are no gas stations and there's only one or perhaps two C-141 capable airfields and the port facilities only hold one or two ships,' that is very demanding" (Healy 1992).

DIFFERENTIATION OF POWER

The differentiated nature of power is the second factor that increases the chance that a declining hegemon will confront several competitors for leadership. Rarely does a single state have the necessary financial resources or the manpower to dominate all categories of military power (i.e., land, sea, and air); states tend to favor one category of defense over others. This differentiated characteristic of power reduces the probability that a single state can dominate all regions of the globe simultaneously. Instead, the differentiated nature of power limits the number of regions that the hegemon can control effectively.

The simplest differentiation in the nature of power is between continental and maritime powers. The advent of the railroad in the last thirty years of the nineteenth century reduced the historical advantage that maritime powers had over land powers. The quick Prussian defeat of France in 1871 demonstrated that railroads were a fast, cheap, and efficient means of land transportation. Until this point, the most efficient means to move goods was by ship, even if it required circuitous routes. In addition, the development of the railroad made it possible for land powers to have secure internal lines of communication and made such states less vulnerable to a naval blockade (Mackinder 1904, 434). As a land power, Russia's Czar Nicholas II wrote that "the strongest fleet in the world can't prevent us from settling our scores with England precisely at her most vulnerable point [i.e., India]" (Friedberg 1988, 217). When the assistant to Britain's First Lord of the Admiralty was asked to determine what naval means existed to attack Russia, he responded, "Russia's geographical position is such that she is very unassailable to a sea power with a small army" (Neilson 1991, 716). The differentiated nature of military power makes it difficult for a naval power to dominate the hinterlands and for a continental power to dominate overseas territories.

Viewing a hegemon's decline as global, simultaneous, and uniform oversimplifies the hegemon's dilemma. A hegemon is likely to confront different emerging contenders that ascend at differential rates and challenge the hegemon's leadership in disparate parts of its empire. The more far-reaching a hegemon's empire, the greater the number of potential challenges it will confront. The dilemma for such a hegemony is how to restore the balance between its global commitments and its economic and military resources without undermining its productive capacity or eroding its military security. Excessive peacetime defense expenditure to keep pace with the military spending of several rapidly rising contenders will divert resources from domestic investment, limit the scope of future economic growth, and eventually weaken the hegemon's productive strength to construct and then maintain a modern military force. Further, accommodating a revisionist challenger to lower the cost of preparing for war against several contenders will empower a future rival who will endanger the leader's security.

THE PLAN OF THE BOOK

Chapter 2 develops the second image reversed plus a second image argument used in this book. Chapters 3, 4, and 5 examine three case studies of hegemonic decline. Chapter 3 examines Britain in the decades prior to World War I (1889–1912). By the turn of the century, Britain faced challenges from imperial Germany, Russia, and France (until 1904), and liberal United States, Japan, and France (after 1904). Within Britain, free traders pushed for a largely cooperative grand strategy, emphasizing freer trade, reduced defense spending, arms limitation agreements, and retreat from empire (devolving leadership over the Americas to the United States, the northeast Pacific to Japan, and the eastern Mediterranean to France). Cooperation reinforced the strength of the free-trade faction by lowering the economic and military cost of hegemony, while maintaining or improving commercial and financial access to the locale, which benefited finance, export-oriented industry, and fiscal conservatives (new loans to Japan, greater access to France's empire, naval retrenchment). Many free traders joined the economic nationalists in favor of punishing imperial Germany, France (until 1904), and Russia even though this response meant heightened defense spending and preferential trading, strengthening the latter coalition. Concerns about economy and the fear that punishment would empower the economic nationalists meant that free traders moderated the scale of punishment by slimming down the naval building Estimates, proposing a number of arms limitation agreements with these states, and negotiating alliances to reduce tension. Free traders used the distributional gains from cooperating with the United States, Japan, and France to further broaden and strengthen their domestic coalition by enacting a number of social and economic reform schemes.

Chapter 4 examines Britain in the interwar period (1932–39). During the 1930s, Britain confronted imperial Germany, Italy, and Japan, as well as a liberal United States. This reversal in the nature of the foreign commercial policy of the rising contenders from a mix of liberal and imperial contenders prior to World War I to mostly imperial contenders prior to World War II had the domestic effect of empowering the economic nationalist coalition while weakening the free-trade faction. Britain punished these contenders by abandoning the gold standard in 1931 and adopting imperial preferences in 1932 at the Ottawa Conference, enacting colonial quotas, and increasing defense spending after 1935. Although greatly diminished in strength, the entrenched free traders were able to moderate the economic nationalists' agenda. The free traders feared that another war like the Great War would permanently strengthen the economic nationalists, thereby extinguishing "gentlemanly" financial capitalism in Britain (resulting in state regulation and management of the economy, curbing the influence of traditional finance and the City of London, and strengthening employers' associations). Concerned for their coalition's survival, free traders pushed for a self-reinforcing strategy of cooperation by (1) containing Britain's military rearmament and more generally imposing fiscal orthodoxy, which was dictated by the "Treasury view"; (2) granting economic concessions and reaching arms limitation agreements and territorial agreements with Germany, Japan, and Italy, and pressing for collective security and, more broadly, the League of Nations; and (3) pushing for free trade within the Sterling Area (which required fiscal discipline at home). One consequence was that Britain's military, industrial, and economic preparation for war was delayed. Combined with the challengers' reneging or not renewing arms control agreements, this meant that Britain's military capability was insufficient to defend its global commitments. By the mid- to late 1930s, the free traders' and Treasury's influence over rearmament had collapsed, and the economic nationalists advanced their preferred grand strategy of rearmament, protectionism, state intervention, government controls, and producer cartels. Empowering economic nationalists meant a clash with a liberal United States, whose goal was to reverse Britain's system of imperial preferences and to dismantle the empire, restoring international liberalism.

Chapter 5 examines Spain during part of the reign of Philip IV (1621–40) and his count-duke, Olivares. Spain confronted imperial France, England, and the United Provinces (Netherlands), as well as the Ottoman Empire and Sweden. Economic nationalists favored restoring Spain's power by punishing these contenders through increases in the army and navy, new fortifications, exclusive trading companies, and offensive military operations on land and at sea. Many liberals, including Castile's Cortes (or parliament, which was responsible for imposing new taxes), Castile's merchants, the aristocracy, and industry, called for lowering the cost of hegemony by accommodating the United Provinces, England, and France (especially renewing the Twelve Years' Truce with the United Provinces, which expired in 1621).[21] Total warfare on several fronts had the intended domestic effect of weakening the primary internal constraints on the Crown's hard-line grand strategy. Punishment everywhere undermined the opposing liberal coalition, especially the Cortes of Castile, thus granting the Crown fiscal autonomy and wresting control over public revenue. Yet, prolonged and excessive spending eroded Spain's fiscal strength and ultimately its military power, while the stress from the search for new sources of revenue contributed to revolts in Catalonia and Portugal in 1640.

Chapter 6 examines the issue of great power tenure and the policy implications of this argument for the United States in the coming decades. The hegemon's international environment can enhance or undermine its ability to extend its great power tenure. I examine whether the strategy of cooperation or punishment is more successful in decelerating a hegemon's rate of descent and prolonging its tenure as a great power. I conclude that a ruling economic nationalist bloc or a free-trade coalition that confronts only imperial contenders can select from a range of strategies that will either wear down the hegemon's economic staying power or undermine its security. In contrast, a ruling free-trade faction that confronts at least some liberal contenders can safeguard the hegemon's economic strength and its national security, ensuring the state has ample economic and military capability to protect its national interests.

My argument sheds light on a current policy debate over how the United States should classify which states are friends and foes, how to rank its global commitments, and how to allocate its national resources between its economy and military security. Some scholars and policymakers have called for the United States to maintain the current "unipolar moment" by discouraging all potential contenders. A more circumscribed version of primacy calls for a policy of selective engagement in the core and retrenchment from most of the Third World. I contend that in order to strike the proper balance between its economy and security, in regions with liberal contenders the United States should retrench and assist in their ascent. In its remaining commitments, where there are no liberal successors, the United States should stand firm and hasten the emergence of liberal powers.

SELECTION OF CASES

This book uses the comparative case method, specifically the structured focused comparison (George 1979). The cases show how the hegemon's commercial environment can empower supporters of the free trade or economic nationalist faction and the subsequent effect on the state's grand strategy. I use the process-tracing method to reveal the impact of the international environment on domestic actors and interest groups, relying mostly on secondary historical literature (King, Keohane, and Verba 1994, 226–28; Van Evera 1997, 64–67). I examine the initial domestic distribution of coalitional power and then see how the environment alters this internal balance, looking for evidence of actors and interest groups defecting and accruing benefits or losses. This includes new political parties that will rise up, mobilizing activists and generating new supporters, greater public attention for their agenda and votes in elections, new lobbying and peak organizations that deploy resources (outside government, inside government, and in the empire), and additional public and private resources. Chapter 2 discusses problems of how preferences are translated into policy outcomes.

I have selected cases with similar characteristics. The class of cases consists of great powers that have extensive global commitments and encountered contenders for leadership in different parts of their formal and/or informal empire in peacetime and wartime, rather than focusing solely on the latter. For each case, the selected time frame reflects the period in which the hegemon began to confront competitors for leadership. In the three cases I have selected (Spain, 1621–40; Britain, 1889–1912; Britain, 1932–39), the beginning date marks the period in which the hegemon's leadership is challenged. For Spain, 1621 marks the end of the Twelve Years' Truce and the preparation for preventive war against the Netherlands. For Britain, 1889 signifies the enactment of the Naval Defence Act in response to challenges by France and Russia. Finally, for Britain, 1932 marks the end of the Ten Year Rule and the beginning of rearmament. These periods often occur well before the complete collapse of the hegemon's empire; the leaders sustained themselves for long periods of time after the initial challenge. The adoption of a regionally differentiated framework of world politics means each case study consists of subcases that examine the dyadic nature of the relationship and how the hegemon responded in the specific locale. The number of subcases will vary based on the extensiveness of the hegemon's empire and the number of competitors it confronts.

These cases provide variation while controlling for competing explanations. First, the international environment varies across these cases. Britain from 1889 through 1912 faced a mix of liberal and imperial contenders, from 1932 through 1939 it confronted mostly imperial contenders, and Spain confronted only imperial contenders. I examine official trade policies to assess the commercial orientation of the rising states. While I have a dynamic explanation for the hegemon's foreign commercial policy, I have fixed strategies for the contenders'.[22] The rationale is that the contenders have already picked their strategy, knowing the hegemon and its strategy. I do acknowledge in the text that within a contender both a free-trade and an economic nationalist coalition will compete to advance their preferred grand strategy. As such, the free-trade coalition within the hegemon will reach out and try to strengthen domestic moderates in the imperial contenders in order to temper a protagonist's foreign (and domestic) policy. However, explanations for how contenders select their foreign economic policy and for reversals in the contenders' commercial policy are largely exogenous to this model.

Second, the hegemon's grand strategy also varies (within and across cases) from cooperation to punishment. Grand strategy includes a state's diplomatic activity, resource extraction, trade policy, and military doctrine. Cooperation entails greater access to markets, participation in collective security arrangements, arms limitation and reduction agreements, and territorial concessions. Punishment involves extraction of additional resources for defense expenditure and protectionism. While Britain (1889–1912, 1932–39) and Spain (1621–40) confronted rising challengers, hegemonic war did not occur in all instances of power transition. In contrast to long cycle, power transition, and deterrence theorists, hegemonic decline as such is not always associated with great power war. Balance of power theory is challenged by differential treatment of the same state due to rapid changes in its foreign commercial policy, not its military capability.

I have excluded cases in which the hegemon lost its empire in a single catastrophic instance. Under such conditions, the declining power was not confronted with the dilemma of balancing its resources and its obligations. For this reason, Napoleonic France was rejected because its vast empire was virtually dismantled by the end of the Napoleonic Wars. I have also excluded cases in which the hegemon's empire was protected or defended by another great power (e.g., suzerainty). Again, under this condition, the hegemon will not have to make crucial decisions about redressing imbalances. I excluded the nineteenth-century Ottoman Empire (the Sick Man of Europe) since Britain defended the Turks against dismemberment by Russia and France (known as the Eastern Question).

CAUSES OF HEGEMONIC DECLINE

The causes of hegemonic decline can broadly be divided into endogenous and exogenous sources. Endogenous causes of decline are attributed to economic and political mismanagement. They include entrenched economic interest groups, decay in morals and the loss of moral virtues, poor leadership, rigid social structure, corruption, and economic mismanagement.[23] In these instances, mismanagement directly contributes to the hegemon's demise. For instance, the decline of the Ottoman Empire is often attributed to poor leadership (Palmer 1993). After a wave of fratricide, the sons of the sultan were kept in the palace, in separate quarters called *kages* (cage), and succession was to go automatically to the oldest living son. Yet, he remained isolated from politics for the bulk of his life until his time to rule. This system ensured no sultan from the seventeenth century forward would have any knowledge of or training in government affairs until he came to power. It is often noted that after 1566, thirteen incompetent sultans ruled in succession.

Exogenous causes of decline will require the hegemon to adjust its foreign policy to its new environment.[24] These environmental shifts include the advent of new technology that makes current products obsolete (mainly military, such as Britain's Dreadnought of 1906), new forms of transportation and communication (for instance, some attribute the decline of Venice and the Ottoman Empire to shifts in trade routes), and demographic growth.[25] Even changes in the organization of the state (e.g., the bureaucratization of France in the 1790s or the creation of the Bank of England) will contribute to uneven rates of growth, forcing other states to adjust or suffer decline.[26]

There exists a fundamental difference between these two sources of decline. Endogenous causes of decline, such as mismanagement, will directly contribute to the demise of the great power while exogenous causes will result in decline even in the absence of mismanagement. Domestic and external barriers can prevent or restrict a declining hegemon from adapting its policies to the shift in its environment.

CHAPTER 2
Second Image Reversed Plus a Second Image

The prime argument of this book is that a declining hegemon's grand strategy is guided by the character of and changes in the commercial environment that it faces. In this chapter I analyze when domestic actors and interest groups are likely to be influential in order to better understand how declining states select their grand strategy (Vasquez 1993, 207–10). I look at the initial domestic political context within the hegemon and then see how the commercial nature of the rising states alters the internal balance of power. By creating domestic winners and losers, the commercial composition of the protagonists will enable the supporters of either the free-trade or economic nationalist bloc. Empowered members will lobby the government for either a more conciliatory or belligerent grand strategy to further advance their coalition's economic and political clout while pushing back the opposing faction's. Any reversals in the commercial orientation of the rising states will again alter the domestic balance of power, rolling back the gains of the empowered coalition and shifting the hegemon's grand strategy. The consequence is that the hegemon's grand strategy is driven less by the concern for interstate relative gains, the reputation for predation, or the strategic value of the locale, than by its international environment and the domestic coalitional outcomes.

COMMERCIAL STRATEGIES FOR HEGEMONS AND CONTENDERS: LIBERAL OR IMPERIAL FOREIGN COMMERCIAL POLICY

Foreign economic policy, as opposed to domestic trade policy, reflects the commercial order that a state will impose on its overseas formal and/or informal empire and any spheres of influence that it comes to dominate or control. A *liberal foreign commercial policy* entails a preference for an open door trading order.[1] A liberal economic strategy will ensure equal access to the area's resources and markets, allowing for the freer movement of goods, services, and capital. A hegemon that adopts a liberal strategy will establish the rules and norms of international behavior to advance freer trade and will enforce them when necessary.[2] Such a hegemon will oppose protectionism, disruption in trade, and restrictions on capital flows. An *imperial foreign commercial policy* translates into an exclusive economic order in any region the state dominates, favoring a commercial policy of economic self-sufficiency and economic autarky. Preferential trading arrangements will shut out foreign commercial competition and investment, ensuring exclusive access to the markets and resources in the locale. A hegemon that adopts an imperial strategy will use its rule-making authority to create monopoly rents for favored domestic groups by restricting the operation of the market.[3]

In shifting from a hegemonic to a multipolar distribution of power, the erstwhile hegemon will confront liberal contenders, imperial contenders, or some combination of these challengers.[4] The more far-reaching and extensive the hegemon's global commitments, the greater the number of potential entrants it is likely to encounter. A *liberal contender* is a state that has a strong preference for a free-trade regional order. Satisfied with the present liberal international order and its rules, a liberal state will continue such an arrangement in any region it dominates because "it offers the best chance of obtaining the goals [it has] in mind" (Organski 1968, 366). An *imperial contender* is a state that seeks to create its own mercantilistic position in the region to advance its interests. Such a contender will establish an exclusive commercial order in any locale that it dominates, whether the locale is currently an open or closed door regional order. Thus, a regional trading order will be quite different under liberal versus imperial governance.

Three points should be stressed about liberal and imperial commercial strategies. First, a state's domestic political system and its foreign commercial policy do not need to correspond. It is possible to have a politically liberal, commercially imperial hegemon, as well as a politically autocratic, commercially liberal hegemon (Diaz-Alejandro 1981). Second, a state's international economic orientation can change over time, moving toward a liberal or imperial commercial policy. Third, a state's foreign commercial policy may differ from its domestic trade policy. A state that is protectionist at home might impose an open door policy on regions it dominates. The reverse is also possible.

Examples of imperial challengers include czarist Russia and Napoleonic France. The Cold War between the United States and the Soviet Union traces its origins to the rivalry between liberal and imperial protagonists. According to Walter LaFeber, "[The Russians,] after annexing land in Asia, tried to control it tightly by closing the markets to foreign businessmen with whom they could not compete. This highlighted the problem between the two countries in the 1890s: the United States believed its prosperity increasingly required an 'open door' to trade in China's rich province of Manchuria, but the Russians were determined to colonize and close off parts of Manchuria" (1997, 2). According to Edward Fox, "The tensions of the Cold War can be understood at least in part as an extension of the land-water dichotomy that first emerged in seventeenth-century Europe: to the east, the vast land-based territorial state of the Soviet Union is heir to the administrative-military tradition, while across the Atlantic to the west, the United States reveals its origins and membership in the oceanic trading community" (1991, 2).

Imperial Napoleonic France posed a threat to Britain's regional trading order. Napoleon's Continental System (Berlin Decree of 1806) outlawed the importation of British goods to the Continent with the intention of expanding French economic control over Europe and weakening Britain's economic power (Kaiser 1990, 251–53; Fox 1991, 93). Napoleon intended to give French industry a Continental monopoly, while bankrupting Britain by cutting off its markets for exports. For Britain, Continental trade was vital to its economic health. Commenting on Napoleon's exclusive Continental System, Robert Gilpin notes, "at issue in the clash between industrial Great Britain and Napoleonic France were two fundamentally opposed systems for organizing the world's economy" (1981, 134).

DOMESTIC COALITIONS

THE POLICY PREFERENCE OF THE FREE-TRADE COALITION

The policy preference of societal actors and interest groups is shaped by their domestic and international orientation.[5] As Peter Gourevitch notes, "what people want depends on where they sit" (1986, 56). Within a hegemon, free-trade and economic nationalist coalitions will compete to advance their clashing agendas for the declining state's grand strategy and to capture the associated distributional benefits.[6] The free-trade coalition is defined as the internationally competitive sectors plus outward-leaning allies. The supporters of the free-trade faction include domestic groups who benefit from international economic exposure or have strong international ties. Internationalists favor greater openness and stability and will press their government to enact policies that promote such market characteristics. Supporters of the free-trade coalition include fiscal conservatives, export-oriented firms, large banking and financial services, central banks, smaller firms oriented to global markets, skilled labor, finance-oriented government bureaucracies, and other interests that perceive little benefit from economic autarky, heightened defense spending, and increased hostilities. The grand strategy preference of this faction includes (1) accommodating imperial contenders and retrenching in regions with emerging liberal contenders in order to lower the political, economic, and military costs associated with hegemony, (2) ensuring efficient industry has access to foreign capital, markets, and resources, and the fear of retaliation and trade wars if an imperial commercial policy is adopted, (3) favoring fiscal and monetary orthodoxy, with an emphasis on limited state intervention, balanced budgets, and low taxation, and (4) enhancing security through low-cost defense arrangements, membership in intergovernmental organizations (IGOs) and nongovernmental organizations (NGOs), collective security arrangements, and international arms limitation and arms reduction agreements.

The free-trade bloc advocates fiscal orthodoxy and, more broadly, macroeconomic stability. This translates into limited government intervention in the economy, open trade, balanced budgets, tight monetary policy, and deregulation of financial markets and exchange rates.[7] Free traders hold that the economic role of government should be limited, rejecting central planning and deliberate industrial development by protectionism at home and abroad (which will benefit specific domestic producers). Instead, free traders back divesting state control over the economy, while expanding the role of market forces and the private sector.

Free-trade supporters favor reforms to liberalize trade such as abandonment of public sector trade and production monopolies, deregulation of trade and currency regimes, and retreat from state planning. They advocate freer competition both domestically (opposing monopolies, cartels, trusts) and internationally (opposing imperial preferences and protectionism).[8] In addition to rejecting protectionism, free-trade supporters will resist domestic policies that threaten international competitiveness such as inflation, balance of payment deficits, an overvalued exchange rate, and currency instability. They warn that high government expenditure will decrease competitiveness of national products in the international market because budget deficits and inflation will put pressure on interest rates and the exchange rate.

Free traders oppose extracting and mobilizing societal resources for defense expenditure. Such policies are rejected because they raise the cost of capital, curtail savings and product investment, and reduce foreign exchange, all necessary to sustain economic growth (Lawson 1994, 153; 1996, 154–55; Solingen 1998, 27; Sachs 2000). Given the opportunity, free traders are prone to slim down the military and retreat from global commitments in order to restore the imbalance between the state's capabilities and obligations. In emphasizing the role of finance and the state's limited financial means, the members of the free-trade faction favor relying on low-cost defense arrangements such as the navy, air force, and/or nuclear weapons to protect the nation's interests over a more costly conscripted standing army. They counter that such national security strategies will divert the least amount of manpower and resources from domestic industrial production, while unrestrained defense spending will result in high inflation, budget deficits, confiscatory taxes, and economic controls that will ultimately bankrupt the state. A strong navy and air force are deemed essential to protect the sea-lanes of communication, trade links, and trade routes to secure imports and exports. Free traders will also triumph economic sanctions and naval blockades to weaken the economy of the adversary and bring about their economic collapse. Finally, the free-trade faction emphasizes collective security arrangements, participation in IGOs and NGOs, and international law to protect the nation's interests.[9] This is not to say that free traders do not extract resources for military security but that they keep it below a level that will undermine the state's international competitiveness. While low peacetime military spending can create vulnerabilities, during wartime such states can extract from a wealthy tax base.

Finally, the economic health of the state requires international stability and a favorable investment climate. Free traders are open to negotiated settlements of conflicts with liberal and imperial contenders. They favor reduced hostilities, settlement of disputes, and arms limitation agreements to lower the political, economic, and military costs of preparing for war. Arms races and hostility spirals are especially dangerous since they will divert resources from productive domestic investment to military spending, undermine prosperity, disrupt trade flows, and contribute to increased protectionism. Free traders will appeal to liberal members in opposing states, attempting to strengthen their position, in order to moderate an adversary's foreign and domestic policies.[10]

THE POLICY PREFERENCE OF THE ECONOMIC NATIONALIST COALITION

Pitted against the free-trade coalition is the inward-looking economic nationalist faction. The nationalist coalition is defined as the noninternationally competitive sectors and domestic-oriented groups. The composition of the economic nationalists include the military, settler pressure groups, unskilled labor, inefficient industry and agriculture (both at home and in the empire), import-substituting manufacturing, labor-intensive industry, public sector managers and workers, colonial and empire-oriented state bureaucrats and civil servants, pro-empire interest groups, small businesses that compete with imports, and state trading companies.[11] The desired grand strategy of the economic nationalist coalition calls for (1) protecting inefficient industry from foreign competition through trade restrictions, enhancing the role of the public sector through state planning, and creating domestic production monopolies, (2) increasing military preparedness and engaging in offensive military operations, and (3) defending and strengthening economic and military ties to the empire.

Inefficient industry and agriculture will favor preferences that restrict the access of overseas competitors to the empire. Protection against cheaper imports by high tariffs means that they will enjoy sectoral monopolies in domestic markets. Such industry will favor capital controls, opposing overseas lending because it will strengthen foreign competition. The military will favor the economic nationalists' agenda of greater military preparedness and maintaining the empire over the free-traders' agenda of retrenchment (Waterbury 1989, 44, 48; Lawson 1994, 148–53; 1996, 147–50; Solingen 1998, 32–48). The danger for the military is that retreat will translate into a scaled-down military and a reduction in overseas missions.[12] State bureaucrats (civil servants) with strong ties to the empire, and especially colonial offices and administrators, will favor an imperial coalition fearing dismantlement of state enterprises. Finally, workers in state enterprises, the public sector, and inefficient industry who risk being laid off as enterprises streamline due to foreign competition or face a reduction in salary will join with economic nationalists (Lawson 1994, 151–52). Economic nationalists are likely to use strategic myths such as economic self-sufficiency, imperialist ideologies, and national security to sustain themselves politically (for example, inefficient industry and agriculture will be defined as strategic for national defense) (Snyder 1991, 17).

Economic nationalists favor a military posture that calls for offensive ground-force systems, lobbying the government for national military conscription to support a substantial standing army (Gaddis 1982, 90–95). The institutional bias of the military-industrial complex and the national-security apparatus is to produce a military doctrine that assures victory. As a result, there is a tendency to adopt offensive rather than defensive strategies (Jervis 1978; Posen 1984, 47–58; Van Evera 1984; 1999, chap. 6). The benefit for the military and intelligence agencies is an increase in their budget, role, and mission. Outside of the government, private and government-owned defense industries, workers, military bases, and partisan leaders who represent these areas receive direct economic benefit from the maintenance of a strong defense and high military budget.

The economic nationalist coalition favors an exclusive economic order in any region that the hegemon dominates through the creation of a system of imperial preferences such as a commonwealth, exclusive spheres of influence, a customs union (*Zollverein*), or a "fortress" concept.[13] Imperial preferences will protect inefficient and state industry from international commercial competition and investment, while ensuring exclusive access to the markets and resources in the locale. Economic nationalists regard colonial and overseas markets as an important source of national power and will press for closer ties to the empire, occupied territories, or settlements, and perhaps expanding these holdings. Such locales are deemed essential for sustaining the policy of self-sufficiency and autarky, which they emphasize for strategic reasons such as the danger of economic dependence and the loss of control over destiny, even if this reduces a country's overall income.

Economic nationalists will view state planning as the engine for enhancing domestic industry. Economic nationalists support an active government that controls prices, licensing, purchasing, and wages. They will lobby for tariffs, duties, and subsidies to protect inefficient and infant industry from foreign competition. Economic nationalists will also recommend technological and financial assistance for national agricultural production and the creation of vast stocks of raw materials. As well, economic nationalists will encourage the collaboration and amalgamation of industry into big business, along with corporatist labor arrangements to compel labor's cooperation with management and the government (especially prohibiting labor strikes). As Stephan Haggard and Robert Kaufman note, one consequence is that "companies dependent on government contracts and credit are threatened by economic liberalization such as devaluation, budget cuts, restrictions on domestic credit, and reforms that reduce protection and government support" (1989, 222). Where such firms are prominent and can mobilize resources through peak organizations, political parties, and the media they will challenge the free trader's imposition of fiscal and monetary orthodoxy (220–24).

Rejecting fiscal orthodoxy, economic nationalists favor an expansionary monetary policy, protection of state-owned industry, and distribution of rents to private and state industry.[14] State enterprises such as the military-industrial complex, state managers, and the public sector will capture a large share of societal resources. In favoring immediate military preparedness, the military-industrial complex is especially prone to sacrifice national wealth and long-term economic capacity. Refusal to compromise with a historical enemy and an inflexible position at peace talks is associated with diligence and self-sacrifice (Lawson 1994, 152).

INTERNATIONAL FACTORS SHAPING THE HEGEMON'S GRAND STRATEGY

International forces will have a second image reversed plus a second image or an outside-in and subsequently an inside-out effect on the hegemon and its grand strategy.[15] Within the hegemon, the supporters of the economic nationalist and the free-trade coalitions will struggle to advance their preferred agenda for the declining state's grand strategy. The commercial composition of the rising contenders will ratchet-up the relative power of either the free-trade or the economic nationalist faction. The strengthened faction will lobby to advance its preferred coalitional grand strategy of cooperation or punishment, capturing the associated distributional gains. Concerns about the distributional consequence (from ratchets, reversals, and rollbacks) will mean that the entrenched coalition in threat of being rolled back will adopt a self-reinforcing strategy that will further bolster their own coalition's relative power (and block the opposing coalition from being empowered). Such action can undermine the nation's interest, and it risks shortening the hegemon's great power tenure. Any subsequent reversals in the commercial nature of the rising contenders can roll back the gains of the ratcheted coalition, altering the domestic balance of power and the orientation of the hegemon's grand strategy.

RATCHETS

In encountering new and old challengers on disparate fronts, the commercial nature of these protagonists will affect the structure of opportunities within the hegemon. By creating new incentives, inducements, restrictions, and constraints, these international stimuli can alter the domestic balance of political and economic power among members of the free-trade and economic nationalist blocs. The beneficiaries will try to accelerate and expand the internal redistribution of power, while the losers will seek to retard and halt it.

If the hegemon confronts mostly liberal contenders, this will empower the constituents of the free-trade coalition, while if it encounters mostly imperial states, this will enable the supporters of the economic nationalist faction (table 1).[16] Free traders will prefer cooperating with liberal contenders, and in some instances imperial contenders (even if this is not in the national interest), strengthening efficient industry, the financial sector, consumers, and fiscal conservatives, while weakening the economic nationalists. Free traders will resist punishing liberal states, because such action will harm their own position while augmenting the strength of the competing economic nationalist coalition, who will push the hegemon to adopt a more forceful stance towards rising imperial and liberal contenders. Economic nationalists will favor punishing imperial contenders and even liberal contenders (where cooperation is possible), benefiting inefficient and state industry, settler organizations and empire-oriented institutions, state bureaucrats, the military-industrial complex, and state trading companies, while weakening the free traders. Economic nationalists will resist cooperating with liberal contenders because such action will enhance the opposing free traders who will lobby for a more conciliatory grand strategy. Thus, cooperation with contenders will have the domestic effect of ratcheting-up the strength of the constituencies of the free-trade coalition, while punishing contenders will have the internal result of empowering the economic nationalist faction.

It is important to disaggregate the coalition's interests from the nation's interests to understand the stakes involved. The coalitional interest is to bolster its own faction's relative power over the opposing bloc's. The national interest is to restore the hegemon's balance between its finances and security without undermining its productive power or eroding its military security. In some instances the coalition's and the nation's interests will coincide, pointing in the same direction, and the chosen grand strategy will advance both interests. For ruling free traders, in confronting liberal contenders, cooperation will advance the nation's interests by lowering the cost of hegemony (safeguarding the leader's productive strength), and it will boost its own coalition's power. For economic nationalists, in encountering imperial contenders, punishment will ensure that the state has sufficient military capability to defend its global commitments (protecting the hegemon's national security) and, concomitantly, it will enhance their faction's strength.

A dilemma arises when free-trade supporters confront imperial competitors and economic nationalist members confront liberal contenders. Ruling free traders that confront imperial states will be pushed to advance their coalitional interests of cooperation, but the national interest calls for punishment. While punishment will mean that the hegemon has sufficient military capability, this strategy will meet strong resistance from constituents of the free-trade faction because it will boost the opposing economic nationalists who will press for a more aggressive grand strategy toward liberal and imperial contenders. Economic nationalists that encounter liberal contenders will be compelled to advance their coalitional interest by punishing liberal contenders, but the national interests call for cooperation. While cooperation will safeguard the hegemon's economic capacity the constituents of the economic nationalists will challenge this strategy since it will strengthen the free-trade faction who will lobby for a more accommodative and international grand strategy. As discussed in the next section, a faction that advances its coalitional interest but harms the national interest will shorten the hegemon's great power tenure.

Concerns about the distributional effects of compromise can block cooperation across cleavages. Compromise is most likely to occur when one coalition is preponderant (i.e., there is a large difference in the relative power of the free-trade and the economic nationalist coalitions). Some issue areas of compromise include monetary, investment, defense deployment and procurement, and trade policies. Compromise is possible because gains by the weaker coalition will not upset the domestic balance of coalitional power. Compromise between coalitions is least likely to occur in states in which free traders and economic nationalists are near parity in power. Each coalition will fear that the other will gain more from collaboration, upsetting the domestic coalitional balance of power and altering the hegemon's grand strategy (which will further undermine their position). As such, jockeying between the newly empowered coalition and the defenders of the old arrangement can result in an incoherent and volatile grand strategy (Frieden 1988, 60; Stein 1993a; Solingen 1994, 141–42).

Coalitions that come to power get stronger through two processes. One is through the defection of members from the other faction, who will bring their constituents, organizational skills, and resources. For instance, in confronting imperial contenders, some members of the free-trade coalition will defect to the economic nationalist coalition in support of greater military preparedness, enhancing the latter faction. In confronting liberal contenders, some economic nationalists will join the free-trade camp. As one author notes with the decline or loss of state rents, flexible rent seekers will restructure operations to secure new markets for export to replace lost market shares at home, becoming supporters of free-market trade practices (Lusztig 1998, 42). But the domestic process of strengthening or weakening a coalition involves more than merely the shift of members from one coalition to another. The domestic coalition that accrues the benefits from cooperation or punishment will use these gains to expand its political clout and exert pressure upon the hegemon's grand strategy.[17] Interest groups will deploy resources to gain particularistic benefits, whether through lobbying, donations, or the promise of votes.

There are several constraints on the ability of the strengthened coalition to convert its interests and preferences into policy outcomes.[18] Collective action and free-rider problems can make it difficult for large logrolled coalitions to organize and voice their preferences (Hardin 1982;

TABLE 1. The Domestic Coalitional Consequences of International Politics

	Contender's Foreign Commercial Policy	
Hegemon	Liberal	Imperial
Free Trade	1. *Cooperation* Strengthen free traders; weaken economic nationalists	3a. *Cooperation* Strengthen free traders; weaken economic nationalists. 3b. *Punishment* Strengthen economic nationalists; weaken free traders
Economic Nationalist	2a. *Punishment* Strengthen economic nationalists; weaken free traders. 2b. *Cooperation* Strengthen free traders; weaken economic nationalists	4. *Punishment* Strengthen economic nationalists; weaken free traders

Olson 1982). Newly empowered factions will also have a disadvantage in implementing their preferences. In the case of empowered economic nationalists, according to Judith Goldstein (1993), if orthodox policies have become entrenched in state institutions, these institutions will resist protectionism and expansionary fiscal policies (for either social or defense spending). The same type of institutional barriers will confront empowered free traders if imperial policies have become entrenched. Finally, economic nationalists will have certain advantages in organizing because they can create rents through tariffs and imperial preferences, rewarding specific groups or compensating losers (while dispersing costs among a larger set of groups).[19] Empowered free traders will reduce protectionism and thereby diminish custom duties and revenue for state patronage (Lawson 1996). Yet, in enhancing the nation's aggregate welfare, free traders will create more wealth to go around and to be redistributed to reward supporters, making coalition building easier (Stallings 1992, 51).

Cell 1. Cooperation: Strengthen Free Traders

In cell 1 (table 1), the liberal nature of the rising contenders will guide the hegemon to cooperate; free traders will respond to these external pressures by pushing to cooperate with the liberal powers.[20] Economically, cooperation entails greater access to markets through such actions as a reduction in protectionism (tariffs, quotas, nontariff barriers or NTBs), elimination of exchange controls, abolition of preferential trading orders, and membership in IGOs and NGOs. Militarily, cooperation involves participation in collective security arrangements and arms limitation and reduction agreements. Cooperation can also translate into territorial concessions.

For free traders, cooperation with liberal states will have the internal result of advancing their faction's outward-oriented policies and the nation's interests. There are many domestic beneficiaries that prosper from a reduction in trade protection, military spending, and interstate hostility. The winners include export-oriented industries, the financial sector, fiscal conservatives, and consumers (while the losers who are harmed include inefficient industry, pro-empire organizations, trading companies, and the military). Efficient industry and invisible exports will benefit from increases in trade, foreign lending, and exports due to reduced protectionism, deregulation of markets, and a stable business climate. For fiscal conservatives and finance-oriented government bureaucracies, cooperation translates into lower levels of defense expenditure, increased savings and foreign exchange earnings, and "cheap money," advancing the private sector. By-products of fiscal and monetary restraint are lower inflation, reduced taxation, balanced budgets, and currency stability, further benefiting the export sectors. Consumers will benefit from cheaper imports.

Free traders will lobby to retrench from locales with emerging liberal contenders in order to further reduce the costs of hegemony, safeguarding the nation's economic capacity. Historically, free traders have aided in the ascent of liberal states, thereby expediting the hegemon's retreat from the locale. According to Rosecrance and Taw, "Dutch capital largely financed British commercial and industrial growth at the end of the seventeenth and the beginning of the eighteenth century. Similarly, British investment provided an essential stimulus to the growth of the United States both before and after the Civil War" (1989, 190). By ceding governance over a region to a liberal contender, either formally or informally, the erstwhile hegemon will retain access to its traditional markets, investments, and sources of raw materials in the locale, without bearing any of the overhead costs associated with regional hegemony and without strengthening the war-making capacity of a rival.[21] These economic, military, and political costs will be borne by the new regional leader (Osgood 1973; Organski 1990). In lowering the expenditure on hegemony, the erstwhile leader will safeguard its core macroeconomic objective of sustaining economic growth, which will also reward supporters. The peace dividend due to the decreasing costs of hegemony can be distributed to entice fence-sitters, used to compensate the economic losers from free trade, or channeled into public and private investment (while reducing taxes and government spending).[22] Further, the hegemon can gather its freed-up military and economic resources in its remaining commitments, strengthening its immediate military capability without extracting additional resources for defense.

In addition to devolving governance, the hegemon can build up a regional surrogate to lower the cost of leadership (a state that is not powerful enough on its own to dominate the locale). By creating and maintaining the regional surrogate, the great power will continue to have leverage over the surrogate's behavior. Mark Gasiorowski defines surrogacy as "a mutually beneficial, security oriented relationship between the governments of two countries that differ greatly in size, wealth, and power" (1991, 2). The Nixon Doctrine is an example of this strategy, which entailed building-up Iran and South Vietnam to police U.S. interests in the Persian Gulf and Southeast Asia, respectively, and bolstering Israel in the Middle East.

Economic, not political, differences exist between commercially liberal states.[23] Disputes include who will bear the burden of regional leadership, since each state favors economy over high military spending. Free traders will reject punishing liberal states. Beggar-thy-neighbor economic policies and increased defense expenditure will empower the economic nationalists while weakening free traders. The danger of punishing a liberal contender is that it can create the false illusion of incompatibility among liberal states. If the state retaliates, the outcome is a costly and self-defeating hostility spiral, crisis, and perhaps war, even though there is no aggressive intent. The risk from a hostility spiral among liberal states is twofold (Jervis 1976; Glaser 1992). First, in punishing a liberal contender, both states might embark on a costly and extensive military buildup. A hostility spiral between liberal states will undermine macroeconomic prosperity by disrupting trade flows, diverting resources from domestic investment to military spending, and contributing to policies such as tariffs, investment restrictions, currency devaluations, and sanctions. The long-term effect can be a decline in international competitiveness. Second, in discouraging a liberal contender from assuming greater regional responsibility, the leader will miss an opportunity to lower the costs of hegemony without strengthening the war-making capacity of a rival.

Cell 2. Punishment: Strengthen Economic Nationalists; Cooperation: Strengthen Free Traders

In cell 2, the liberal nature of the rising states will encourage economic nationalists to push for punishing these contenders. Punishment entails extraction of additional resources for military expenditure, protectionism, preferential trading orders, exchange and currency controls, and foreign aid reduction.

For economic nationalists, punishing liberal contenders will have the domestic consequence of advancing their coalitional interests by ratcheting-up their relative factional power, while weakening the opposing free-trade coalition. Punishment will strengthen inefficient industry and import-substituting industries, empire-oriented bureaucrats, settler organizations, the military, and the recipients of state-sanctioned monopoly rents from preferential trading arrangements. For inefficient industries and state-run enterprises, punishment translates into protection from international competition, preferring a settled share of the domestic market. For the military-industrial complex and the national-security apparatus, a hostility spiral means increased allocation of national resources and an enlarged role and mission. External threats are used to bolster the myth of national security through empire and offensive military operations. State managers and empire-oriented bureaucrats will use external threats to push for stronger links to the empire and perhaps territorial expansion. Punishment benefits the public sector due to expansionary fiscal policy. Finally, belligerence will dampen moves by internationalists, export-oriented industry, and the private sector to further escalate their collaboration with counterparts in other states. The danger of this response is that if the contender refuses to capitulate in its challenge, the outcome is a costly hegemonic war.

Economic nationalists will oppose cooperating with liberal contenders. While cooperation will advance the national interests by lowering the cost of hegemony, it will also bolster the power of the opposing free-trade coalition. Cooperation is possible because the liberal contenders' concern about economy means that they are unlikely to use the gains from trade to initiate an arms race. However, cooperation will place severe strain on the economic nationalists' bloc. Constituents such as protected state-run enterprises and import-competing industry will resist cooperation since they will bear the burden of trade liberalization, increased foreign access to their markets, and a reduction in government controls and rents. A reduction in tension will weaken the security apparatus and the military-industrial complex by diverting the resources away from defense expenditure (and undermining the myth of national security). State-affiliated managers and colonial bureaucrats are threatened by the dismantlement of state-owned enterprises and the public sector monopolies and monopsonies, devaluations, budget cuts, deregulation, lowering of tariffs, lowering of social welfare spending, and retreat from empire that accompany accommodation.

Cell 3. Cooperation: Strengthen Free Traders; Punishment: Strengthen Economic Nationalists

In cell 3, free traders will respond to external pressures by pressing for cooperation with imperial powers. For free traders, cooperation will have the domestic outcome of boosting their own faction's relative power. Concern for economy, which reflects its constituents' interests, especially lower peacetime military spending and opposition to protectionism, means that free traders favor extending military, economic, or territorial concessions in order to moderate a contender's ascent and demands.[24] The types of concessions most acceptable to the hegemon are the ones that impede further increases in the military and economic power of the contender, and open access to the contender's markets. If the hegemon can convince the rising contender to moderate its military buildup, then it can lighten the unbearable burden of preparing for war against multiple challengers; the leader will not need to divert resources from industry and investment toward the military. An arms limitation agreement can also prevent a costly arms race. Thus, cooperation can moderate the competitor's military ascent or territorial expansion without the expense of a military buildup or preventive war.

Free traders will resist punishing imperial contenders. While punishment will advance the national interests by assuring that the hegemon has ample military capability to protect its global commitments, it will also ratchet-up the strength of the contending economic nationalist faction. While some members of the free-trade faction will defect to the ranks of the economic nationalists (especially exporters who fear the loss of overseas markets since such a contender will impose a closed door commercial order in the locale), the bulk of the outward-oriented free-trade supporters will lobby against immoderate military and commercial punishment.[25] Free traders will contest offensive military proposals and will try to lower military budgets, while proposing arms limitation agreements and diplomacy to reduce tension. Free traders will seek to limit the retreat from fiscal orthodoxy and will oppose calls for higher tariffs and duties for fear of foreign retaliation (they also recognize that the long-term risk from protection is a decline in the proportion of the economy that is involved in the international economy). Finally, free traders will warn of the danger of the misallocation of societal resources due to the decline in competition and the encroachment of state intervention, protectionism, and sector monopolies.

Cell 4. Punishment: Strengthen Economic Nationalists

In cell 4, the imperial nature of the rising states will direct the hegemon to react by punishing contenders; economic nationalists will petition to punish the imperial states. For economic nationalists, punishment will have the internal result of advancing their coalitional interests by augmenting their relative power and also of advancing the national interest by ensuring that the state has adequate military resources. Punishment is the preferred response since economic nationalists favor preserving or creating their own preferential commercial order and extracting societal resources for greater military preparedness. Punishment benefits inefficient industry, empire-oriented bureaucrats, settler organizations, the military, and the recipients of state-sanctioned monopoly rents from preferential trading arrangements. If both the hegemon and the contender select punishment, then the outcome is a hostility spiral. This spiral entails beggar-thy-neighbor economic and trade policies or an arms race. The ultimate outcome is a hegemonic war.

THE FORMATION AND REFORMULATION OF A HEGEMON'S GRAND STRATEGY

The commercial nature of the rising states will guide the hegemon's grand strategy by ratcheting-up the supporters of either the free-trade or the economic nationalist coalition. The benefited coalition will use these gains to further expand its domestic political power in order to advance its preferred grand strategy by applying pressure on the government, while the victims will be weakened politically and economically (Rogowski 1989, 4–5). To further enhance its relative position, the empowered coalition will push the hegemon to adopt a more accommodative or belligerent posture.

The redistribution of power within the domestic arena can reorient the hegemon's grand strategy. An economic nationalist coalition that cooperates with liberal contenders will empower the opposing free-trade faction (table 1, cell 2b). In upsetting the domestic balance of power, strengthened free-trade supporters will press for a more accommodative grand strategy, favoring a comparatively softer response and militating toward a more flexible stance. Free traders have an interest in economic liberalization and the formation of closer ties to the outside world. Concerned for fiscal orthodoxy and a greater reliance on market forces, they will lobby for a reduction in protectionism and expansion of the private sector. Their policy package will include retreat from empire, liberalization of trade and exchange rate policies, improved efficacy of government spending (austerity measures, devaluations, military budget cuts, reduced subsidies and price supports, and curtailed public sector or "white elephants"), reduction in bloated state apparatuses, changes in tax policies (releasing resources for private investment), and replacing bureaucratic control by market mechanisms (administrative reform and privatization) (Evans 1992, 139–42). Such actions will escalate free-trader activities, further undercutting the position of the economic nationalists.

A free-trade coalition that punishes imperial contenders will empower the contending economic nationalist bloc (table 1, cell 3b). Enhanced economic nationalists will push for a more belligerent stance toward rising contenders. Expanding the role of economic nationalists who have a desired agenda for increasing military security, preferential trading arrangements, and retaining the empire will hurt outward-oriented domestic actors such as investors and providers of capital, and will dampen the chances for international collaboration.

REVERSALS AND ROLLBACKS

Changes or reversals in the foreign commercial policy of a contender can again alter the hegemon's domestic coalitional balance of power, the distributional gains, and ultimately reorient the leader's grand strategy. Reversals will have the effect of rolling back the economic and political gains of the empowered or entrenched coalition.

The reversal in the foreign commercial policy of imperial contenders toward a liberal commercial policy will roll back the gains of the economic nationalist coalition. Enhanced free traders will press for a more accommodative grand strategy. They will call for improving the domestic business climate and will push for easing international tension and the settlement of disputes in order to improve the international environment for trade. The free-trade bloc will roll back the advances of the economic nationalist coalition through restoration of freer trade, fiscal orthodoxy, and retreat of the state from intervention in the economy. They will especially emphasize the role of monetary discipline, volunteerism, and market mechanisms to prevent wasteful expenditure and inflation, while rejecting central planning and a command economy that will benefit specific domestic producers. Concomitantly, economy-minded free traders will push for a return to a defensive military posture, emphasizing air, naval, and nuclear forces and enhancing security through economic sanctions, collective security, and arms control. These programs will strengthen members of the free-trade coalition such as efficient industry, visible and invisible exporters, supporters of fiscal orthodoxy, and finance, whereas opponents of liberalization stand to lose.

The reversal in the foreign commercial policy of liberal contenders toward an imperial commercial policy will roll back the gains of the free-trade coalition. Strengthened economic nationalists will push for a more belligerent grand strategy. State managers and civil servants will favor planning, and empire-oriented bureaucrats will use external threats to push for closer ties to the empire. Inefficient industries and state-run enterprises will favor protection from foreign competition (Pollard 1969, 53). The military-industrial complex and the national-security apparatus will push for greater military preparedness.

SELF-REINFORCING SUBOPTIMALITY

Concerns about the distributional consequences from ratchets, reversals, and rollbacks can affect whether the supporters of the economic nationalist and free-trade factions will respond nationally or coalitionally to external pressures. For free traders that confront liberal states and for economic nationalists that confront imperial states, cooperation and punishment will respectively advance their faction's interests and the nation's interests. The dilemma occurs when free traders confront imperial contenders and economic nationalists encounter liberal contenders. These external pressures will push the faction that is under threat of being rolled back to advance its desired coalitional agenda, which will harm the national interest. In such instances, the entrenched or ruling coalition will adopt a *self-reinforcing* strategy that will ratchet-up its faction's relative power by capturing the associated distributional gains, but will undermine the nation's interest by either eroding the hegemon's economic capacity or undermining its military security, shortening the leader's great power tenure.[26] Self-reinforcing strategies are most likely to be selected when the threatened coalition faces a severe setback to its relative power if it advances the nation's interest over its faction's interests.

An Economic Nationalist Coalition That Confronts Liberal Contenders

An economic nationalist coalition that confronts liberal contenders will be pushed to advance its factional interest of punishment even though the national interest calls for cooperation (which would lower the cost of hegemony, safeguarding the hegemon's productive strength; table 1, cell 2b). Economic nationalists will oppose cooperation because it will bolster the associates of domestic free traders who will push the hegemon to adopt a more accommodative stance rather than intransigence. The danger in punishing liberal contenders is that it risks undermining the hegemon's economic base (private and public resources) for future military security.[27] As Robert Gilpin (1981) and Paul Kennedy (1987) warn, excessive and sustained peacetime military expenditure will divert resources from domestic investment, limit future economic growth, and erode the financial basis that the declining hegemon has to construct and maintain a modern military force.[28]

A three-step argument links military spending and economic decline (Melman 1974; Gilpin 1981, 156–85; Kennedy 1987, 514–35). First, military spending to defend global commitments diverts resources from wealth-creating activity, such as domestic investment, research and development (commercial, not military), education, the infrastructure, equipment and factories, and the like (as will nonmilitary government consumption such as entitlement programs and private consumption). Second, a shift in resources away from productive investment slows the expansion of the existing stock of capital and national wealth available for investment, and it impedes the rate at which technology and innovation spread throughout the economy. Finally, by constraining reinvestment, innovation, and production, military spending reduces the state's long-term productive capacity, which precipitates economic decline. One problem with this argument is that the long time-lag between extraction and decline makes it difficult to ascertain whether military spending is the primary culprit in economic decline.[29]

Too heavy a burden on the economy cannot be borne indefinitely without ruining the descending state's future capacity to create a modern military. In the case of Spain, prolonged levels of domestic resource extraction contributed to Castile's lag in growth industries of the period such as textiles, metallurgy, and shipbuilding (Lynch 1992, 219). More recently, some argue that America's policy of "peace through strength" forced the USSR into an arms race, undermining its productive strength and the source of its military power. At the extreme, in 1916, Germany embarked on the Hindenburg Program, which entailed converting almost the entire German industrial system to munitions production. The outcome was the short-term increase in production at the price of making certain that the German wartime economy would collapse in a few years, undermining its ability to field a large military force (Barnett 1976, 13).

High defense spending in peacetime will drain the hegemon's war chest. Britain's leaders viewed England's fiscal strength and economic stability as the "fourth arm of defence" on which the three branches of the military services (and traditionally Britain's allies) depended. For this reason, Britain's Exchequer feared that excessive taxation and/or borrowing during peacetime would leave little room for expansion during wartime. Exorbitant taxation might also provoke social unrest and domestic instability, especially if certain groups feel they have been unfairly targeted or if there is a decline in the country's standard of living. For instance, France's Louis XVI's attempt to levy higher taxes contributed to the French Revolution, Spain's Philip IV's attempt to increase taxes in Catalonia and Portugal resulted in a revolt (1640), and the strain of excessive extraction during World War I contributed to revolutions in Russia (1917) and Germany (1919).

A Free-Trade Faction That Confronts Imperial Contenders

Free-trade supporters that confront imperial contenders will be pressured to advance their coalitional agenda of cooperation, although the national interest calls for punishment (to ensure that the hegemon has sufficient military capability to defend its global commitments; table 1, cell 3b). Free-trade constituents will oppose punishing imperial contenders because that will empower the affiliates of the economic nationalists who will push for a more hard-line policy. The problem for free traders is that an imperial contender will prefer punishment. Within imperial contenders there is pressure from empire, military-industrial complex constituents, and cartelized business to resist agreements that limit or downsize defense endowments and territorial aspirations. Opposition is especially likely if the agreement entails maintaining the current liberal commercial order in the locale, thus rejecting the economic nationalists' preferred choice of an exclusive trading order. The danger for such economic nationalists is that cooperative agreements, even a softer stance, can upset the internal struggle for power between free traders and economic nationalists. Cooperation will undercut the influence and institutions of economic nationalists while economically and politically strengthening the members of the liberal coalition. For this reason, economic nationalists will act politically and lobby the government to reject such concessions.[30]

The danger (to the hegemon) in advancing the free traders' coalitional interests of cooperation is the risk of undermining the lender's military security. As imperial contenders encroach, they are likely to reject and perhaps violate cooperative economic, political, and military agreements.[31] E. H. Carr notes that "weaker states will renounce treaties concluded by them with stronger states so soon as the power position alters and the weaker state feels itself strong enough to reject or modify the obligation" (1964, 190). Imperial states desire an alternative commercial arrangement than the existing liberal regional trading order. Since cooperation is unlikely to achieve their final objective, such states will see preemptive war as inevitable, moderating their behavior until they perceive a good chance of overturning the status quo. The combination of allocating too few resources to defense by the hegemon, failed or lapsed arms reduction agreements, and/or illegal rearmament by the challenger means that the declining power will have insufficient military capabilities to defend its global commitments.

GREAT POWER TENURE

A policy question that I address in an extended discussion in chapter 6 is why some states are more successful in managing their decline. A hegemon's allocation of its national resources will influence how long it can remain in the ranks of the great powers. In shifting from a hegemonic to a multipolar distribution of power, the grand strategy of a declining state is to remain in the ranks of the great powers as long as possible. As a great power, the former hegemon can preserve the existing international order, which is compatible with its commercial and security interests. While the hegemon might not remain *the* leader, it can be *a* leader. In falling from the ranks of the great powers to a second-rate power, the erstwhile hegemon's influence in the international system will also decline, becoming regional or even local in nature. As a second-tier power, the former hegemon's influence will be limited, counting on the remaining great powers to protect its commercial and security interests.

The hegemon's international environment can enhance or undermine its ability to prolong its great power tenure. In aggregating a hegemon's response across regions, a dominant free-trade coalition (that confronts at least some liberal contenders) is in a better position to lengthen the hegemon's great power tenure than where economic nationalists rule. Decision makers must consider both the financial and security ramifications of a foreign policy strategy in selecting how to balance capabilities and commitments. If the hegemon favors either economic or security concerns it can hasten its fall from the leading states to a second-rate regional power.

RULING ECONOMIC NATIONALISTS

For ruling economic nationalists, in the long term, there are no good strategies that will safeguard both their fiscal and security interests. Their preference for punishment will weaken the state by undermining its economic base for future military spending, while an accommodationist strategy in order to reduce the costs of hegemony will erode the leader's military security (besides strengthening the opposing free traders). Imperial contenders will likely renege or defect on any agreement that limits arms buildup or territorial expansion so as to encroach on and challenge the hegemon for leadership over the locale. In lacking sufficient economic capacity or military capability, as the hegemon falls from the ranks of the great powers, its corresponding influence over the international system will also decline, becoming regional or local.

RULING FREE TRADERS

A ruling free-trade coalition that confronts some liberal contenders can prolong the state's great power tenure.[32] If the hegemon devolves regional hegemony to liberal powers, the leader will lower the costs of leadership without harming its economic base. By amassing these freed-up resources in its remaining commitments, the hegemon will strengthen its immediate war-making capacity without extracting additional funds, thereby protecting its military security. These actions will ensure the erstwhile hegemon has ample economic and military capability to protect its commercial and security interests. In retaining its great power status, the hegemon can continue to influence the rules of the game to advance its national interests. Failure to retrench when the free-trade bloc has the opportunity, even in strategic locales, means adopting a suboptimal policy that risks harming the hegemon's fiscal health through prolonged high levels of defense expenditure.

CHAPTER 3

Liberal Contenders and Britain's Grand Strategy of Cooperation, 1889–1912

In the sixty or so years after the Napoleonic Wars, Britain came to dominate many regions of the globe. These spheres of formal and informal influence comprised the Far East, especially China; central Asia, including the "Jewel in the Crown," India, and the buffer territories of Persia and the Gulf, Afghanistan, and Tibet; the Mediterranean (the Straits of Gibraltar and the Turkish Straits); southern and eastern Africa; and Central and Latin America. While it did not dominate Europe, Britain was the historic balancer on the Continent. To defend its far-flung interests, Britain's Royal Navy commanded the high seas as well as most of the strategic sea-lanes of communication. As Admiral Fisher gloated, "Five strategic keys lock up the world!" (Kennedy 1976, 244). They were Singapore, the Cape, Alexandria, Gibraltar, and Dover, and they all belonged to England. An extensive global network of coaling stations, cable stations, and naval bases supported Britain's naval and commercial supremacy.

By the last decade of the nineteenth century, the dilemma for London was how to respond to the simultaneous and multiplying dangers, given Britain's limited national resources and extended global commitments. Britain confronted multiple contenders for regional hegemony that were ascending at differential rates and challenging Britain in disparate parts of its formal and informal empire. Britain faced intense industrial competition and naval construction challenges from Germany, the United States, Russia, France, and Japan in the Far East; France and Germany in the Middle East and Africa; France and Russia in the Mediterranean; Germany on the Continent; Russia in central Asia; and the United States in Central and Latin America.

Within Britain, members of the opposing free-trade bloc and the economic nationalist faction vied to shape how London would select which contenders to punish, where to cooperate, and how to allocate societal resources between the nation's economy and its security. Their agendas clashed on key issues such as naval construction, army reform, and national conscription; tariffs and imperial preferences; fiscal orthodoxy and state intervention in the economy; social and economic reforms; international arms control and arms reduction agreements; and the empire. The members of the economic nationalist coalition included uncompetitive firms and export-oriented staple industries (steel, iron, textiles), farmers and landowners (cheap cereal poured in from Russia, Eastern Europe, and the United States), the military services (War Office, Admiralty) and supporting lobbying organizations (the Navy League), the Conservative Party, pro-empire organizations, and colonial bureaucrats (the Colonial Office and the India Office).[1] Economic nationalists favored a grand strategy of punishing rising liberal and imperial contenders through (1) tariff reform to heighten trade barriers against foreign competition and imperial preferences to protect British industry and imperial markets, (2) closer economic and military ties to the empire, and (3) greater military preparedness. Economic nationalists warned that failure to punish contenders would tempt states to challenge Britain's domestic and empire markets, sea-lanes of communication, and home defense. Preempting the backlash from the free-trade faction over the cost of higher naval Estimates, the First Lord of the Admiralty, Lord Selborne, wrote in 1901, "Compare our burthen of taxation, our debt, & our wealth with that of most of our continental neighbours, and it is impossible for me to believe that we are approaching the end of our resources" (Boyce 1990, 126).

In opposition, members of the free-trade coalition included invisible exports such as overseas investments, shipping, insurance, financial institutions and other commercial services (merchant banking such as the Bank of England, known broadly as the City), the Liberal Party (constituents included the middle and working class), Radicals, the Treasury, and top civil servants. Free traders favored a grand strategy of accommodating and cooperating with rising contenders, especially commercially liberal powers, through a program of (1) an open world economy (by the elimination of duties and a reduction of protectionism and tariffs), (2) fiscal and monetary orthodoxy (the Gladstonian tradition of limited government expenditure on defense and social welfare, low taxation, minimal state interference in the economy, and free trade) and safeguarding the gold standard, (3) military retrenchment, the sharing of mutual interests with partners or allies, the settlement of existing conflicts to reduce tension, and international arms control agreements, and (4) retreat from empire (both formal and informal) in order to lower the cost of hegemony. For free traders, London's failure to reduce the cost of hegemony would erode Britain's prosperity, the underpinning of its war chest.

The commercial composition of the rising contenders guided London's grand strategy toward cooperation; the nature of the foreign commercial policy of the rising contenders pushed the free traders to advocate a policy of conciliation. Britain confronted a mix of liberal (United States, Japan, and France after 1904) and imperial (Germany, Russia, and France before 1904) contenders for regional hegemony. The free traders cooperated with the liberal contenders, devolving leadership, extending loans, reducing protectionism, and assisting in their naval ascent. Within Britain, cooperation bolstered efficient industry, the City of London, the Liberal Party, and fiscal conservatives. Free traders opposed economic and military punishment of liberal contenders because such a policy risked a costly hostility spiral. Punishment would also augment the power of the members of the economic nationalist coalition such as the military, inefficient industry, and empire-oriented interests who would push London to adopt a more belligerent grand strategy.

Many free traders joined the economic nationalists in favor of punishing imperial Germany, France (until 1904), and Russia even though this response translated into increased defense spending and protectionism, strengthening the latter coalition. In accommodating imperial states, free traders feared losing commercial and financial access to the locale while strengthening the war-making capacity of a rival. Yet, the free traders moderated the scale and the nature of the economic nationalists' program for punishing imperial contenders by slimming down the naval building Estimates, proposing a number of arms limitation agreements with these states, and negotiating concessions to reduce regional tension.

The domestic repercussions of Britain's grand strategy of cooperation ratcheted-up the strength of the supporters of the free-trade faction while further weakening the economic nationalist coalition.[2] An increase in trade activity, growth in foreign lending, reductions in government appropriations, and gains in export performance strengthened the free traders' core constituency. The General Election of 1906 was fought largely on the issue of imperial preferences and tariff reform. The election resulted in an overwhelming defeat for the Conservative Party, which stood for protection, imperial preferences, and higher defense spending, returning to power the free-trade Liberal Party. Conservatives suffered further defeats in the two elections of 1910 over the issue of tariff reform. Free traders used these distributional gains and the savings from lowering the cost of hegemony to attract new supporters by enacting a number of costly social and economic reform programs (1909 Old Age Pensions Act, 1911 National Insurance Act) that were attractive to the working and middle classes. Thus, the commercial nature of the rising contenders transformed the domestic distribution of power, affecting Britain's grand strategy.

This chapter examines the domestic and foreign consequences of the commercial nature of the rising contenders that Britain confronted between 1889 and 1912. The first section uses the differentiated framework developed in chapter 1 to discuss the complex nature of the challenges that Britain encountered. The second section discusses the commercial nature of these rising contenders. The third and fourth sections examine the members and policy stance of the opposing free-trade and economic nationalist coalitions, and their response to challenges by the United States, Germany, Japan, France, and Russia in disparate parts of Britain's empire. The final section discusses the distributional consequences of Britain's grand strategy of cooperation.

THE EMERGING CONTENDERS FOR REGIONAL HEGEMONY

Scholars who examine Britain's geostrategic environment prior to World War I often focus on Great Britain's position in a single region, such as the Americas, Europe, Central Asia, or the Far East, or a challenge by a single protagonist—most often the German challenge in Europe and Britain's home waters. Since Britain had the largest navy in the world, when confronted with a single contender, London could have concentrated or diverted its fleet from other stations in its empire, gaining local superiority and overwhelming the challenger's fleet. However, during this period, Britain encountered Germany, Japan, the United States, Russia, and France, rising at uneven rates and in disparate parts of its empire. With its extensive empire, Britain had many frontiers to defend, and resisting all these new pressures imposed a severe strain on resources. In oversimplifying Britain's predicament, it is difficult to understand the nearly impossible dilemma that both free traders and economic nationalists faced in how to balance Britain's military capabilities and global commitments without eroding the state's economic strength or undermining its national security[3]—for even economic nationalists recognized that Britain's fiscal health was a component of its military power. As the First Lord of the Admiralty stated, "Its Credit and its Navy seem to me to be the two main pillars on which the strength of this country rests, and each is essential to the other" (Sumida 1989, 23). Likewise, many free traders with global interests recognized the importance of a strong navy to defend trade routes and strategic sea-lanes of communication.

First, Britain confronted disparate contenders for regional leadership across its empire. During the three decades before World War I, Britain faced intense industrial and naval competition from the United States in Latin America, especially in Central America; Japan, Russia, the United States, Germany, and France in the Far East and Pacific; Russia in Central Asia; Russia, France, and Germany in the Middle East; France and Russia in the Mediterranean; and France and Germany in Africa. In addition, Britain faced a rapidly rising Germany on the European continent.

Second, differential rates of industrial growth allowed contenders for regional leadership to encroach on Britain's position at uneven rates, with some states rising earlier and faster than others. The United States was the first power to surpass Britain in a number of key industrial sectors such as steel production, coal consumption, and energy use.[4] In 1890, an emerging United States produced more steel than Britain (by 1913 more steel than the rest of the great powers combined), and by 1900 the United States surpassed Britain in relative shares of world manufacturing. By 1900, Germany was the second power to eclipse Britain in a number of industrial sectors. While Russia remained a relatively backward power, it underwent rapid industrialization in the first decade of the twentieth century. Although Japan did not enter the ranks of the great powers until after World War I, it greatly increased its industrial and military capability during this period.

Finally, Britain's regional leadership was challenged by competitors at uneven rates across these locales. As early as the 1870s, Russia posed a threat to Britain's interests in Central Asia, mainly India, and to the buffer states of Persia and Afghanistan (Yapp 1987). During the mid-1880s, Britain confronted France in both Africa and southern China. By the early 1890s, and especially after the conclusion of the Franco-Russian Alliance in 1894, both France and Russia encroached on Britain's naval supremacy in the Mediterranean. The scramble for empire in China did not begin in earnest until after the Sino-Japanese War in 1894–95 when Germany, Russia, and France carved out sections of the collapsing empire. Around the same time, the United States and Britain had a number of disputes in North and Central America, as the United States was attempting to exert greater control over events in its backyard. In Britain's home waters, Germany emerged as a major naval challenger around 1904.

Thus, Britain's rate of decline was far from global, rapid, or simultaneous in nature. Had Britain confronted a single emerging contender, it could have concentrated its existing resources in one locale, overwhelming the challenger's fleet. Instead, Britain confronted an emerging United States, France, Russia, Germany, and Japan, growing at differential rates and challenging its hegemony in disparate regions and at different junctures in time. The predicament for Britain's leaders was how to align the nation's ends and means without undermining either its productive capacity or military security.

LIBERAL CONTENDERS

Britain confronted a mix of ascending liberal and imperial contenders between 1889 and 1912. The foreign commercial policy of a contender reflects whether the state will impose an open or closed door economic order on any locale that it comes to dominate. As liberal contenders, the United States, Japan, and France (after its reversal in 1904) would maintain Britain's Open Door policy in the respective locales; while imperial Germany, France (until 1904), and Russia would impose an exclusive commercial order in any locale they controlled.

The United States

In the case of the United States, although protectionist at home, President William McKinley sought to ensure equal access for the United States to overseas commercial opportunities, especially in China (LaFeber 1963, 284–325). Presidents McKinley and Theodore Roosevelt, among others, were driven by the belief that foreign markets were necessary to relieve a glutted U.S. market and that the U.S. economy would stagnate if it failed to expand (the United States had just come out of a severe depression) (Becker 1984, 185). With the close of the American frontier in the 1890s, U.S. leaders redirected their focus from continental expansion to the creation of a free-trade empire.[5]

America's free-trade outlook was actualized in the Open Door Notes, which became the basis of U.S. foreign policy (Williams 1972). In 1899, President McKinley and Secretary of State John Hay issued the first of two

Open Door Notes, supporting Britain's Open Door policy in China. Hay distributed a note to Britain, France, Germany, and Russia calling on the major powers to declare equality of commercial treatment in their spheres of influence (the Chinese government would operate the tariffs equally across all the spheres) (McCormick 1967). Specifically, the Notes called upon the great powers to give formal guarantees of equal commercial access to both treaty and nontreaty ports, and assurance of uniform (nondiscriminatory rates) harbor dues and railroad rates in their spheres. The preamble to the British note emphasized that the open door would help maintain the integrity of China.

Britain, France, and Germany agreed to adhere to the main points. Japan had not been approached because it was not thought to have a sphere of interest. After asking to be invited, Japan adhered to the declaration. Russia's ambiguous reply (refusal to sign but verbal consent) was interpreted by Hay as evidence of adherence although Russia's intentions were far from clear.[6]

In 1900, after the Boxer Rebellion against Western penetration, Hay issued a second Note to prevent Britain, France, Russia, or Japan from using the uprising as an excuse to carve up China. The states agreed to "preserve Chinese territorial and administrative entity, protect all rights guaranteed to friendly powers by treaty and international law, and to safeguard for the world the principle of equal and impartial trade with all ports of the Chinese empire" (Clymer 1975, 148). Hay asked for no formal replies because he expected "Russia was opposed to it, and would probably reject it" (McCormick 1967, 160).

The U.S. support for Britain's Open Door policy in China was intended to keep the fabled "China Market" open for future U.S. trade. U.S. leaders believed their economic strength and efficiency would allow the United States to dominate the region commercially (and eventually the world marketplace), as long as it remained open to all (Williams 1972, 28–57). U.S. opposition to the partition of China by special concessions and exclusive spheres of influence drew it closer to Britain (and, as discussed later, Japan) in opposing Russian ambitions in Manchuria and French and German expansion in China. The State Department recognized, "a threat to the British position was also a threat to American interests. Only Great Britain, and possibly Japan, shared the American enthusiasm for the open door" (LaFeber 1963, 321). For Britain, the Open Door Notes signaled U.S. support for the objectives of Britain's Open Door policy in China.

Japan

As a late developer, Japan initially favored an exclusive sphere of influence to protect its markets and investments from more competitive and efficient producers such as Britain and the United States.[7] While Japan had commercial ambitions in Manchuria and Korea, the Triple Intervention demonstrated to Tokyo that it could not compete with Russia, France, and Germany to acquire its own share of China's crumbling empire (LaFeber 1963, 312–13). Due to the subsequent scramble for China, and especially Russia's expansion in Manchuria and Korea and its attempt to dominate Peking, Japan feared that it would be excluded from China, and that Korea would be occupied and subsequently closed off to Japanese trade and investment.[8]

Japan supported Britain's Open Door policy in the Far East to prevent Russia and Germany from annexing Chinese territory. Further Russian expansion pushed Japan into fully embracing the Anglo-American position of protecting China's territorial integrity and the continuation of the Open Door policy (Nish 1966; Beasley 1981; McKercher 1989). In 1899, Japan signed the American Open Door Notes. During the Boxer Rebellion (1900), Japan collaborated with the great powers to prevent a further partition of China by the imperial powers. In 1902, with the signing of the Anglo-Japanese Alliance, Japan endorsed the Open Door policy in China again. The Alliance committed both states to "maintaining the independence and territorial integrity" of China and Korea and "securing equal opportunities in those countries for the commerce and industry of all nations" (Beasley 1987, 77).

France

Britain increasingly viewed France as a satisfied rising contender, especially after 1904 (Rock 1989, 91–122). France sought to reserve its colonial markets for itself and to use these markets to absorb gluts in products of metropolitan manufacture (Fieldhouse 1966; Ashley 1970; Lebovics 1988). The Méline Tariff of 1892 firmly established the policy of tariff assimilation (over the practice of imperial preference).[9] France's colonial policy of economic assimilation called for the incorporation of its colonies into the metropolitan tariff—which meant the establishment of the French tariff on foreign imports into the colony, as well as a free exchange of goods between the colony and France (Clough 1939; Smith 1980). Yet, some colonial possessions, such as Morocco, remained "nonassimilated" because of international agreements, like the 1904 Entente Cordiale with Britain, which allowed London to maintain commercial freedom in parts of France's empire (one of London's conditions for acceptance of the entente was the protection of British trade in Morocco).

IMPERIAL CONTENDERS

Germany

While the United States and Japan, and to a lesser degree France, supported Britain's Open Door trade policy abroad, Germany sought to carve out its own exclusive sphere of influence in the center of Europe (Fischer 1974, 46–56; 1975). According to David Calleo, Germany's economic expansion consisted of two sequential commercial phases: the first was characterized by an "economically liberal, territorially satisfied Germany, submitting to comparative advantage in agriculture as well as industry, and counting on free trade both to supply its factories and to sell their products. The second option was a mercantilist and imperialist Germany, seeking self-sufficiency, and hence needing hegemony over a space commensurate with its growing production and population" (1978, 18–19).

Beginning in 1897, Britain viewed Germany's global policy of *Weltpolitik* or world policy and its correlate, the Continental policy of *Mitteleuropa*, as a threat to its open trading system.[10] *Weltpolitik* called for a more active foreign policy (Craig 1978, 302–38). This included a search for new overseas markets and exclusive colonial possessions for markets and raw materials, a large North Sea fleet to protect its trade and to reflect its rising stature (*Risikoflotte* or risk fleet), Continental expansion, and increased tariffs to make Germany more self-sufficient.[11] Several geopolitical arguments were put forth for greater German economic self-sufficiency: Germany needed to maintain a capable indigenous agriculture; growing German dependence on foreign foodstuff made Berlin vulnerable to cutoffs in time of war; industrializing states would steadily consume their own raw materials, leaving little for export; Germany bordered two increasingly hostile neighbors and could not rely on their exports; and Britain might damage German trade by imposing imperial preferences (Calleo 1978, 20–22).

Of greater concern to Britain was Germany's Continental policy of *Mitteleuropa*. As a late entrant in the race for colonies, there was extensive discussion in Germany that Central Europe was its natural territorial sphere in the world (despite Britain's eventual willingness to cede to it some colonies in Africa). *Mitteleuropa* was a mercantilist and expansionist plan that called for a closed central European economic system or customs union headed by Germany.[12] This *Zollverein* was intended to serve as a "United States of Europe" under German leadership, targeted at the three other great empires of Britain, the United States, and Russia. Calleo (1978, 17–18) points to Bismarck's bilateral alliance with Austria-Hungary in 1879 as the first step in creating a self-sufficient German-dominated bloc in Central Europe. As part of a larger mercantilist scheme, Leo von Caprivi, Bismarck's successor, sought to create a liberal European trading bloc (the New Course). According to Fritz Fischer, "Behind Caprivi's trade policy was the idea of closer tariff links in Mitteleuropa so as to keep out the British Empire, Russia, and above all the United States" (1975, 6).

By 1912, Germany aimed to become a world power by creating an empire consisting of four parts (Fischer 1975, 259–66). These included (1) permanent control of Belgium and direct annexation of the French iron areas in the west; (2) permanent control of the entire area between Germany and Russia in the east; (3) *Mitteleuropa*, or the creation of a Central European Customs Union dominated by Germany that would include the partners in the Quadruple Alliance, Holland, and the Scandinavian countries, as well as defeated powers such as France; (4) *Mittelafrika*, which called for a German belt all the way across Africa. Other regions into which Germany would exert its influence included the Near East (the Baghdad Railway). However, only a secure position in central Europe could provide the economic base for Germany's global empire. London feared that Germany's foreign policy of *Mitteleuropa*, like Napoleon's Continental System a century before, was directed at Britain. Germany's exclusive *Mitteleuropa* policy would destroy Great Britain's extensive and profitable Continental trade, thereby threatening the economic base of its military power.

Russia

Like Germany's, Russia's economic expansion concerned Britain. As early as the 1840s, Britain perceived Russia as the most likely challenger to its free-trade system (Seton-Watson 1967; Brawley 1993, 127). Britain feared Russia's imperial expansion because it threatened its Open Door commercial policy in Asia and the Pacific. Russia's rejection of the American Open Door Notes further confirmed London's fears. British leaders widely accepted that "where the czar sets his Custom House he there proclaims the policy of 'Protectionism'" (Marder 1940, 238). Russia's finance minister, Count Witte, claimed openly his determination to exert "control over the entire movement of international commerce in Pacific waters" (LaFeber 1963, 320). Domination was possible through Russia's burgeoning railroad network in central Asia and the Far East.

Britain's officials feared that Russia, as a powerful country with a backward economy, would close off foreign competition in any region it dominated.[13] As a relatively backward state, Russia had a disadvantage in Open Door competition with more efficient producers. Accordingly, "after annexing land in Asia, [the Russians] tried to control it tightly by closing the markets to foreign businessmen with whom they could not compete" (LaFeber 1997, 2). Thus, Russia would exclude British economic interests from Manchuria, and as Russia expanded it would make China its vassal, threatening Britain's interests in other parts of China as well.

In summary, Britain confronted a mix of emerging liberal and imperial contenders for regional hegemony. The United States, Japan, and France supported Britain's Open Door commercial policy. Imperial Germany and Russia sought to carve out or partition off exclusive spheres in Europe, central Asia, and the Pacific. Moving from a hegemonic to a multipolar distribution of power, the commercial nature of the rising contenders guided Britain's response, acting upon its allocation of national resources and its great power tenure.

BRITAIN'S GRAND STRATEGY

In confronting new and old challengers, within Britain the members of the economic nationalist and the free-trade coalitions competed for control over the state's grand strategy and the associated distributional spoils. Economic nationalists favored punishing contenders through trade protection and tariffs, imperial trading preferences, stronger military ties to the empire, and increased defense expenditure for the army and especially for the navy. Punishment would have the domestic effect of ratcheting-up the political and economic power of inefficient industry, the military, agriculture, the Conservative Party, and pro-empire organizations and colonial bureaucrats. Strengthened economic nationalists would press the government for a more belligerent stance toward contenders, harming the interests of free traders. Free traders favored cooperation with contenders, especially liberal states, by reducing protectionism, retreating from empire, lowering defense expenditure, and engaging in international arms limitation agreements. Cooperation would have the internal outcome of augmenting the relative strength of the City of London, efficient industry, and fiscal conservatives, while undercutting the position of the supporters of the economic nationalist faction.

THE MEMBERS OF THE FREE-TRADE COALITION

While Britain's share of world trade in its staple industries (visible exports) was on the wane by the 1890s, it was compensated by London's emergence as banker and common carrier to the world (Drummond 1981; Kennedy 1983, 93–94). It is noted that "the period 1880 to 1914 was one of precarious equipoise, when the power of finance, growing increasingly cosmopolitan, reached a transitory equality with that of land, whose agricultural base was slowly undermined by the free-trade internationalism on which the City flourished" (Cain and Hopkins 1993b, 131). Britain maintained its balance of payments by capturing a large share of the world's shipping, insurance, returns on investments abroad, and banking and commercial services (Longstreth 1979, 160–64; Pollard 1989, 235–58; Cain and Hopkins 1993b, 161; Tomlinson 1994, 41, table 2.3). The openness of the global economy, Britain's fiscal orthodoxy, and the gold standard encouraged the growth of the service economy. In the 1906 elections, instead of listening to the protectionist sectors, voters and Parliament heeded export-oriented commercial, financial, and shipping interests (Checkland 1983; Friedberg 1988; Brawley 1993).

The members of the free-trade faction included the Labour and Liberal Parties, the Radicals, a complex of international financial services (banking, shipping, insurance, broadly defined as the Bank of England and the City of London), export-oriented firms, state bureaucracies such as the Treasury and the Foreign Office, the trade unions (TUC), and many top civil servants wedded to Gladstonian orthodoxy, who perceived little gain from economic isolation. The free-trade coalition had a common interest in freer trade (ensuring that both the visible and the invisible sectors had access to foreign markets), fiscal orthodoxy and laissez-faire economic policy, military retrenchment (especially abandonment of the two-power naval standard, or at least cutbacks in naval construction), retreat from empire (overseas possessions were "costly, burdensome and unnecessary," which required expensive garrisons and periodic intervention; Friedberg 1988, 31), and international agreements on disarmament to escape from costly spiraling arms races. The free-trade coalition was deeply suspicious of any attempts at uniting the empire economically and anxious to avoid arms races, either of which could contribute to protectionism (Cain and Hopkins 1993b, 204–9).

Free trade was linked to both cheaper food and cheaper raw materials. Opposition to trade protectionism included labor, which favored freer trade to keep consumer costs down.[14] The lower middle and working classes remained wedded to the traditional doctrines of low-cost imports of food, known as the "cheap loaf," and other commodities (Pollard 1989, 243). Labor was joined by manufacturers of finished goods and consumers of imported raw materials who wanted to keep the costs of inputs low (including coal, shipbuilding, and segments of the cotton industry). For such free traders, trade retaliation would lead to a commercial war of spiraling duties and counterduties, disrupting the flow of goods, services, and money (Kavanagh 1973).

Labour and the Liberal Parties

Both the Labour and the Liberal Parties were wedded to the policy agendas of freer trade, retreat from empire, and reduced defense spending.[15] During the 1906 general election, the Liberal candidate, Sir Henry Campbell-Bannerman, campaigned on the Manchester slogan of "peace, retrenchment, and reform," using the issue of Unionist naval spending to rally his Liberal Party (Williams 1991, 78). The Liberal Party favored military retrenchment in order to release resources for social reform programs (Emy 1972; French 1982a; Howard 1982; Williams 1991). Such savings would be possible by downgrading the two-power naval standard to a 60 percent standard and reducing international tensions. Members of the Liberal Party opposed the costly prospect of raising and dispatching a Continental-size army to France. Instead, reflecting Balfour's strategy, the navy would be used for home defense and to keep the sea-lanes open for imports of vital food and raw materials, while the army was responsible for imperial defense. As prime minister, Campbell-Bannerman (1905–8) warned, "A policy of huge armaments keeps alive and stimulates and feeds the belief that force is the best if not only solution of international differences" (Howard 1982, 145). Even as the threat of war approached, Liberals called for using the existing small volunteer army and Royal Navy, which would not draw on the manpower and factories devoted to civilian production.

The City of London

As the commercial and financial center for the world economic system, the City identified its interests with the free-trade coalition. The City of

London included international banking, financial services, shipping, insurance, overseas merchanting, and income from capital invested overseas. They called for freer trade by reducing tariffs and duties, the elimination of regulation by the state, and ensuring that the sterling maintained its position as the reserve currency for the world monetary system and as the major vehicle for international economic transactions.[16] The bankers claimed that free trade was essential for London's dominance of money markets (Daunton 1989, 149). With London at the center of the free-trade system, the City's prosperity was assured, but required a growing and open world economy. For the City, a deficit in the balance of trade with the United States and Europe could be covered by British surplus in trade with India, Australia, the Near and Middle East, Equatorial Africa, Central and South America, China, and the Far East (Capie 1983, 23, table 2.7).

The City responded harshly to the economic nationalists' call for tariff protection. They retorted that British firms were not aggressive enough and that the failure to maintain traditional markets resulted more from commercial indifference than from the lack of government support, foreign protection, or overseas dumping (Friedberg 1988, 74). Instead, the City highlighted the complementary effect of foreign industrialization for British economic growth, challenging the negative assumptions from increased competition (Feinstein 1996). As foreign industry expanded, it raised incomes abroad for the purchase of British products and services. Indirectly, industrialization increased the demand for raw materials, which meant that suppliers of primary commodities were able to increase their purchases from Britain. For free traders, protective tariffs would simply preserve industry's inefficiency. Yet the City was criticized routinely by economic nationalists for neglecting domestic industry and pursuing international economic policies to the detriment of manufacturing industry.

The Bank of England

The political power of the City extended through private organizations such as the Bank of England and key state bureaucracies such as the Treasury, who were responsible for managing the economy.[17] As the guardian of the gold standard, the Bank of England was the most important element in determining the money supply in Britain (Pollard 1989, 244–50; Tomlinson 1990, 25–28). The Bank of England was a private enterprise, and the government had no direct access to its decision making. Yet the government asked for and frequently took the advice of the Bank of England on questions of monetary policy and related issues. The gold standard meant that domestic currencies were convertible into gold at a rate of exchange (which fluctuated within narrow limits). International economic transactions could be made in principle with any national currency whose value was determined in relation to gold. But most transactions were conducted in sterling rather than gold, due to Britain's dominant economic and political position. For the gold standard to function smoothly, trade had to flow freely, unimpeded by restrictive tariffs and duties. Once more, confidence in the stability of sterling was essential, for it increased the desire to purchase British goods and services.

The Treasury Department

As the watchdog over government finance, the Treasury Department was responsible for striking a balance between the competing demands of government expenditure (civil and military) and maintaining the health of the economy. In order to accomplish this goal, the Treasury was in charge of levying and creating new taxes as well as approving each department's annual budget Estimate. The intention of Treasury control over government expenditure was to ensure that a department's Estimates were economical (see the appendix for a discussion of the concept of Treasury control). As one chancellor noted, "The function of the Chancellor of the Exchequer is to resist all demands for expenditure made by his colleagues, when he can no longer resist, to limit the concession to the barest point of acceptance" (Kynaston 1980, 57).

The philosophy of the Treasury was steeped in the Gladstonian tradition of limited government expenditure on defense and social welfare, low taxation, minimal interference in the economy, and freer trade (Emy 1972, 105–7; Tomlinson 1990, 28–30). The rationale was that Britain's fiscal strength was a third leg of defense, upon which the army and the navy would rely in the event of a prolonged conflict. As the prospect of a Continental war emerged, Britain would serve as the financial backer of the Triple Entente. According to David French, a strong British economy would allow the allies to "sustain the burden of war while the enemy is rapidly consuming his resources" (1982a, 34–35). Too much extraction in peacetime would divert resources from domestic investment, limit the scope of future economic growth, and ultimately undermine Britain's productive capacity to construct a modern military and to wage a prolonged war. In living beyond its means, the Treasury warned that Britain risked draining the financial war chest (its wealth and its international credit) that it would need to mobilize for war. For this reason, the Treasury Department opposed any measures that translated into an increase in foreign commitments or overseas expenditure, especially imperial expenditure.

In peacetime, the Treasury's priority was to restore Britain's war chest by lowering direct taxes and by repayment to the Sinking Fund.[18] First, the Treasury's ability to levy direct taxes (taxes on income such as rent, profits, or wages) and indirect taxes (taxes on commodities such as alcohol, tea, and tobacco) meant that it could extract immense revenue on short notice. The Treasury opposed new or increased direct taxation for fear that it would leave little room for expansion during wartime. Low peacetime taxation translated into low civil and military expenditure. Second (in peacetime), the Treasury resumed repayment to the Sinking Fund, a debt repayment program.[19] Debt repayment from previous wars to the Sinking Fund ensured that Britain could borrow large sums at relatively low interest rates during a future emergency. Each budget set aside a fixed amount for payments of the interest on past debt and allocated a sum toward the Sinking Fund for the redemption of the principal. The Treasury recognized that failure to meet past responsibilities would damage the nation's credit rating, thereby increasing the cost of borrowing during future crises. In protecting Britain's war chest, there was little room to increase its rate of resource extraction for military spending during peacetime.[20]

The Radicals

Finally, international disarmament was one of the primary goals of the free traders, including the Liberal Party and the Radicals. The Liberal Party favored multilateral agreements to limit armaments in order to lower the costs associated with leadership (Howard 1982, 148). The Radicals "subscribed to the ideal of universal disarmament, friendly relations with all countries, open diplomacy, and the settlement of international disputes by arbitration" (Morris 1971, 367).[21] They called for a new League of Peace and argued that Britain could not expect relatively weaker navies to make the first move toward naval disarmament. Instead, Britain with its naval supremacy would have to make the first steps unilaterally.

Other members of the free-trade bloc included the Foreign Office. Anxious to reduce Britain's commitments in distant parts of the world, the Foreign Secretary tried to remain on good terms with the rising contenders (Steiner 1963, 73–75). The Foreign Office explored the possibilities of negotiations with Germany, France, Japan, Russia, and the United States.

There were some differences of opinion among the members of the liberal coalition. The Treasury regarded the Liberals' social policy as dangerous because it required a constantly rising level of public expenditure, and sooner or later protective tariffs would have to be introduced to pay for their social programs (by 1914 many Unionists again clamored for tariff reform to pay for defense spending). The Treasury also opposed the Liberals' progressive taxation. Their fear was that taxes would harm industry and enterprise, and would undermine Britain's reserves necessary to pay for a major war in the future.

THE SUPPORTERS OF THE ECONOMIC NATIONALIST COALITION

In response to commercial and military challenges from the United States, France, Russia, Germany, and Japan, the economic nationalist coalition called for tariff barriers, imperial preferences (to roll back U.S. and German penetration of the empire), stronger empire links (commercial and military), and increased defense expenditure (revision of the two-power naval standard to a three- or even a four-power standard and a big army) to thwart these competitors. The economic nationalist coalition included inefficient industry, arable agriculture and landowners, state bureaucrats such as the Chamber of Commerce, the military services, supporters of the Conservative Party, and pro-empire organizations and colonial bureaucrats.

Chamberlain and Tariff Reform

Industry hurt by the import penetration of foreign manufactures lobbied for heightened tariff barriers and imperial preferences. The most influential organization in the tariff reform movement was Joseph Chamberlain's Tariff Reform League, established in 1903.[22] Other pro-imperial preference groups included the National Fair Trade League, the Imperial Federation League, the British Empire League, the United Empire Trade League, and the Tariff Commission. Chamberlain's Tariff Reform League consisted of a coalition of industrialists (Birmingham manufactures), metal and engineering trades, the woolen industry, and workers hurt by foreign competition (Ramsden 1978, 6–20; Friedberg 1988, 33–38; Pollard 1989, 235–56). New industries such as glass and chemicals that faced stiff foreign competition also supported Chamberlain's Tariff Reform campaign.[23] Finally, farmers and landowners, who claimed cheap imported food was destroying agriculture, joined the coalition.[24] With the support of the National Agricultural Union, especially wheat growers, farmers sought protection to secure more homegrown food production, emphasizing the national security risk of Britain's dependence on imported food in the event of war. They also called for the national government to establish granaries in which supplies of wheat could be stored in peacetime for use during emergencies.[25]

Economic nationalists called for punishing competitors through the implementation of imperial preferences. Chamberlain's rationale for protectionism included (1) retaliating against European and U.S. protectionism, tariff walls, and trusts that excluded British goods; (2) preventing cheap imports, due to foreign dumping, from destroying Britain's agricultural sector and weakening its industry; and (3) blocking foreign competition from cutting into Britain's traditional overseas markets in Africa, Latin America, and Asia.[26] Tariff reform would combine protection for British industry with imperial preferences and thereby strengthen economic links within the empire. Such a commercial federation would serve national security purposes by ending Britain's dependence on food imported from potentially hostile powers such as Russia.

In 1903, as colonial secretary in the Conservative coalition government, Chamberlain proposed the creation of a system of imperial preferences. Imperial preferences would impose 10 percent import duties on foreign goods, giving an advantage to colonial products, while forging the empire into a single commercial unit.[27] Within the empire there would be free trade (Imperial Free Trade Area or "Imperial Zollverein"), but each member could impose whatever duties seemed suitable on the products of foreign powers. This meant preferential treatment for food imports from the British colonies, while Britain would use the empire as "relief" from international trading competition.[28]

Economic nationalists complained that Britain's clearing and merchant banks, brokerage houses, insurance companies, and investment trusts had a bias toward capital, undermining domestic manufacturing firms.[29] For many economic nationalists, the Bank of England represented the narrow section of overseas finance, and the gold standard policy was intended to advance finance rather than general industry and trade (Williamson 1984). Economic nationalists argued that the export of capital harmed home industry and commerce (Pollard 1985, 489). For this reason, Chamberlain opposed Britain's financial services since foreign loans "promoted the industrialization of the world behind tariff barriers: a process destined to knock Britain's traditional exports out of business" (Skidelsky 1976, 167).

Chamberlain led a double-pronged campaign for tariff reform among the electorate and within the Conservative Party.[30] Among the electorate, tariff reformers promised higher and more stable levels of employment for the working class (Green 1995, 205). Chamberlain claimed that imperial unity would bring both direct and indirect material benefits to the working class such as more regular employment (due to the prosperity of British industry and full employment over cheap imports), higher wages, and old age pensions (French 1982c, 209; Tomlinson 1990, 20). The revenue from tariff reform was also touted as a source of funding for social welfare programs designed to link the working-class voter to the Conservative Party. Without empire unity, Conservatives countered that Britain would be a "fifth ranked nation" lacking the resources to promote social reform (Green 1995, 204). But tariffs would also mean more expensive food.

The Conservative Party

Chamberlain also sought to establish the Conservative Party as the party of empire (Green 1995, 69–77). For Chamberlain, between 1902 and 1906, the tariff campaign offered Conservatives a chance to reestablish their credentials as such a party. The Conservative Party's southern base was increasingly connected with the empire through colonial employment and investment in railways and governments. As a consequence, "the motivations of the leadership of the Tariff Reform League . . . were more empire-minded than often allowed" (Thompson 1997, 1033). The majority of Conservatives feared for the continued safety of the empire, and they demanded stronger measures of national defense, arguing that the agenda of the free-trade coalition was weakening industry at home and in the empire and sapping Britain's military strength. Tariff reform would address these problems by protecting industry while concomitantly generating additional revenue, through tariffs and indirect taxation, to fund the increased defense expenditure. In the 1906 election campaign, the Conservative Party represented the free traders, and especially, the Liberal Party, as utopian internationalists. Balfour campaigned on the fear that a Liberal ministry would forfeit Britain's security in the name of economy (Morris 1971, 378). The implication was that "only Conservatives could be trusted with matters of national and imperial defence" (Green 1995, 203).

Prominent among the Conservative Party membership, the diehards (landed Conservative aristocrats in the House of Lords) were active in organizations designed to promote a big army and navy, national service, and tariff reform.[31] The diehards were fearful of Britain's decline as an economic, military, naval, and imperial power. Their primary concern was what would happen to Great Britain if the Royal Navy ever lost command of the seas. The diehards believed that the free-trade coalition's agenda weakened Britain's defense at a time of great danger of war and the possibility of foreign invasion. The diehards' principal lobbying organization was the National Service League (1902), one of the most militant of the lobbying organizations. They campaigned for compulsory military training to produce a large standing army in the prewar years. Yet the diehards were thwarted by budgetary debates over who would pay for increases in military, administrative, and infrastructural outlays.

Other important lobbying organizations supported by Conservatives and diehards included the Navy League (established in 1895) and the Imperial Maritime League (1908) (Marder 1940, 49–55). The Navy League was convinced that only tariff reform, a big army and navy, and closer imperial unity would ensure Great Britain's place among the great powers.[32] Absent in the rosters of these organizations were members of the free-trade coalition, such as bankers, labor representatives, and members of the leading City houses.

The Military Services

In conjunction with visible exports, the Tariff Reform League, the Conservative Party, and lobbying organizations, many members of the armed services (navy, army) called for increased defense spending to maintain Britain's naval supremacy. The Admiralty was intent on retaining command of the sea. By revising the traditional two-power naval standard to a three- or four-power naval standard, Britain could maintain its command of the high seas and its local supremacy in the Far East, the Mediterranean, and the Americas. The Admiralty warned that failure to increase Britain's military capability would tempt the rising contenders to challenge Britain's empire, sea-lanes of communication, and home defense. In response to the free traders' concern for economy, the Admiralty countered that resources must be found for the navy, since defeat at sea would be far more ruinous than any damage to the economy due to increased government expenditure (Monger 1963, 9–10). After the Agadir crisis (1911), the War Office firmly embraced the ideal of a Continental Commitment. The military was determined that the British Expeditionary Force (BEF) should be sent to France to cooperate with the French army on the Franco-Belgian frontier. In 1913, the Unionists (with one Liberal sponsor) introduced a bill calling for compulsory training to replace voluntary recruiting for the Territorial Army, but faced opposition from both the Liberal and Labor parties (French 1982a, 25).

Economic nationalists capitalized on the fear of invasion to rally popular support for increased expenditure for home and empire defense and imperial preferences. During much of the Boer War (1899–1902) and especially the "Invasion Scare of 1900," economic nationalists fanned the fear that France or Germany would send an invasion fleet across the Channel and that Britain was unprepared to deter such an attack.[33] Economic nationalists used fears about the security of wartime food supplies to persuade the government to introduce tariff reform and closer ties to the empire. The president of the Navy League (the former president of the National Agricultural Union) warned that Britain's dependence on imported food meant that in the event of war, interruption would lead mobs to "take to riot and pillage under the stress of hunger" forcing the government to surrender (French 1982b, 210). Economic nationalists also threatened that a Liberal ministry would sacrifice Britain's security in the name of economy and by 1917 there would be a strong Labour Party in the House of Commons that would refuse to defend the empire.

There were few links between the free-trade and economic nationalist coalitions. No important bankers joined Chamberlain's Tariff Reform League (Longstreth 1979, 162), while the directorate of the Bank of England was dominated by the leading City merchant banks and merchant houses, with few industrialists. Of the thirty-five firms represented on the Board of the Bank of England between 1890 and 1914, thirteen (37 percent) were merchant bankers, seventeen (49 percent) were merchants, and five operated in other spheres (Pollard 1989, 245). When the Treasury called on outside experts, this usually involved people from the City or ex-chancellors of the Exchequer (Tomlinson 1990, 34). Industrialists distrusted the Bank of England's freedom of action, calling for a new central bank with purely administrative control, lower interest rates, a politically managed low exchange rate to enhance export competitiveness, and a "National Investment Bank" to bypass City markets.[34]

A TAILORED RESPONSE

The agendas of the economic nationalist and free-trade coalitions clashed on the key issues facing Britain such as naval construction and army reform, trade protection and imperial preferences, finances, international arms reduction agreements, and the empire. The commercial nature of the rising contenders guided Britain's grand strategy toward cooperation. Free-trade constituents, such as efficient export-oriented industry, fiscal conservatives, and invisible exporters, pressed for cooperating with liberal contenders. Many free traders had a commitment to a strong navy to protect shipping and trade, and thereby joined with economic nationalists such as the military, inefficient industry and agriculture, and pro-empire organizations in punishing imperial contenders (Smith 1991, 30). Yet, free traders moderated the extreme economic and military programs of the economic nationalists for reasons of economy and for fear of strengthening the opposing coalition, who would pressure for a more belligerent grand strategy. Many in the City were especially concerned that tension and hostility spirals would trigger a financial crisis, which would threaten orthodoxy, result in gold flight, and lead to new or increased tariffs to raise revenue. The domestic consequences from cooperation reinforced the strength of many members of the free-trade faction, while further rolling back the constituents of the economic nationalists. As Cain and Hopkins (1993b, 111) note, "Arable agriculture was the first outstanding victim of Britain's mid-century commitment to the international division of labour, one momentous consequence of which was the decline in the wealth and influence of the landed aristocracy who had hitherto been the dominant component of gentlemanly capitalism." Free traders used the distributional gains from cooperation to further broaden and strengthen its domestic supporters.

IMPERIAL FRANCE AND RUSSIA: THE NORTH SEA, THE MEDITERRANEAN, CENTRAL ASIA, AND THE FAR EAST

Russia and France were the first entrants to challenge Britain's hegemony, encroaching on London's position in its home waters in the North Sea, the Mediterranean, Central Asia, and the Far East. In Britain's home waters and in the Mediterranean, beginning in 1888, both Russia and France launched new naval construction programs. In 1891, the two powers agreed to an entente that stopped just short of a military alliance. In 1894, the two powers formed the Dual Alliance, a formal military alliance. The Admiralty projected that this naval combination would cause Britain's naval superiority over France and Russia in 1894 of five first-class battleships to fall in 1895–96 to mere equality, drop behind in 1896–97 by two, and plummet by seven first-class battleships in 1897–98 (Marder 1940, 191).

In the Far East, Russia reinforced its position in 1898 by leasing ice-free

Port Arthur for its expanding Far Eastern squadron and by sending battleships from its Baltic Fleet, further raising the specter of a partition of China. In addition to Russia's naval expansion, in 1887 Russia began to survey for a Trans-Siberian railway, inaugurating construction in 1891. Britain estimated that the Trans-Siberian Railway could deliver 35,000 reinforcing troops each month. In 1896, Russia secured the right to construct the Chinese Eastern, which would link the Russian Trans-Siberian Railroad to Vladivostok. Instead of following the more difficult but all-Russian route (along the Amur River), Russia annexed the northern part of Manchuria allowing Russia to shorten its route and to facilitate its penetration into Manchuria, where British trading interests were paramount.

In Central Asia, in 1895, in the aftermath of the Russo-British crisis, Russia extended the Trans-Caspian Railway along the Afghanistan border to Tashkent, threatening India.[35] In 1901, Russia began construction on a railroad line that would connect Orenburg to Tashkent. When completed in 1904, Russian railheads would be within 400 miles of Kabul, greatly increasing India's vulnerability to an overland attack and diplomatic blackmail. Britain estimated that Russia could transport as many as 60,000 men in one month and 200,000 within four months.

The Naval Defence Act and the Spencer Act

London's response to these challenges was a mixed strategy of punishment, in the form of the Naval Defence Act of 1889 and the Spencer Act of 1894, and cooperation, in the form of the Anglo-French Entente (1904) and the Anglo-Russian Agreement (1907). In the Naval Defence Act, the First Lord of the Admiralty, George Hamilton, formally called for Britain to maintain a two-power standard, or a navy "at least equal to the naval strength of any two other countries" (Marder 1940, 106). For Hamilton, the two-power standard was based on modern battleships, but extended to first-class cruisers too.

The navalists convinced the government that the best way to protect Britain and its empire was to maintain a two-power standard as an absolute minimum. Britain's Admiralty argued that by building more ships than France and Russia's combined naval programs, and by building them faster, the Naval Defence Act (1889) and the Spencer Act (1894) would discourage the naval aspirations of these rising states, and also deter future naval challenges.[36] The Naval Defence Act would bring Britain's fleet up to a two-power standard by constructing ten battleships, forty-two cruisers, and eighteen torpedo-gunboats over five years, at a cost of 21.5 million pounds (Marder 1940, 143). As Hamilton noted, "If there are any nations abroad who do wish to compete with us in naval armaments, the mere enunciation of this scheme will show to them the utter futility of their desire" (Sumida 1989, 15). In 1894, under First Lord of the Admiralty John Spencer, Britain enacted another five-year naval program authorized by the Spencer Act. The Spencer Act, which approved the construction of seven first-class battleships, six second-class cruisers, and thirty-six destroyers to be completed by 1899, would "show once and for all that such competition was futile" (Marder 1940, 204). Proponents of a bigger navy rationalized that in deterring current and future naval challengers, these expensive naval programs would save money by allowing Britain to reduce its naval spending in the long run.

The navalists were joined by London's financial interests, who supported punishing France and Russia through increased naval construction (Smith 1991, 36–42), while ship owners feared that in the event of war, trade would be entrusted to ships sailing under neutral flags. The City of London was concerned about the Royal Navy's ability to inspire commercial confidence—to protect overseas shipping (especially supplies of vital foodstuffs and raw materials), commerce, and colonies against imperial France and Russia—even though their support strengthened members of the opposing economic nationalist faction. The danger was that if Russia consolidated its power in the Far East, and its power would be immense after the completion of the Trans-Siberian Railroad, it could close the open door at will (LaFeber 1963, 322). The government turned to the City to broker the loan for the Naval Defence Act. Reflecting the rise in the political influence of invisible exporters (and the relative demise of the aristocracy), to pay for the naval increase, the chancellor of the Exchequer rejected a registration tax on imports and exports, a tax on the activity of the Stock Exchange, and a tax on shipping tonnage. Instead, in 1889, the chancellor taxed the landed interests in the form of an estate duty (Smith 1991, 40).

With the support of free traders, the Liberal government (1892–95) moderated the size of the Spencer Act, authorizing construction of seven battleships (Friedberg 1988, 156). The chancellor of the Exchequer, George Goschen, argued the case for frugality, challenging fleet expansion. Prime Minister Gladstone supported a "little navy" since foreign powers would regard an increase in the naval Estimates as an act of defiance (Marder 1940, 196–205). Gladstone resigned from the government (1894) in opposition because he believed the increase would lead to an arms race and ultimately to financial disaster.

The Liberal government was replaced in 1895 by the Conservative Unionist Administration, which ordered additional battleship construction beyond the Spencer Act. Economic nationalists such as the Navy League doubted the adequacy of even this additional construction in the face of the Franco-Russian menace. By October 1902, the Admiralty hedged upward the two-power standard to a formula of "equality plus a margin" over the next two strongest naval powers.[37] Such a goal could only be achieved by laying down three battleships in each of the fiscal years from 1903–4 to 1906–7. In support of Selborne's naval proposals, Joseph Chamberlain called for Britain to build five ships for "any three battleships built by any naval combination against this country" (Friedberg 1988, 155).[38] The sinking of the Russian fleet in the Straits of Tsushima (1904) meant that Russia sank into fourth place among the naval powers, and that France and Germany were the world's second and third strongest naval powers. Many free traders clamored that the two-power standard might soon become obsolete. Yet Selborne countered, "It is an error to suppose that the two Power standard . . . has ever had reference only to France and Russia" (Williams 1991, 74).

Free traders denounced the high level of defense expenditure as leading "straight to financial ruin" (Sumida 1989, 23). Successive chancellors of the Exchequer, including Hicks Beach, C. T. Ritchie, and Austin Chamberlain, pressed for cooperation with the contenders based on the need for economy and, especially, the need for a reduction in military and naval Estimates. Sir Michael Hicks Beach (1895–1902) opposed an increase in the two-power standard, arguing that Britain could ill afford to keep pace with the naval construction of three emerging states without undermining its fiscal strength. His rationale was that no more revenue could be extracted from an already overburdened populace and that Britain's financial problems would not end with the conclusion of the costly fighting in South Africa. In a letter to Selborne in January 1901, he warned that "I would never undertake the impossible task of building against more than two principal naval powers" (Boyce 1990, 107). Later in the same year he cautioned that the possibility of a tax being raised above the wartime level "could not be borne" (Monger 1963, 9). Liberals supported the goals of the 1899 Hague Conference to discuss disarmament and peace, including naval force limitations for a fixed period, which met stiff resistance from Conservatives and navalists (Marder 1940, 341–43).

The Foreign Office, led by Marquess of Lansdowne, and later by Sir Edward Grey, aligned with the chancellor of the Exchequer to reduce the cost of hegemony. The foreign secretary approached each of the contenders to reduce hostilities, including Germany, France, Russia, the United States, and Japan alone or in combination with other powers (Monger 1963; Steiner 1977). The foreign secretary was cautious to ensure against being dragged into a war by a new partner.

France's Shift in Foreign Commercial Policy (1904): The Entente Cordiale

By the turn of the century, Britain increasingly viewed France as a rising satisfied power. In 1902, France capitulated in its naval challenge; France's naval minister, Camille Pelletan, ended the naval race with Britain (Marder 1940, 470–72; Rock 1989, 99–100). Pelletan ordered a halt to the construction of battleships, canceled fleet maneuvers, cut the Mediterranean fleet, and suspended work on the modernization of out-of-date battleships.[39] In the aftermath, Britain and France began to negotiate the Anglo-French Agreement of 1904. One of the conditions of the Anglo-French entente, which recognized French predominance in Morocco, was the protection of British trade rights in the region.[40]

Economic nationalists such as the Board of Admiralty, Director of Naval Intelligence, and the War Office opposed the entente with France (Monger 1963, 130–33). The Service Departments argued that the entente weakened Britain's position since London would have to rely on Paris to protect Britain's interests along the strategic Moroccan coast, the entryway into the Mediterranean Sea. The prospect of a French base on the Moroccan coast within easy striking distance of Gibraltar and the Straits was alarming enough (Williamson 1969, 8). Of greater concern, the Conservative government and navalists correctly foresaw the free traders' demand to exempt France from the two-power standard (Wilson 1981, 33–34; Williams 1991, 75). Doing so would mean a reformulation of the basis of Britain's shipbuilding, entailing a real diminution of naval strength.

To the dismay of the economic nationalists, the entente was intended to remove all outstanding sources of friction and reduce Britain's naval presence in the Mediterranean. British financiers also emphasized the financial risks of Anglo-French hostility. Large French holdings in short-term British assets could be withdrawn from England, causing the price of sterling to fall, pushing up interest rates, and even causing some danger of financial collapse (Rock 1989, 116). Closer relations would avert such a scenario, while providing French support of the pound during times of financial weakness. In 1906 and 1907, the Bank of France lent the Bank of

England reserves to counter the effects of heavy withdrawals of gold from London. Radicals supported the entente because it represented the first step toward a greater union of nations and the "end of that Imperialist spirit which caused such bitter enmity between the two nations" (Weinroth 1970, 657). The extension of the Anglo-French Agreement to include additional states such as Russia and Germany would ensure international stability.

The 1907 Anglo-Russian Entente in Central Asia

The rivalry in Central Asia represented a conflict between a sea power (Britain) and a land power (Russia). To defend India, the India Office, the War Office, the Viceroy of India, and the Government of India proposed significant army reinforcements. The original Estimates of 100,000 reservists were raised to 143,000, and by 1905 the estimate was 158,000 reservists. The number of camels alone needed to transport supplies exceeded 5 million (Mahajan 1982, 175; Yapp 1987, 663–64; Gooch 1994, 288). Economic nationalists also called for the construction of an extensive railway system ensuring that any conflict with Russia occurred beyond the Indian frontier (Monger 1963, 95–96).

After 1906, the Liberal government with the support of the free traders opposed the anti-Russian strategy in Central Asia, favoring an agreement to check Russian expansion (Williams 1966, 368–69). Pledging economy and military retrenchment, the Liberal government preferred to negotiate with Russia rather than to prepare against it, diminishing the risk of war while furthering international cordiality. As a naval power, the Liberal government never considered it financially feasible to deter the Russian "steamroller" through solely military means. The City championed the rapprochement with the czar because it would facilitate financial investments in Russia, while protecting Britain's commercial and financial interests in Persia. As well, a large percentage of French capital was tied up in Russia, making the French financial sector dependent upon the continued health and stability of the czarist regime. Weakening the czarist regime would have an impact on the financial markets of France and hence Britain (Rock 1989, 114–15). Through an Anglo-French loan in 1906, intended to encourage a liberal turn in Russia's internal development, Britain hoped to strengthen Russian liberals.[41] Meanwhile, a loan of 2.225 billion francs from France to Russia was floated almost exclusively by the City of London (Rock 1989, 115).

In opposing the War Office's proposal for an increased troop buildup and an expensive railway to transport the troops to the frontiers of Afghanistan, Britain could only restrain Russian expansion through concessions, resulting in the 1907 Anglo-Russian Entente. The objective of the Anglo-Russian agreement was to check Russia's advance to India and the Gulf. The entente settled a number of colonial disputes but contained no special assurances of friendship or cooperation and did not devolve regional hegemony (unlike Britain's cooperation with the United States, Japan, and France). For free traders, the newly established relationship would facilitate the City's financial investments in Russia and promote international cordiality (Weinroth 1970, 665–66). The Radicals favored the Convention because it "diminished very sensibly the risks of a European war" (666), while economic nationalists complained bitterly that Britain had conceded too much in Persia for too little and that a lasting settlement with imperial Russia was impossible.[42]

LIBERAL UNITED STATES: THE HAY-PAUNCEFOTE TREATY

In 1901, Britain ceded leadership over the Western Hemisphere to the United States with the signing of the Hay-Pauncefote Treaty.[43] As J. A. S. Grenville notes, "The signature of the Hay-Pauncefote Treaty in 1901 marked—and the British cabinet was in no doubt about this—the conscious British recognition of the eventual United States supremacy in the Western Hemisphere and thus entailed a fundamental change in the relations of the two countries" (1955, 48).[44] In the Clayton-Bulwer Treaty (1850) the United States and Britain agreed that neither state would build an isthmian canal exclusive of the other, nor limit the navigation rights of other powers in such a canal nor fortify it. The Hay-Pauncefote Treaty revised this agreement by granting the United States the exclusive right to build, operate, and defend an isthmian canal, resulting in a major reinterpretation of the two-power standard (Williams 1991, 71).

Revision of the Clayton-Bulwer Treaty was unanimously opposed by the army and the navy chiefs for strategic reasons (Grenville 1955, 51–52, 66–67; Bourne 1967, 342–51). Both countered that the construction of the canal would impair Britain's naval supremacy by allowing the United States to "transfer its ships quickly from one Ocean to the other," giving Washington an immense advantage in an Anglo-American war (PRO, Adm. 1/7550A, 12/31/00). Other members of the economic nationalist coalition favored blocking the export of British investment capital to the United States because it facilitated the growth of foreign competition in

Britain's home market and its empire. The Colonial Office, the West India Committee, and members of the CID (Committee of Imperial Defence, established in 1902 to coordinate policy among departments) resisted the reduction and elimination of garrisons in Canada and the West Indies, calling for the retention of troops at Bermuda, Jamaica, St. Luca, and Halifax (Wells 1968, 339).

On economic grounds, free traders such as the Board of Trade favored the revised treaty and the construction project (PRO, FO. 55/392, 1/3/1899). Their rationale was that the canal would benefit Britain more than any other country (including the United States) due to the magnitude of its overseas trade. Specifically, they estimated that 60 percent of shipping passing through the canal would fly the British flag (Grenville 1955, 52). For English financiers, stable Anglo-American relations were vital since the United States was a profitable outlet for surplus British capital. English capital was an essential component in the early development of U.S. industry, especially the construction of its vast railroad network. In 1899, British investors held about $2.5 billion in U.S. stocks and bonds or 75 percent of the U.S. securities in foreign hands (Rock 1989, 45).

Free traders, including the Foreign Office, recognized that by relying on the United States to protect British interests against hostile European powers, London could withdraw from Central America and the Caribbean, thereby lowering its defense expenditures (Bourne 1967, 350). As one author notes, "Britain was finding the cost of maintaining a two-power standard navy too great, and since the United States also wanted to keep the oceans open for trade and had no rival territorial ambitions, the control of some seas could be left to the U.S. navy" (Mackintosh 1969, 249). London could redistribute naval and army forces from colonial garrisons in the Caribbean Sea (Barbados, Trinidad, Bermuda, and Jamaica) and Canada (Halifax, Esquimalt, and the Great Lakes) to its home waters and the Mediterranean and in so doing strengthen its immediate military capability without extracting additional resources for defense. Indirectly, this treaty accelerated America's naval ascent by allowing Washington to shift fleets from one ocean to another (especially the Pacific, which might prove a counterweight to Russian pressure) (Bourne 1967, 350).

Free traders opposed punishing the United States because they feared an unnecessary and costly hostility spiral of duties and counterduties. Such a spiral would weaken the invisible services and disrupt the close commercial and financial connections that existed between Great Britain and the United States, while enhancing the economic nationalists.

LIBERAL JAPAN: THE ANGLO-JAPANESE ALLIANCE

In the Far East, free traders pursued an Anglo-German naval agreement, an Anglo-German-Japanese agreement, an Anglo-Russian agreement, and an Anglo-Japanese Alliance (Monger 1963; Steiner 1977). In 1902, with the failure of the former, Britain and Japan signed the Anglo-Japanese Alliance, devolving leadership over the Pacific to Japan (Nish 1966). The objectives of the alliance were "the integrity of China, the maintenance of the open door, and equal opportunity throughout the Empire."[45] The Anglo-Japanese Alliance entrusted Japan with the preservation of naval security in the northeast Pacific, while the British fleet continued to safeguard the sea routes to Australia and New Zealand and to protect British interests in Hong Kong and Singapore. During World War I, the foreign secretary, Lord Curzon, admitted, "I suppose it is not to be denied that our alliance with her [Japan], and the assistance of her naval forces, assured the complete safety of our possessions in the Pacific" (Barnett 1972, 252).

Economic nationalists attacked the stance that Britain could rely on Japan or the United States to defend its national interests (Monger 1963, 310). The Board of the Admiralty argued that "as the responsible naval advisers of the Government, [the Admiralty] cannot base their plans upon the shifting sands of any temporary and unofficial international relationships."[46]

For free-trade constituents, there were many benefits of entering into a naval alliance with Japan (Nish 1985, 11–14). These included allowing Britain to maintain a local naval supremacy over the Dual Alliance in the Far East, while reducing its Far Eastern naval station; checking imperial Russia's expansion; maintaining the open door in China; and expanding trade with Japan, Britain's new ally.[47] The City of London played a central role in the formation of the alliance due to the complementarity between Japan's industrialization and the City's export trade of capital goods and services (Nish 1966, 11–13). Since the 1870s, Britain had been the leading exporter of capital goods to the Japanese market and was the first country to replace its "unequal treaty" with Japan in 1894. In 1897, Japan adopted the gold standard, cementing the Anglo-Japanese financial relations and dependency on the City of London for government loans. Free traders were eager to see Britain's ally receive all the financial support it needed in order to encourage Japan's industrial development (Kynaston 1995, 349–50). According to Shigeru Akita (1996, 52), "the interest of the City of London played an important role in setting out an economic and political framework under which it [Japanese industrialization] took place." The assumption was that "the more Japanese cotton industries developed and construction of railways progressed, the more British machinery and railway materials tended to be imported" despite the competition to British merchants (53).

For British investors, the Anglo-Japanese Alliance provided a sense of safety for their investment of Japanese loans and for the emerging Anglo-Japanese financial relationship (Akita 1996, 57). The alliance was supported by British financiers such as the London consortium or the London Group (Parr's Bank, Yokohama Specie Bank, Hong Kong Shanghai Bank) who facilitated Japanese government loan issues and who advanced loans to Tokyo at good rates (Warner 1991, 46–61; Akita 1996, 56). The Bank of England also gave the City considerable assistance in supplying Japan with money.[48]

In addition to promoting Japan's industrialization, Britain accelerated Japan's naval ascendance to assure that Tokyo could assume greater regional responsibility, to the consternation of the economic nationalists. This was accomplished through construction of much of the Imperial Navy in British shipyards and by British loans. The City of London also floated five huge war loans for the Japanese government during the Russo-Japanese War.

While supportive of the objectives of the alliance (territorial status quo and Open Door policy in China) and with economy in mind, Sir Michael Hicks Beach, the chancellor of the Exchequer, and some liberal free traders criticized the military pact on several points. Their concern was that an alliance against Russia might provoke a costly tension spiral, contributing to a counterbalancing Far Eastern Triplice (France, Russia, Germany) or encouraging Japanese forwardness (Weinroth 1970, 654–55). For reasons of economy, free traders such as the Treasury preferred improved relations with each of these states rather than a treaty against them (Steiner 1959, 32).

Renewal of the Anglo-Japanese Alliance

In 1905, the Anglo-Japanese treaty was renewed and expanded to include as a *casus belli* an attack by any one power on the "Asiatic possessions" of either Japan or Britain.[49] The extension of the treaty with Japan solved the problem of Britain's inability to defend India in the instance of a Russian invasion. As part of the renewal of the Anglo-Japanese Alliance,

Japan agreed to commit 100,000 troops to the defense of India and the adjacent territories as well. There was even talk of inviting America to join.[50] While the government of India and the War Office resisted the idea of Japanese troops operating on the North-West Frontier, for free traders the renewal and extension of the treaty meant reductions in the army. The War Office feared that "drastic reductions [in the army] would be 'greatly augmented' if a Radical government believed it could rely in war upon an unlimited supply of Japanese troops" (Williams 1991, 79). Yet, Sir George Clarke commented that Britain would "pull off another great coup" by getting Japan to assume some responsibly for the defense of India (Neilson 1991, 717).

The ramification of retrenchment in the Americas and the Far East was a drastic reduction in military spending. Austin Chamberlain, the chancellor of the Exchequer (1903–6), exacted further concessions from Arnold-Forester, the secretary of state for war, and Selborne, for leaner defense budgets. Chamberlain warned both services, "In my opinion, they [reductions] must be sought in both the Army and Navy Estimates. Neither alone will be sufficient; and however reluctant we may be to face the fact, the time has come when we must frankly admit that the financial resources of the United Kingdom are inadequate to do all that we should desire in the matter of Imperial defense."[51] In 1904–5, the army cost 31.6 million pounds, and by 1905–6 this amount had been reduced to 29.1 million pounds and continued to decline until 1913–14 (Sumida 1989, table 15). Savings resulted from withdrawal of a number of colonial garrisons between 1904 and 1906 (West Indies, Bermuda, Canada), reducing British forces in Canada, and a cap on Britain's defense spending in India.[52]

More drastically, beginning in 1904, Britain underwent a second round of reductions in naval spending, evoking loud protests from the Navy League, the military members of the CID, and even the commanders in chief of far-flung naval stations such as China who argued that the free traders were letting down Britain's guard, resulting in complacency (Marder 1940, 483–514; Williams 1991, 64–65). Selborne and his First Sea Lord, John Fisher, reduced naval expenditures by creating a smaller and less expensive fleet and by scrapping obsolete ships (known as the Fisher Reforms).[53] This savings was accomplished by implementing four reforms: creation of a nucleus crew system, the redistribution and further concentration of fleets in home waters (which was aided by the telegraph and faster ships) to meet current needs (which had been going on since

1901), the decommission of ships of minimal fighting value (scrapping 154 ships), and the introduction of the all-big-gun battleship and battle cruiser (Williams 1991). In the aftermath of the Fisher naval reforms, Britain's naval Estimates declined every year from 1904–5 to 1909–10, falling from 41 million pounds in 1904–5 to a low of 32.7 million in 1907–8, not surpassing the 1904–5 level until 1910–11.[54] Expenditures on battleships and cruisers fell from 10 million in 1904–5 to a low of 6.9 million in 1908–9, not reaching a new high until 1912–13 (Sumida 1989, table 8).

IMPERIAL GERMANY

As early as 1902 and perhaps as late as 1906, Germany challenged Britain in the North Sea. London's initial concern was that German naval construction would hold the maritime balance between the British and Franco-Russian fleets (Ropp 1962, 212; Kennedy 1980, 251). John Lambelet contends that "there is good evidence that initially the British authorities did not take Germany's plans seriously and did not realize that the Germans meant what they said, until some time between 1903 and 1906" (1974, 2). Arthur Marder has found no evidence that the German threat caused any modification of British plans before 1904. Marder maintains that Britain's 1904 fleet distribution was a sign of changes in technology and that a "redistribution of British naval strength was long overdue" since it had been "determined in the sailing-ship era when sea voyages were long" (1940, 491). New armored cruisers with greater speed meant that ships did not need to be distributed widely across the globe, while modern telegraph systems meant that ships could be instantly signaled to steam toward a region.

Shortly after entering office in 1906, with the support of many free traders, radicals, and the "economists," the Liberal government pushed for improved relations with Germany to enable the government to cut expenditures without endangering Britain's naval superiority. Between 1906 and 1908, free traders made substantial reductions in naval expenditures, while resisting economic nationalist taunts to engage Germany in an arms race and tariff retaliation. By 1912, many free traders retreated from their call for cooperation, siding with moderate economic nationalists in their support for increased naval Estimates (Howard 1982, 147).

Reflecting their cause for economy and military retrenchment, the Liberal government redefined the two-power standard. After 1904, France and Germany were the world's second and third strongest naval powers.

With the growing amity of France, Prime Minister Campbell-Bannerman diluted the two-power standard. He called for a naval standard that would secure Britain not against any combination of powers, but against "any reasonable combination" (Williams 1991, 93). To further reduce defense expenditures, Asquith renounced the use of Defence Loans Acts that allowed the government to borrow to pay for long-term defense projects during peace. He argued that they encouraged "crude, precipitate, and wasteful experiments" by defense departments (Peden 1991, 23). Economic nationalists bemoaned excluding France, since it would destroy the two-power standard, forcing an immediate reduction in British naval strength.[55] Lord Tweedmouth, the First Lord of the Admiralty, insisted that the entente with France was temporary (Monger 1963, 311–12). The prime minister's reply was that "France + Germany is a myth" (313). By April 1909, conceding defeat, the Admiralty unofficially based its policy on a standard of equality with Germany plus a margin of 60 percent (Germany and the United States were the two next strongest naval powers and were viewed as unlikely allies) (Robbins 1977, 19; Sumida 1989, 191). This policy was officially adopted in March 1912, replacing the two-power standard.

The German Navy Law amendment of 1907 shortened the life span of German battleships, resulting in a faster tempo of naval construction. In response to the German naval challenge, the Liberal government's Estimates called for three battleships in 1907–8 and only two battleships in 1908–9, departing from the 1905 Cawdor naval program of constructing four battleships annually (Monger 1963, 310; Morris 1971, 379). The Liberal cabinet postponed the building of one further battleship from the 1907–8 Estimates as a goodwill gesture toward the forthcoming Hague Peace Conference of 1907 (and promised to drop the battleship if the Conference was successful), hoping that it would produce an international agreement on naval arms limitation.[56]

Anxious to avoid an international naval race, free traders focused on improving relations with Berlin. London bankers financed Germany's booming industries and its foreign trade (which economic nationalists countered pressed heavily on certain British industries). They argued that tension between the two countries would result in the collapse of British banks (Kennedy 1983, 95). For free traders, the solution was to strengthen exporters in Germany, who were also complaining of the tension in Anglo-German relations, and who would press the government in Berlin for improvements (Steiner 1977). Meanwhile, Radicals pointed toward the electoral gains of the Social Democrats and the antiwar elements that would stem Germany's foreign policy. They believed that "the fortunes of the anti-war elements were on the upgrade; whether they secured control of the Reischstag or not, their enhanced numerical force promised to stem the tide of German aggressiveness" (Weinroth 1970, 663). Free traders also criticized economic nationalists for exaggerating the naval threat to panic the cabinet, doubting the likelihood that Germany could fulfill its target construction for each year.[57] The chancellor of the Exchequer, Lloyd George, dismissed the economic nationalists dire projections of German strength, scoffing, "I believe the Admiralty are procuring false information to frighten us" (Williams 1991, 157). Free traders were correct in their doubt of the navalist claims on German naval construction. As Howard notes, "By 1912 the German navy had, not 21 dreadnoughts, not 17, not even 13, but only 9, with the British riding high with a comfortable total of 15" (1982, 156–57).

Spurred on by the German Supplementary Law of 1908, the Conservatives and their navalist supporters clamored for at least eight battleships for the building program of 1909–10, and even more for 1910–11. The Board of Admiralty and the First Lord of the Admiralty, Reginald McKenna, called for a minimum of six dreadnoughts in the former period. They warned that failure to increase the tempo of naval construction would give Germany a naval lead by 1912. Challenging the unofficial 60 percent standard, the Sea Lords, diehards, Imperial Maritime League, National Service League, and Tariff Reform League reiterated their earlier demands for a new and upwardly revised "two-keels-to-one" standard over Germany (Williams 1991, 175). The Navy League, with the support of the First Sea Lord, Fisher, demanded, "we want eight and we won't wait" (Schmidt 1986a, 36). They opposed the free traders' repeated calls for international arms limitation agreements because negotiations signaled British naval weakness at home and abroad.

In response to the German Supplementary Law of 1908, the Liberal administration, the chancellor of the Exchequer (David Lloyd George, who also stressed the need for rapprochement with Germany), and President of the Board of Trade (Winston Churchill, who also agreed that the German challenge was much exaggerated) favored building only four battleships, not six or eight.[58] Determined to avoid unnecessary naval expenditures, Lloyd George and Asquith called for a compromise solution of the construction of four dreadnoughts to be built immediately and four more if Germany attained such a level of construction.[59]

Eager to achieve a relaxation in the naval competition, the free traders' solution to a costly naval program was an Anglo-German naval agreement. Free traders engaged in several attempts to secure a naval arms control agreement, despite the heavy criticism from economic nationalists. For the 1907 Hague Conference, the Radicals advanced a plan that would limit expenditure on armaments for five years, and at the very minimum a naval truce (Germany refused to discuss the question of naval disarmament) (Morris 1971, 376). One Radical critique of Britain's approaches to Germany was that London called for a cessation of naval competition when it enjoyed a preponderance of battleships and had just invented the dreadnought with its superior firepower, armor, and speed (Morris 1971, 372, 384; Weinroth 1971, 102–4). Instead, Britain's naval supremacy meant that London had to take unilateral steps toward disarmament.

Other attempts at the limitation of armaments included the Grey mission of 1909–10 and the Haldane mission of 1912 (Kennedy 1980, 451–52). Britain even called for a "holiday" from the Anglo-German Naval Race to reduce their antagonism with the goal of easing the burden of naval expenditures. According to John Maurer (1992), an informal agreement on naval armaments (reciprocal restraint) was reached after 1912, dampening the naval arms race and reducing the burden of military expenditures. It was based on an agreement of a 10:16 German-British naval ratio.[60] Yet London refused to pay the Kaiser's price of a naval holiday, which was a pledge of neutrality in the event of a Continental war (Robbins 1977, 18). Navalists responded, "Our disarmament crusade has been the best advertisement of the German Navy League and every German has by now been persuaded that England is exhausted, has reached the end of her tether and must speedily collapse if the pressure is kept up" (Steiner 1977, 49).

In 1912, further lowering the cost of hegemony, Winston Churchill, the new First Lord of the Admiralty (1911–15), publicly announced the government's commitment to maintaining a 60 percent margin of superiority over Germany's existing dreadnought program. This fleet program meant that if Germany increased its battleship construction, Britain's would outstrip the German naval effort. As Churchill wrote, "Nothing, in my opinion, would more surely dishearten Germany, than the certain proof that as the result of all her present and prospective efforts she will only be more hopelessly behindhand" (Maurer 1992, 103). Hard-line economic nationalist critics argued that maintaining such a margin left the navy unable to fulfill its role of defender of Britain's global imperial interests, especially in light of continued expansion of the Austrian and Italian fleets.

The German Navy Laws of 1912 and 1913 increased further the size of the German fleet and its war readiness. Many free traders retreated from their earlier support for naval retrenchment, siding with the more moderate economic nationalists in their support for increases in the 1912–13 and 1913–14 naval Estimates. In the remaining two years before the war, Britain completed twelve additional dreadnoughts and ten capital ships while Germany built nine dreadnoughts and six capital ships.[61] In 1914, free traders and economic nationalists reached a compromise calling for the passage of the 1914–15 naval Estimates in return for promises of cuts in the 1915–16 Estimates.

LIBERAL FRANCE: THE ANGLO-FRENCH NAVAL AGREEMENT

In 1912, Winston Churchill announced the Anglo-French naval agreement with great support from economy-minded free traders who had lobbied for a further reorganization and redistribution of British naval forces. The Anglo-French naval agreement transferred leadership over the eastern Mediterranean to France, allowing Britain to concentrate its Mediterranean fleet in the North Sea and the upper reaches of the Channel. Devolution meant Britain could maintain its naval supremacy in its home waters while ensuring its commercial and imperial interests in the Mediterranean.

Many economic nationalists, including navalists and the War Office, rallied against the Anglo-French naval agreement. They disliked the prospect of dependence on France and lamented the loss of British influence in the Mediterranean (Lee 1971, 277; Robbins 1977, 19; Williams 1991, 277). A former First Lord of the Admiralty (McKenna) countered that "our colonies and our trade will depend not on British power, but on French goodwill" (Kennedy 1976, 268). Economic nationalists favored more battleships, calling for the construction of a new battleship squadron in the Mediterranean, regardless of the cost (Williamson 1969, 277). One Admiralty memo claimed: "Ten more British dreadnoughts laid down in 1912–13 would make the British position secure in both home waters and the Mediterranean from 1915 onwards without extraneous help" (Williamson 1969, 268). While free traders would never assent to such a program, successful Admiralty lobbying meant that Britain would maintain a battle fleet equal to a one-power standard in the Mediterranean, excluding France (Robbins 1977, 19–20).

For free traders, the Anglo-French Entente was the "cheapest, simplest and safest solution" (Williamson 1969, 270).[62] Opposing the high level of defense expenditure, free traders undermined the economic nationalists' illusion of receiving the necessary funding to maintain a two-power standard in the Mediterranean (Italy and Austria) and a 60 percent margin against Germany. Some free traders opposed the Anglo-French Entente for fear it might be transformed into a binding commitment to assist France in wartime. Their concern was that an Anglo-French alliance would result in a costly conscript army and threaten Germany by hemming it in (Robbins 1977, 6).

DISTRIBUTIONAL CONSEQUENCES

Members of the free-trade coalition were able to use the economic and political distributional gains from cooperation to expand their domestic clout, while undercutting the supporters of the economic nationalists. For the economic nationalists, the expansion of world trade and the rise in British exports of goods, capital, and services proved counterproductive to their campaign. Free traders diverted to the working class the sustained gains from robust trade activity and export performance (after 1900), record volumes of lending, investment, and capital exports (which reached new heights between 1910 and 1913), and the peace dividends from the reduced cost of empire and economies at the War Office and Admiralty. By advancing their agenda of social legislation and reform, the free-trade coalition further expanded their base of support among the working and middle classes for freer trade policies and openness of the economy. Free traders lobbied effectively for increased government spending on social services, health, education, pensions, and insurance. As George Monger quips, "Old Age Pensions were financed by the *entente cordiale*" (1963, 313).

The social reforms advanced by the free-trade coalition included the 1909 noncontributing Old Age Pensions Act, the 1909 discriminatory and redistributive tax system, and the 1911 National Insurance and Unemployment Act (Peden 2000, 56–63). The 1909 Old Age Pensions Act reduced the heavy burden on working-class families for caring for the old. The National Insurance Act (1911) provided for state-supervised contributory insurance schemes against ill health for wage earners and against unemployment for some trades most subject to fluctuations in the trade cycle.

Increased social and defense spending reached a head in Prime Minister Lloyd George's "People's Budget" of 1909, prompting two debates between the opposing coalitions. For most Conservatives, the answer to the revenue shortage was an end to free trade. They advocated stiff tariffs as a new source of revenue. For Liberals, tariff reform was rejected as a way to finance social welfare reform given their commitment to freer trade. A second debate ensued on the limits of tolerable taxation for particular groups of taxpayers (Emy 1972, 106–9, 112–13). Liberal politicians argued that the bulk of increased taxation should be borne by the wealthy, not the middle class. Liberals called for Britain to reduce or abolish indirect taxes and to increase direct taxation to meet higher levels of government expenditure for social programs. In addition to increases in direct taxation, they called for a graduated income tax, the differentiation between earned and unearned incomes, and the taxation of land values, all directed at the wealthy. Conservative politicians argued that direct taxes should be kept as low as possible, instead preferring indirect taxation as the main source of revenue. Even Sir Robert Giffen, who claimed Britain could sustain higher levels of government expenditure, called for increased indirect, rather than direct, taxation (Murray 1980, 22–23).

To meet an estimated deficit, the People's Budget raised direct taxes rather than indirect taxes through an income tax and by levying a new tax called a supertax to be paid in addition to income tax by all those with an income of over 5,000 pounds per year. While their working- and middle-class supporters gained significant tax reductions, the burden of new taxes imposed in the 1909–10 and 1914–15 budgets fell on the opposing aristocracy, by taxing unearned income (Emy 1972, 122–23, 129; Murray 1980, 9–10). What roused the fury of the landed classes (the Conservative opposition and the House of Lords) was Lloyd George's proposal for the valuation of land, with a view to future taxation on profits from increases in land values. These moves were resisted by Conservatives since they derived much of their political support from the landed class and sought to protect its constituents against substantial new taxation. The fallout from the House of Lords obstruction was the Parliament Act of 1911, eliminating the Lords' veto over money bills and reducing the Lords' veto over other bills to a power to delay for two years.

CONCLUSION

The existing literature on Britain's grand strategy prior to World War I emphasizes the role of geopolitics, domestic characteristics, and individual idiosyncrasies. It is often argued that Germany's differential rate of economic growth, naval construction, and quest for empire disrupted the European balance of power (Marder 1940; Mowat 1968; Howard 1972; Kennedy 1976). To restore the balance, Britain was pressured to cooperate with every other major state.[63] Other arguments concerning the influences on Britain's grand strategy include specialized bureaucracies (such as the CID and the Foreign Office) and individuals (such as Prime Minister and Foreign Secretary Lord Salisbury's faith in the efficacy of Splendid Isolationism) (Steiner 1963; Sumida 1989; Boyce 1990; Ferguson 1994). National similarities and differences such as political, ideological, and societal characteristics are also emphasized to explain Britain's response. High societal homogeneity (among other factors) between Britain and the United States contributed to their rapprochement, while low societal homogeneity between Britain and Germany played a role in their bitter antagonism (Rock 1989). Other arguments maintain that Britain's more flexible constitutional system meant that London could react to Germany's naval challenge by punishment, since it could mobilize a greater share of societal resources for naval spending than Berlin.[64] Finally, some accounts view Britain's grand strategy as a failure, blaming domestic and individual constraints. Entrenched images meant that decision makers held to wrongheaded beliefs that England could not increase government expenditure and raise taxes without damaging its economy, leading Britain to prematurely surrender its worldwide naval supremacy by redistributing and concentrating its fleet (Friedberg 1988).

This literature ignores the effect of Britain's international environment on its grand strategy. The commercial nature of the rising contenders empowered domestic free traders and thereby directed Britain's response. Within Britain, members of the free-trade and economic nationalist blocs competed to shape Britain's grand strategy and to capture the domestic distributional gains. With the goals of economy, a reduction in international tension, and the promotion of a stable business climate, the free-trade coalition advocated a grand strategy of cooperation. This strategy called for freer trade, military retrenchment, fiscal orthodoxy, retreat from empire in locales with liberal contenders, and international arms limitation agreements. In opposition, the economic nationalist coalition supported a hard-line grand strategy of punishment by means of imperial preferences and protectionism, retention of the empire, and increased military preparedness.

In confronting liberal contenders, supporters of the free-trade faction pressed for cooperation. This translated into freer trade, access to new markets, new loans, and devolution of regional hegemony over the Americas to the United States, the northeast Pacific to Japan, and the eastern Mediterranean to France. The domestic consequence of cooperation was the strengthening of the City of London, shipping, insurance, and other commercial services, invisible exporters, efficient industry, fiscal conservatives, and the Liberal Party, while punishing these liberal contenders risked creating a hostility spiral and ratcheting-up the relative power of the opposing economic nationalists.

In confronting imperial France, Germany, and Russia, free traders sided with economic nationalists in punishing these states, despite the coalitional consequences. Free traders feared that imperial contenders would carve out an exclusive sphere of influence in the locale, blocking Britain's future access to its traditional interests in the region. Due to concerns about empowering the economic nationalist faction and for reasons of economy, the free traders moderated the excessive economic, commercial, and military policies of the economic nationalists by proposing arms limitation agreements and diplomacy to reduce hostilities with imperial states.

Free traders used the rewards from cooperation to further broaden and reinforce their domestic coalition. Cooperation strengthened the core supporters of the free-trade coalition by contributing to an expansion in trade, foreign lending, and exports. These gains and the savings from devolution and reduced military Estimates allowed the free traders to fund costly social and economic reform programs that attracted new supporters for their agenda.

As World War I approached, economic nationalists clamored for expanding the army and navy, as well as state intervention in the economy to direct resources, railroads, and manpower from civilian production to support the armed services. In 1912, a government subcommittee recommended that on the outbreak of war the government should assume overall control of the railways to ensure that the best use was made of them in the national interests. As late as 1914, entrenched free traders effectively moderated the punishment of Germany, favoring a policy that David French (1982c) titles "business as usual." This strategy opposed mobilizing for war, it rejected expanding the navy or army, and it blocked dispatching a Continental-size army to France. Instead, free traders chose the cost-savings response of a naval blockade of German ports and economic pressure (contributing to economic depression in Germany) to force Berlin's defeat.[65] The navy was favored over the army since a larger army would divert manpower and resources from factories devoted to supplying Britain's Continental allies (who were to conduct the fighting). As Maurice Hankey (the secretary to the CID) wrote in 1913, "the transport service would be demoralised, the mills, mines, and agriculture would all be short of labour at a time when it was specially required" (French 1982a, 34). "Business as usual" also rejected government controls and intervention in the business sector (insurance for shipping or state control over the railways) to marshal the nation's resources for war, instead favoring a laissez-faire policy toward government intervention. Free traders, especially Treasury officials, did not believe that the government had the right to interfere in the market because it would benefit a narrow group, contributing to a state subsidy, while others suffered from wartime costs.

The strength of the free traders, especially the City of London and invisible goods, was predicated upon global prosperity. This meant that the free trade coalition was highly vulnerable to the shock of war and the collapse of international credit and the global trading order (Kennedy 1983, 95–98). As discussed in the next chapter, World War I empowered the economic nationalists. The predominance of the free-trade coalition in 1914 accounts for Britain's reliance on the cost-saving measures of a naval blockade of German ports, deployment of the British Expeditionary Force to assist France, and financial and industrial quartermaster to the Allies, requiring limited economic, industrial, and manpower mobilization.[66] By 1916, increased state intervention in the economy, heightened military spending, and protection for industry and agriculture ratcheted-up the strength of the members of the economic nationalist coalition, while rolling back merchant banking, fiscal conservatives, and international financial services. Enhanced economic nationalists escalated Britain's involvement from a Limited Liability strategy to a Continental strategy, calling for conscription of a mass army, total warfare and military offensives on the Western front, and a knockout blow against Germany, requiring state control over the economy, along with industrial and manpower mobilization (French 1986).

CHAPTER 4

Imperial Contenders and Britain's Grand Strategy of Restrained Punishment, 1932–1939

In the decades after World War I, Britain was a leading world power (McKercher 1991). New regions in the Near East (namely, the former Ottoman Empire) were included in Britain's empire. Germany had been disarmed under the Versailles Treaty, and its navy was scuttled at Scapa Flow after the Great War. Other potential contenders for regional leadership such as Italy and Japan were relatively quiescent. France gave priority to its army and to the construction of the defensive Maginot line over its navy. Russia had been greatly weakened by the revolution, civil war, and Stalin's purges of the officer corps. The United States returned to a policy of near-isolationism, concentrating its efforts in the Americas. In sum, Britain was in the enviable position of "not wanting to quarrel with anybody because we have got most of the world already, or the best parts of it, and we only want to keep what we have got and prevent others from taking it away from us" (Pratt 1975, 3).

However, by 1930, Britain's global interests were under siege in disparate parts of its empire and by several contenders for regional hegemony. Britain faced Japan, the Soviet Union, and the United States in the Far East, Germany on the Continent, and Italy in the Mediterranean. As well, Britain encountered nationalist challenges within its empire in Egypt and India, and a civil war in Palestine. The Spanish civil war (1936) posed a threat to Britain's passage to its Far Eastern empire through the Straits of Gibraltar and the strategic Balearic Islands. Economically, Britain's traditional exporting industries were succumbing to foreign competition, while Britain's growing dependence on trade with its empire meant, more than ever, that London needed to protect its foreign commercial interests (Capie 1983, 17–22).

Within Britain, two large and logrolled coalitions battled over which contenders to accommodate, where to punish, and how to appropriate the nation's resources between its political economy and its national security. Critical differences existed between the supporters of the free-trade and economic nationalist blocs on the issues of the restoration of the gold standard, rearmament and arms limitation agreements, peacetime state planning and intervention in the economy, loans to China and Germany, collective security and the League of Nations, and imperial trade preferences. The constituents of the free-trade coalition included the Labour Party, invisible exporters and the City of London (shipping, banking, insurance services), the Bank of England, fiscal conservatives, state bureaucrats and supporting civil servants, exporters and importers who relied heavily on foreign raw materials and markets, and the working class. The free-trade coalition's preferred grand strategy called for cooperation. In the aftermath of World War I, free traders lobbied for the restoration of the gold standard, international banking, and the currency system; a return to fiscal orthodoxy including balanced budgets, reduced government spending, lowered taxes, and retreat from wartime state intervention in the economy; freer trade and the elimination of wartime tariffs and duties; and reliance on collective security, arms control, and arms reduction agreements. Free traders viewed the easing of international tension and the settlement of disputes between nations as essential for improving the international climate for trade. For reasons of economy, they emphasized disarmament, collective security, sanctions, and the League of Nations to promote international peace and European stability rather than relying on the balance of power and rearmament. The domestic consequence of such an agenda would ratchet-up the strength of efficient industry, the City of London, the Bank of England, and bureaucrats such as the chancellor of the Exchequer. Free traders argued that punishing contenders through rearmament or protectionism would result in commercial and military retaliation, undermining Britain's recovering fiscal strength by prolonging defense expenditures.

In opposition, the members of the economic nationalist coalition included inefficient industry, empire-oriented lobbying organizations, colonial bureaucrats, the services (air force, army, navy), and peak business organizations. The economic nationalists' preferred grand strategy was to punish the rising contenders. Their policy package favored massive rearmament (two-power naval standard, Continental army, and air force with reserves), peacetime state intervention in the economy (termed National Efficiency), abandonment of the gold standard (the gold standard meant higher export prices), international binding trade agreements (covering production, prices, and the allocation of markets), and imperial preferences that would link the empire and the domestic economy. The internal result of such an agenda would enhance inefficient industry, the military services, settler groups, and empire-oriented bureaucrats. Economic nationalists condemned Britain's "lead" in disarmament (the Washington Disarmament Conference meant that Britain would not complete any new capital ships for ten years). They warned that failure to increase Britain's defense expenditure would leave Great Britain vulnerable to attack, undermining its national security. Economic nationalists also warned that the restoration of the gold standard or any rollback of wartime protection and subsidies would destroy domestic industry because of the unfair competition, dumping, protectionism, and tariffs of Britain's major trading competitors.

In contrast to the period prior to World War I, during the two decades prior to World War II, the commercial composition of the emerging contenders shifted from a preponderance of liberal contenders to a preponderance of imperial competitors. By 1932, the foreign commercial policy of Germany, Japan, Italy, and to a lesser extent France had turned toward economic autarky and commercial self-sufficiency, while a liberal United States opposed Britain's colonial rule and sought to reverse London's policy of imperial preferences.

Within Britain, the reversal in the foreign commercial policy of the rising states altered the domestic structure of opportunities and constraints. The outcome was the strengthening of the economic nationalist faction and the weakening of the free-trade coalition, swaying London's grand strategy toward punishment. Some free traders defected to the economic nationalist faction. They joined inefficient industry, who renewed their push for a departure from the gold standard (1931), and imposition of imperial preferences (Ottawa Agreement of 1932) and protectionism (quotas and new tariffs). The military services reversed the Ten Year Rule in 1932 and engaged in a large rearmament program after 1935, limited by free-trade opposition and by industrial bottlenecks. The Conservative Party (the dominant force in the national government) led a successful propaganda campaign resulting in the general public becoming more oriented to defense and empire. Manufacturing and business used their strengthened bargaining position to advance state intervention in the economy, industrial rationalization, and industrial cartels and international agreements, eroding the principles of free trade.

The City of London, the banks, the Labour Party, the Treasury, and the Bank of England resisted the economic nationalists' grand strategy of punishment. Outward-oriented free traders feared that another war like the Great War would permanently extinguish gentlemanly financial capitalism in Britain (Cain and Hopkins 1993a). They prophesied that strengthening economic nationalists meant the "establishment of a 'new economic order' in which price-fixing and the control of production and competition would replace the market as the main regulatory mechanism of economic life" (Wurn 1993, 49). Even a massive rearmament program carried such risks, since it would require state intervention in industry and would divert resources and factories from export to rearmament. As the Treasury warned, state intervention in managing the economy was turning Britain into "a different kind of nation" (Peden 1984, 24). For the sake of their coalition's survival, free traders pressed for a self-reinforcing grand strategy of cooperation. Free traders moderated the economic nationalists' agenda by (1) restraining Britain's military buildup and more generally imposing fiscal orthodoxy and laissez-faire economics, (2) lobbying for economic and territorial concessions, and arms limitation agreements with Germany, Italy, and Japan, and (3) pressing for free trade within the Sterling Area (which required fiscal discipline at home). The outcome of the free traders' strategy was the delay in Britain's rearmament program.

The combination of Britain's delayed rearmament and the challengers' defecting or not renewing the arms reduction agreements and territorial concessions meant that Great Britain's military capability was insufficient to defend its global commitments (as discussed in chap. 6). Limits on Britain's industrial capacity also restricted the scale of Britain's rearmament program. As one author concedes, "more ambitious plans without strict Treasury control of priorities would not necessarily have resulted in better-equipped forces by the late 1930s" (Bond 1980, 192). Once rearmament began in 1935, bottlenecks, industrial dislocation, shortages of engineers, supplies, and machine tools to manufacture the equipment, and competition among the services for scarce industrial resources restricted Britain's rearmament program.[1] The solution, rejected by the free-trade coalition until the war, was government compulsion of manpower and industry.[2]

This chapter examines Britain's international environment to explain

London's grand strategy between 1932 and 1939. The first section discusses the contenders for regional leadership that Britain confronted. The next sections focus on how Britain responded to these challenges, the domestic coalitional consequences, and the effect on Britain's grand strategy.

THE EMERGING CONTENDERS FOR REGIONAL LEADERSHIP

Scholars who examine Britain's diplomatic history in the decade prior to World War II tend to focus on Great Britain's position in a single region (i.e., the Continent, the Mediterranean, the Far East, or the empire).[3] Had Britain encountered a single challenger it could have concentrated its considerable resources from the other parts of its empire, without any debate over alternative foreign policy strategies and the related financial and security ramifications. By the 1930s, Britain confronted Germany, Japan, and Italy, rising at differential rates and in disparate parts of its empire, as well as challenges from within its empire. As one author notes, "There is no major discussion of British foreign policy in the 1930s which faces the problems, as the Chamberlain administration had to, as part of a concurrent though rarely concerted attack on Britain's position in Europe, in the Mediterranean and the Middle East, and in East Asia and the Pacific" (Watt 1965, 208). Another states that "British statesmen from Lansdowne to Churchill grappled with one overriding problem: how to maintain Britain's leading position in the world as her relative power declined. Rarely was this task more difficult than in the late 1930's" (Lee 1973, 1).

First, Britain confronted a number of contenders for regional leadership. In the Far East, Britain faced Japan, the United States, and (to a lesser extent) the Soviet Union; in the Mediterranean, Italy; and on the Continent, Germany. Second, differential rates of industrial growth meant these contenders encroached on Britain's empire at uneven rates. Germany was the first power to encroach on and, based on some indicators, to surpass Britain in key sectors such as iron and steel production, energy consumption, and relative shares of world manufacturing (Kennedy 1987, 200–202). Behind Germany, Japan overtook France in the 1930s and was rapidly gaining on Britain's industrial lead. On most economic indicators, Italy remained a distant, third-rate power.

Third, Britain's regional leadership was challenged by rising contenders in different periods during the 1930s. In 1931, with the invasion of Manchuria, Japan was the first power to challenge Britain's regional hegemony. Italy's invasion of Abyssinia in 1935 and its attempt to create a new Roman Empire threatened Britain's passage through the strategic Mediterranean Sea. Although Britain never dominated the Continent, in 1938, beginning with the *Anschluss*, Germany expanded its hegemony over Central and Eastern Europe.[4]

Thus, Britain's decline was far from global, simultaneous, and uniform. Beginning in the early 1930s, Britain confronted Germany, Japan, and Italy on disparate fronts, challenging Britain for regional hegemony. Had Britain confronted a single contender, it could have concentrated its resources in the respective region. Oversimplifying London's predicament makes it hard to understand the difficult problem that Britain faced in striking the correct balance between its rearmament program and its global interests while avoiding financial ruin or leaving the country militarily weak (Kennedy 1983, 27).

IMPERIAL CHALLENGERS

Japan

By the decade prior to World War II, Britain confronted a preponderance of imperial contenders for regional hegemony. The foreign commercial policy of a state reflects whether it will impose an open or closed door commercial order in any locale that it comes to dominate. As imperial contenders, Japan, Germany, Italy, and to a lesser degree, France would create an economically self-sufficient fortress in any locale they controlled. In contrast, a liberal United States favored an open door commercial policy and decolonization. Empowered British economic nationalists clashed with the United States over Britain's imperial preferences adopted at the Ottawa Conference and colonial rule. The United States also viewed Germany's *Mitteleuropa* in central and eastern Europe and Japan's New Order in Asia as an obstacle to the liberalization of global trade.

Until the 1930s, Anglo-Japanese relations were based on decades of cooperation (see chap. 3). As Japan retreated from its support of Britain's Open Door policy in Asia, its commercial and security policies were designed to create an exclusive hegemonic position in the region, beginning with the conquest of Manchuria (1931) and the invasion of Shanghai (1932). During the 1930s, Britain's leaders recognized that Japan wanted to consolidate its hold on north China, dominate the political and economic life of the rest of China, and ultimately extend its control over the rich resources of Southeast Asia. Many in Britain suspected that

Tokyo had long-range designs on Australia and even India. For Britain, Hitler's claim to bring into the Reich merely those neighboring areas with substantial German population seemed less objectionable than Japan's declared goal of a new order in East Asia.

During the mid-1930s, Japan's leaders announced their intention to implement a "Monroe Doctrine for East Asia." The Amu statement (1934), Hiorta's Fundamental Principles of National Policy (1936), and the New Order (1938) all stressed that Japan regarded East Asia as its exclusive sphere of influence (in violation of the Nine Power Treaty) and objected to Western intervention in China (Crowley 1966, 187–210, 279–300). The Asian "Monroe Doctrine" first applied to Japan, Taiwan, Korea, north China, and Manchukuo (the inner ring of Japanese expansion). After 1937, the prospect of Japanese penetration into China south of the Great Wall and into southeast Asia (creating an outer empire) threatened Britain's regional hegemony and the centers of British commercial activity in the Yangtze valley and southern China.[5] By 1940, Japan openly declared its sphere of influence to include East and southeast Asia, known as the Greater East Asia Co-prosperity Sphere, with Japan, north China, and Manchukuo as the industrial base (Beasley 1987, 233–43). The other countries were to provide raw materials and form part of a vast consumer market, building a degree of economic strength that would enable Japan first to meet and contain any counterattack from outside, then to incorporate India, Australia, and Russia's Siberian provinces by further wars (Beasley 1981, 272). The chain of islands stretching from Malaya to northern Australia was of crucial economic and strategic significance to Japan because of the vital raw materials, especially oil (Lowe 1977, 65).

Japan's bid for regional hegemony would block England's future access to its valuable markets, investments, and resources in the locale, especially the potentially lucrative China market.[6] Ann Trotter notes that "Japan's aim was the domination of China and that the failure of western powers to assist China would lead eventually to the formation of a Sino-Japanese bloc which would admit westerners only on sufferance" (1975, 35). The combination of the Depression, the loss of its market share in the Americas and Europe, and the cost of rearmament meant Britain's trade with China was more important than ever to maintain a positive balance of trade.

Free traders viewed Japan as a threat to Britain's existing open regional trading order for three reasons. First, Japan would monopolize trade with

China, especially the Yangtze Valley, in the same manner as it did with Manchukuo, excluding Britain from its profitable trade with China. In 1937, Japan restricted foreign shipping on the Yangtze, eliminating British competition. In 1938, the Japanese Diet approved a bill creating a North China Development Company, with the goal of establishing monopolies in transportation, communications, electricity, and mining (Lee 1973, 121–22). Second, as part of Tokyo's attempt to make north China an exclusive domain, Japan moved to incorporate China into its expanding Yen bloc. Japan unsuccessfully sought to do this by replacing the Chinese currency (the *fapi*) with the Federal Reserve Bank notes. In response, Britain's foreign secretary (Viscount Halifax) advocated a 10 million pound loan to the Chinese currency stabilization fund (Lowe 1977, 58–62). Third, Japan's ultimate objective was autonomy and economic self-sufficiency. Japan's leaders defended the concept of the new order, referring in particular to the growth of powerful economic blocs in the world, such as those associated with the British Empire, the United States and Latin America, and Russia.[7] Monopolization of this sphere would provide the resources and the markets necessary for Japan to build the industrial strength it needed to confront the Soviet Union and the Anglo-American states (Beasley 1987). After 1937, the Greater East Asia Co-prosperity Sphere, stretching from Manchuria to the Dutch East Indies, would grant Japan control over the region's tin, oil, rubber, bauxite, and other strategic raw materials.

Germany

Britain viewed Germany, like Japan, as an imperial challenger seeking to create a closed self-sufficient sphere in central and eastern Europe. Such a sphere would block Britain's future access to the region and strengthen Germany's position when it turned westward. Similar to Japan's, Germany's foreign economic policy evolved from a policy of autarky and self-sufficiency to one of forceful expansion known as *Lebensraum*, or the acquisition of greater living space in eastern Europe.

By 1931, Germany sought to create a self-sufficient sphere in southern and eastern Europe (Stambrook 1972; Boyce 1987). Germany's Chancellor Heinrich Brüning proposed the Austro-German customs union accord of March 1931, reviving the German dream of *Mitteleuropa* and taking the first step toward *Anschluss* with Austria.[8] Free traders fretted that such a sphere would block Britain's future access to central and eastern Europe. As one author notes, "Such an extension would automatically open the door for Germany's absolute control of the commerce of Hungary, Czechoslovakia, Jugoslavia, and Italy" (Foerster 1931, 619). He forewarns, "The creation of a Central European national block would inevitably give rise to a Germanic hegemony on the European continent" (622). Germany was negotiating other tariff preference treaties with Romania and Bulgaria (Stambrook 1972, 116). Britain's concern was that Hitler and the National Socialist Party, which advocated economic self-sufficiency and autarky (as well as both *Anschluss* and *Mitteleuropa*), made substantial gains in the 1930 and 1932 Reichstag elections (Kaiser 1990, 371–72). In related events, during May 1932, the Germans announced their intention to leave the League of Nations World Disarmament Conference, and in 1933, Hitler became chancellor, withdrawing from the League of Nations and accelerating German rearmament.[9]

German economic policy challenged liberal trade principles. Under the direction of Hjalmar Schacht at the Reichsbank, the Germans introduced a complex system of controls and the use of foreign exchange (Newton 1991, 183–84). Trade policy was founded on barter agreements with neighboring and Latin American countries, which provided food and raw materials in exchange for manufactured goods (any difference was made up in inconvertible marks eligible for use only in Germany). By 1936, Hitler supported a policy of economic autarky. Hitler's Four Year Plan was intended to reduce German dependence on foreign suppliers and to conserve available foreign exchange for the importation and stockpiling of strategic materials and food imports (foreign exchange was needed to pay for raw-material imports for rearmament) (Carroll 1968, 122–39). It was urgent to prepare the army and the economy for war in four years. To achieve self-sufficiency, the Plan created rudimentary synthetic oil and rubber industries, as well as increased home production of certain raw materials, such as iron and light metals, which could be substituted for unavailable metals (Weinberg 1980, 23–25). The problem with such a plan was that German dependence on overseas raw materials would always require substantial German participation in world trade (Murray 1984, 5–6, charts 1 and 2).

Neither a policy of participation in the global trading order nor economic autarky could satisfy Germany's economic needs (Craig 1978, 698). For Hitler, the ultimate solution lay only in the conquest of *Lebensraum* (Calleo 1978, 94, 97, 105–7; Deist 1994, 381–82). Hitler proposed to solve Germany's economic problems by conquering Austria and Czechoslovakia in order to clear land for German colonization (Kaiser 1990, 371). A dominated Eastern Europe would serve as a territorial and agricultural base from which Germany could compete with the British Empire and the United States.[10]

Italy

In 1935, like Japan and Germany, Mussolini began to advocate a commercial policy of economic autarky and imperial grandeur under a Third Rome. Known as the "March to the Ocean," it would establish Italian hegemony over the entire Mediterranean, making Italy "the mistress of the Mediterranean" by linking Libya, Ethiopia, and the Sudan via French North Africa (Cassels 1983, 260–68; McKercher 1991, 752). Italian agricultural policy or "the battle for wheat" was aimed at freeing Italy from dependence on foodstuffs from abroad. Yet, Italian autarky was largely impossible since Italy was highly dependent on foreign strategic raw materials and imported energy (Murray 1979b, 45).

Italy's commercial policy of autarky concerned Britain. Free traders warned that an economically backward country like Italy would block Britain's future access to its markets and investments in the region. Unable to compete with more efficient foreign powers, Italy would exclude them from any region that it came to dominate. As one author claims, "Italy was in decline and therefore dangerous" (Pratt 1975, 84).

Finally, by 1930, Aristide Briand, the prime minister of France, was one of the primary advocates of a Pan-European Union, including a customs union or Continental trading bloc (Pegg 1983, 83–86). Supporters emphasized the need for expanded trade between the industrial western states and the agricultural eastern states. Germany opposed the Pan-European Union because it would undermine its own plans for a customs union with the smaller states in south and central Europe. Britain opposed the "United States of Europe" plan because its Continental competitors would gain trade advantages through moderate or high external tariffs (Pegg 1983, 99).

LIBERAL UNITED STATES

Unlike Germany, Japan, and Italy, the United States was a liberal contender. The Reciprocal Trade Agreements Act (1934) authorized the president to lower tariffs, reversing the protectionist trend in American commercial policy (the Fordney-McCumber Act of 1922 and the Smoot-Hawley Tariff of 1930) (Lake 1988, 204–5). One goal of the United States was the restoration of the Open Door economic trading order (Gardner

1969; Williams 1972; McKercher 1993). U.S. Secretary of State Cordell Hull called Britain's protectionist Ottawa Agreements "the greatest injury, in a commercial way, that has been inflicted on this country since I have been in public life" (Gardner 1969, 19). Britain's imperial preference system was seen as a barrier to American recovery from the Depression since foreign markets could provide an outlet for surplus agricultural and manufactured products (Williams 1972, 233).

During World War II, Washington used the Atlantic Charter (Anglo-American declaration of war aims, signed in 1941) and the Lend-Lease Act to pressure London to reverse its imperial preference system, open the Sterling Area, and restore the gold standard (Cain and Hopkins 1993a, 99–102). The United States tried to write a nondiscrimination clause into the Atlantic Charter calling for "access, on equal terms, to the trade and to the raw materials of the world that are needed for their economic prosperity" (Gardner 1969, 46–47). For the sake of good Anglo-American relations, President Franklin Roosevelt agreed to Prime Minister Winston Churchill's request to water down the accord by replacing the clause "with due respect for our existing obligations" (Kimball 1971, 250). The Lend-Lease Act (1942) was less vague: Clause VII called for the "elimination of all forms of discriminatory treatment in international commerce and . . . the reduction of tariffs and other trade barriers" (Kimball 1971, 253).[11] The goal of both clauses was to destroy Britain's imperial economic bloc and to break up the Sterling Area.

In addition to destroying Britain's imperial preference trading system, the United States sought to dismantle the British Empire (at least until the rise of the Cold War) by promoting a policy of self-determination. Part III of the Atlantic Charter called for "sovereign rights and self-government restored to those who have been forcibly deprived of them" (Graebner 1984, 87). Further, Roosevelt repeatedly offered advice to Churchill on the desirable steps toward Indian independence. With such a policy, the United States operated at cross purposes with Britain in the Middle East and Asia.

BRITAIN'S GRAND STRATEGY

In confronting new and old protagonists, within Britain the members of the opposing free-trade and economic nationalist blocs struggled over how to respond to these challenges. Free traders and internationalists preferred cooperation with contenders, translating into an outward-oriented policy of freer trade, disarmament, participation in the League of Nations, fiscal orthodoxy, and resumption of the gold standard. Such cooperation would strengthen efficient industry, the City of London, fiscal conservatives, the Treasury, and the Bank of England. Enhanced free traders would lobby the government to adopt a more conciliatory policy toward liberal United States and even imperial Germany, Italy, and Japan. Constituents of the economic nationalists favored punishing contenders by means of increased military spending, imperial preferences, and abandonment of the gold standard, supported by state intervention in the economy. Punishment would bolster the military, inefficient industry, and colonial-oriented bureaucrats. Strengthened economic nationalists would press for a more belligerent stance toward imperial and liberal contenders alike.

Britain's World War I strategy of punishment greatly empowered the members of the economic nationalist coalition, with domestic economic considerations (state intervention in the economy, industrial protection, closer union with the empire) taking precedence over international concerns.[12] This shift in the domestic balance of political power was apparent by 1916, with the Paris Agreements in which Britain and its allies pledged to deny Germany and Austria most-favored-nation status after the war (Newton and Porter 1988, 50). Gains for the economic nationalist faction included a reversal in the declining trend in agricultural development by the war, which agriculture sought to retain in its aftermath.[13] Wartime protectionism benefited inefficient industry and state managers. The war also enhanced the position of the military services, resulting in new naval construction, an air force with air reserves, and a Continental army. Invisible exports were hurt by the decline in the international service economy, domestic tariffs and duties, and the beggar-thy-neighbor economic policies. The embargo on foreign loans undermined the City and meant that British customers cut off from credit had to make new arrangements, often turning toward New York (Cain and Hopkins 1993a, 41). Concomitantly, the war weakened fiscal conservatives such as the Treasury, who strove to contain expenditure, while the Bank of England's control over the money supply was eliminated with the suspension of the gold standard (1919).

The war challenged traditional economic orthodoxy by enhancing the role of the state, big business, and peak business organizations (Tomlinson 1990, 62–68). By 1918, two-thirds of the economy and nine-tenths of imports were subject to direction by bodies authorized by the government (Newton and Porter 1988, 36; Cain and Hopkins 1993a, 49). Numerous ad hoc commissions and boards were set up to regulate and coordinate business, such as the Ministry of Munitions, Coal Controller, and Shipping Controller. Regulation and management of the economy meant intervention in the conduct of industrial firms, coordination of railways, the manipulation of investment into useful enterprises, the ban on specific exports (chemicals required for the production of explosives), heavy duties to discourage the misuse of limited shipping cargo space (McKenna duties), and currency controls to prevent the loss of foreign exchange.[14] Other state schemes included the central allocation of resources and price fixing of munitions and food, import licensing, railroads, and shipping insurance. As well, the state intentionally encouraged the development of peak industrial organizations and big business in Britain, and the cooperation between capital and labor (Holland 1981, 299–300).

Finally, enhanced economic nationalists, with the support of the Conservative Party, pushed to expand Britain's imperial interests in Asia, Africa, and the Pacific (Beloff 1970). During the war, Prime Minister Lloyd George summoned an Imperial Conference, creating the Imperial War Cabinet, which regarded the western front as little more than a disagreeable necessity (Howard 1972, 64). Lloyd George's War Cabinet included well-known imperialists such as Milner, Curzon, and later Smuts, while Leo Amery was an adviser on Middle East issues. In 1916, Britain and France partitioned the Middle East into respective spheres (Sykes-Picot Agreement), and in 1917, Lloyd George diverted resources to Palestine, ordering General Allenby, the new commander in Egypt, to strike the Turks as hard as possible.

Between 1917 and 1923, strengthened economic nationalists attempted to translate their wartime gains into tariff reform, imperial preferences, and empire self-sufficiency in foodstuffs. Tariff Reformers and newly formed organizations such as the British Commonwealth Union, the British Manufacturers' Association, the National Union of Manufacturers, and the British Empire Producers' Organization provided much of the resources to advance the particularistic agenda of imperial preferences and empire consolidation. At the Imperial Conference (1917) an imperial emigration program was proposed. For national security, segments of industry, especially engineering and provincial businessmen, lobbied for Britain to retreat behind its empire through imperial preferences and imperial self-sufficiency over inter-Allied cooperation (Cain and Hopkins 1993a, 51–52). To slow Germany's industrial recovery and block the renewal of postwar German commercial competition, economic nationalists pressed for reparations in the Versailles settlement. As Liberalism weakened, the Conservative Party was convinced that its hour had come and that imperial economic unity offered far greater benefits (Kennedy 1981; Turner 1988).

CONSTITUENTS OF THE FREE-TRADE COALITION

In the aftermath of World War I, the free traders were no longer the dominant coalition, and their agenda became to roll back the wartime gains of the opposing economic nationalist faction (McRae and Cairncross 1984, 15–16; Newton and Porter 1988, 55–63; Tomlinson 1990, 53–59, 79–89, 113–21). The members of the free-trade coalition generally agreed that the best solution to Britain's dilemma was an easing of international tension, retreat of the state from intervention in the economy, and the freeing of international trade from artificial restraints. Specifically, the Bank of England was determined to restore the gold standard, to control the money supply, and, most important, for London to resume its position as the world's money market. The Treasury's intent was to return free trade, balance budgets, and restore economy in public spending; reduce high wartime tax; and roll back the state as regulator of the economy. Fiscal conservatives argued that wartime protection was corrupting the political process by creating powerful vested interests whose influence would be difficult to resist. They countered that the problem of the staple industries was that they needed to "put their house in order" and address the issue of inefficiency. The City's interest was to restore the international service economy, which would help pay for imports, produce a balance of payments surplus, generate capital for foreign investment, and stimulate demand for British exports. Finally, the Treasury, the Bank of England, and the City of London especially opposed the military's program for peacetime rearmament for fear that it would bring inflation and a subsequent economic crash in Britain's recovering economy.

The members of the free-trade bloc included the Labour Party, Liberals, trade unions, invisible exports, the City of London, the financial community, the Bank of England, fiscal conservatives, pacifists, state fiscal bureaucrats (chancellor of the Exchequer, Treasury advisers, and supporting civil servants), exporters and importers who relied heavily on foreign raw materials and overseas markets, and the working class. The free-trade coalition favored a grand strategy of cooperation through (1) arms limitations and disarmament agreements to prevent a costly arms race, and reliance on collective security to lower the cost of hegemony, (2) retreat from empire and, concomitantly, a reduction in imperial defense, and (3) restoration of fiscal orthodoxy (including balanced budgets, debt-funding, and cuts in public expenditure), a return to the gold standard (which was necessary for a revival of trade), deregulation of the economy, and rolling back state economic management. One of the central strategies of the free trader coalition was to cultivate the growth of moderates within rival imperial states, especially free-trade-oriented business, who would pressure their respective governments for commercial and military restraint.

The Treasury Department

As the central department of finance, Britain's Treasury Department pressed for rolling back state intervention in the economy and the high levels of public spending to prewar norms of policy. The Treasury Department was responsible for the oversight of all government spending, and it had the final say on all issues relating to budgetary control and debt management (Shay 1977; Peden 1979, 38–44; 1983, 374–78; Kennedy 1981, 230–36). The Treasury had influence over what proportion of the national wealth should be allocated to defense and how the services would allocate their resources. First, the Treasury was responsible for levying and creating new taxes. Second, since there was no Ministry of Defence, the allocation of funds was negotiated directly between the Treasury and the three services.[15] This meant that the Treasury also had the function of coordinating among the services, thereby preventing a chaotic competition among the services for scarce resources that would have slowed the rate of rearmament; hence it had a substantial voice over Britain's grand strategy (see the appendix for a discussion of the concept of Treasury control). The autonomy of Britain's Treasury was intended to safeguard the country's fiscal strength by preventing excessive extraction of societal resources for military purposes, while allowing for modest increases in the rate of defense spending.

The theoretical approach of the Treasury's fiscal policy remained rooted in the Gladstonian tradition of limited government expenditure, low taxation (especially direct taxation), adherence to the gold standard, debt reduction, and minimal intervention in the economy in order to safeguard Britain's financial strength.[16] The heart of the Treasury's position was that finance was the "fourth arm of defence," upon which the three branches of the Services (and traditionally Britain's allies) would rely in the event of a prolonged war.[17] To pay for future wars, Britain's leaders intended to use its creditworthiness, the sales of foreign securities, and running down its war chest, which was composed of gold and foreign exchange reserves (Peden 1979, 1984).

In the aftermath of World War I, the priority of the Treasury was to lower direct and indirect taxes. The Treasury opposed high taxation in peacetime because it would leave little room for expansion during war. To protect Britain's international creditworthiness, London renewed its debt repayment to the Sinking Fund. While Britain's tradition of war finance had dictated that the national debt should be kept down to the lowest possible level by paying for wars out of current taxation, and in particular through an income tax, the outcome of war was often high debt. However, failure to meet past debt responsibilities would damage Britain's ability to obtain new foreign loans at reasonable interest rates during an emergency and would erode foreign confidence in Britain's economic stability.

The Bank of England

For the Bank of England, the Treasury's fiscal sibling, the central concern was the restoration of the gold standard, which had been suspended in 1919. The Bank of England was supported by financiers, overseas banking, insurance, shipping, and the Treasury, who viewed a fixed currency and stable exchange rate as essential for the revival of trade (Newton and Porter 1988, 59). The service economy urged the government to return to the prewar gold standard as quickly as possible in order to restore the financial position of the City of London and to help businessmen, particularly exporters (Skidelsky 1976, 30–33). Montagu Norman, the governor of the Bank of England (1920–44), warned that if Britain failed to go back "the world center would shift permanently and completely from London to New York" (Tomlinson 1990, 54). This policy posed a challenge to industry since restoration of the gold standard involved an overvalued pound, especially in relation to the dollar, further disadvantaging British exports (Longstreth 1979, 164–67). Returning to the prewar valuation left the prices of British goods about 10 percent above their real value (Brawley 1993, 155). Suspicion was heightened among economic nationalists by the fact that the inner cabinet of the Bank consisted of directors of merchant banks, acceptance houses, and overseas banks, ship owners, and merchants, but only a few industrialists (Williamson 1984, 108). The Bank of England also advocated the establishment of central banks throughout Europe, which would be free of political control and would cooperate to manage the new financial order.

The City of London

Invisible exports favored a return to free trade and fiscal orthodoxy. While weakened by World War I, beginning in 1921, the City of London (shipping, banking, creditors, bondholders, insurance services, and overseas investment) along with the Treasury and the Bank of England reasserted their authority over economic policy in order to restore the prewar liberal trading system. The City opposed a large rearmament program, fearing that excessive borrowing might lead to inflation and weaken Britain's recovering economy. By the mid-1930s, the City preferred to rely on private industry for rearming, rather than state arms factories. Detractors of wartime duties and imperial preferences included those who relied heavily on foreign raw materials and markets, such as shipbuilding, and the working class, who feared higher food prices.

The Labour Party

The Labour Party also favored financial orthodoxy. The Labour Party functioned as a pressure group for labor and the trade unions, supporting cheap consumer imports and the export orientation of British industry on which much union strength had been built. Labour also supported expenditure on welfare, clashing with the Treasury Department. Yet, as Tomlinson notes, "we cannot see the early 1920s as a period when a growing labour movement fought against prevailing economic orthodoxies" (1990, 67). Labour and its constituents regarded disarmament, collective security, and consultation among League of Nations members (rather than balance of power diplomacy) as the only certain method for preventing war (Gordon 1969, 47–54; Hall 1976, 478–80; Schmidt 1986b, 279–88). They opposed the economic nationalists' rearmament proposals for fear that "unilateral" British rearmament risked igniting another arms race. In the 1935 election, the Labour Party declared that "the best defence is not huge competitive armaments, but the organisation of collective security against any aggressor and the agreed reduction of armaments everywhere" (Shay 1977, 58). Consequently, Labour members urged the government to take all steps necessary to bring the 1932 League of Nations World Disarmament Conference to a successful conclusion.

SUPPORTERS OF THE ECONOMIC NATIONALIST COALITION

In opposition, empowered economic nationalists sought to perpetuate their windfall from punishing Germany and the Great War. Their desired grand strategy was to punish the rising contenders through immediate rearmament, which meant repealing the Ten Year Rule, expanding the wartime duties and tariffs to include imperial preferences, extending state management over the economy, and blocking calls for a return to the gold standard. As the party of protection and empire, the Conservative Party clamored for reserving access to its empire markets for its own industry, while blocking non-empire competition, and correcting the deficiencies in the nation's defenses.[18] Economic nationalists also called for repealing the Ten Year Rule (1919), which instructed the military services (army, navy, air force) to plan their budgets on the assumption that no major conflict would occur for ten years, countering that Britain could afford a large rearmament program.

Industrialists

The members of the economic nationalist coalition included inefficient industry, state managers, members of the military services, state bureaucrats such as the members of the Committee of Imperial Defence, and empire organizations. Inefficient British industry (including iron and steel, the motor car industry, cotton, and coal), industrial lobbying organizations (such as the National Union of Manufacturers or NUM and the Federation of British Industry or FBI), and the Association of British Chambers of Commerce supported tariff reform, imperial preferences, and management of the British economy.[19] More threatening to free traders, by the mid-1930s, the FBI rejected conventional economic beliefs, calling for managed international trade. This entailed binding international agreements or producer alliances between industrial competitors (in Britain, Germany, and Japan) by creating a managed price-system, sector production, and the joint development of markets. Another grievance common to industrialists was the overvaluation of sterling due to the restoration of the gold standard in 1925 (Holland 1981, 288). Industrialists opposed the return to gold because it meant higher export prices, tighter international markets, and scarcer investment capital due to high interest rates (Bright 1985, 222).

The Military Services

The members of the Navy and the Army (Chiefs of Staff, COS) called for immediate rearmament, earmarking greater resources to defense, while complaining about the lax armaments policy.[20] Since 1919, conscription had been abandoned, defense Estimates lowered, and disarmament advanced (in the 1921–22 Washington and 1930 London Naval Treaties). In 1924, strong opposition to armament expenditure by the Labour government halted construction of the Singapore naval base (which was approved in 1921). In 1925, a one-power naval standard was adopted (Peden 1979, 6).

In 1933, the COS provided a detailed report of the existing deficiencies in the defenses of the empire. They argued that only from a position of strength could Britain negotiate with Germany, Japan, and Italy. The military recommended a large rearmament program, including the upward revision of the navy's existing one-power standard to a two-power standard, completion of a fifty-two squadron bomber and substantial reinforcements of the Fleet Air Arm, and an army expeditionary force to defend the Low Countries. In response to the free traders' call for economy and retention of the Ten Year Rules, proponents for higher defense spending argued that the danger of underrating Britain's defense might lead to "defeat in war and complete destruction," while the danger of overrating the nation's financial resources could "only lead to severe embarrassment, heavy taxation, lowering of the standard of living and reduction of social services" (Shay 1977, 201).

British naval men scorned the Washington and London Naval Conferences. Economic nationalists were determined that the country's "lead" in disarmament should go no further. At the Washington Naval Conference, Britain accepted a one-power standard in battleships and established a naval holiday from battleship construction until 1936.[21] As a result, the Admiralty was faced with scrapping twenty capital ships. At the London Naval Conference, delegates agreed to limit cruisers, destroyers, submarines, and smaller auxiliary ships. Because of these treaties, between 1923 and 1934 there could be rebuilding and re-equipping of the fleet on only a minor scale. The military also called for greater imperial defense, including the construction of a naval base at Singapore. Singapore was selected as the site to defend Britain's interests in the Far East. The Admiralty argued it was essential that Singapore be built up to defend itself during the six weeks it might take for the main fleet to arrive.

Empire Organizations

Empire organizations such as the British Commonwealth Union, the Imperial Lobby, and the Empire Industries Association lobbied for imperial preferences, the importance of empire markets, and safeguarding home industries from foreign competition.[22] They called for empire self-sufficiency in foodstuffs and committed Britain to tax empire goods less heavily than foreign goods. There were renewed calls for Britain and the other empire countries to admit empire products free or at lower rates

(New Zealand and Canada were especially eager). Empire organizations protested returning Germany's former colonies and criticized America's anti-imperialist ideology, which they feared and resented (as well as America's economic internationalism).

ENTRENCHED FREE TRADERS AND THEIR SELF-REINFORCING STRATEGY: COMMERCIAL AND MILITARY COOPERATION

The foreign commercial policy of the rising contenders and the domestic distributional consequences guided Britain's grand strategy. In facing imperial Germany, Italy, Japan, and to a lesser extent France, the military, inefficient industry, and colonial bureaucrats pushed for a grand strategy of punishing these emerging contenders. Economic nationalists were joined by free traders who argued that the loss of Great Britain's access to global markets would have a detrimental effect on Britain's wealth and balance of trade. The empowered economic nationalist coalition used these gains to exert pressure to advance their agenda of empire, protectionism, rearmament, and state management of the economy. For the economic nationalists, the 1931 election was an overwhelming victory for pro-tariff Conservatives (forming the national government), replacing the pro-free-trade Labour government (1929–31). The 1935 election of Conservative Prime Minister Stanley Baldwin was a further mandate for their agenda and against Labour's reliance on collective security and economic sanctions, disarmament, and free trade (Robertson 1974; Dunbabin 1975, 591–93).

To preserve their faction's existence, the embattled free-trade coalition lobbied the government for a self-reinforcing grand strategy of cooperation with liberal and imperial contenders. Such a strategy would have the domestic consequence of moderating the rollback of their faction's relative power; it would retard their economic and political demise. Free traders lobbied to restrain the extreme military and commercial programs of the economic nationalists, calling for limited rearmament, naval arms limitation agreements, territorial concessions, and free trade within the Sterling Area. As a number of authors conclude, although rearmament began in earnest in 1935, the shortage of skilled labor (especially engineering) and productive resources in key industries created bottlenecks, thereby further limiting the scope of Britain's rearmament. One proposed solution, which was rejected by free traders, was the creation of a "semi-war" state organization to allocate manpower.[23]

ABANDONMENT OF THE GOLD STANDARD, IMPERIAL PREFERENCES, LOANS, QUOTAS, AND PROTECTIONISM

Encountering predominantly imperial contenders had the domestic consequence of strengthening the economic nationalist coalition while ravaging the service industries of the City of London. Enhanced economic nationalists pressed for an imperial economy: the abandonment of the gold standard, adopting imperial preferences, British tariffs, quotas against Japanese exports, loan and credit embargoes against Germany, and trade sanctions against Italy. Economic nationalists argued that British financial and trade concessions would be used to expand Germany's and Japan's potential for aggression. Other traditional supporters, such as the National Union of Manufacturers, pressed the government to take action against German-subsidized exports, while the Lancashire textile industry pushed for protection from Japanese competition and preferences in the empire (Lowe 1981, 148). FBI-TUC discussions, representing organized management and organized labor, articulated a joint program for the development of imperial preferences (Dintenfass 1991, 84–85).

New converts to the economic nationalist coalition included organized labor (Trades Union Congress, or TUC), shipping, and even bank directors and City financiers, who turned toward protectionism, import controls, and the empire to save themselves (including the chairmen of the "big five" clearinghouses) (Williamson 1984, 119–20; Cain and Hopkins 1993a, 73–75). The Banker's Industrial Development Corporation (BIDC), established with government encouragement and funding from the Bank of England, a variety of banks, and the City institutions, supported industrial reorganization (Newton 1995, 488). The BIDC limited the competition in cotton spindles, while the National Shipbuilders' Security purchased and disposed of redundant shipyards to reduce capacity in shipping. Finally, as other states embraced economic nationalism, the proliferation of bankruptcies and factory closures in Britain caused many free-trade constituents to swing around to a pro-tariff and pro-empire position.

Many free traders were harmed by the global trend toward self-sufficiency and exclusive commercial spheres (Roberts 1991, 65–67). As Eric Francis notes, "London's position as a centre of world banking, insurance, shipping and merchanting had inevitably been seriously affected by the decline in foreign trade, and more especially by the growth of barter, exchange clearing and other forms of direct trading, which by-passed the established channels of international distribution and finance" (1939, 293). In all, earnings fell from 200 million pounds in 1926–30, to 110 million pounds in 1931–33, to 51 million pounds in 1934–38 (Roberts 1991, 68). Relatedly, the marine insurance business conducted by British insurance companies suffered. The merchant banks, which specialized in the finance of international trade and foreign loan issuing, businesses that issued long-terms loans for overseas borrowers, and commodity traders and the commodity markets were also adversely affected.

Abandonment of the Gold Standard

The expanding political clout of the economic nationalist coalition contributed to the abandonment of the gold standard in 1931 and the adoption of imperial preferences in 1932, further weakening the members of the free-trade coalition. The abandonment of the gold standard was a major defeat for the Bank of England, the City of London, the Treasury, and the financial community, thereby marking the end of the Bank's independent authority over monetary policy and, more important, the demise of London's role as the center of international finance (Longstreth 1979, 171–73). With abandonment, the government, advised by the Treasury, replaced the Bank of England as the authority over monetary policy.[24] As one author summarizes, "The thirties thus constituted a decade in which the political power of banking capital was definitely diminished" (Longstreth 1979, 171–72). Free traders were further weakened in 1931 by the imposition of an informal embargo upon capital issues in London for non-empire borrowers. The main City casualties were the merchant banks that for decades had specialized in loans on behalf of foreign clients (Roberts 1991, 66).

Imperial Preferences

Supporters of free enterprise were dealt a second blow when empowered economic nationalists advanced their dream of Empire Free Trade, intensifying the global trend toward autarky.[25] The Conservative Party, empire visionaries, and industry supported imperial preferences in order to protect British industry against non-empire competition. They also hoped to direct British investment toward the empire, encouraging self-sufficiency and expanding the demand for British exports (Tomlinson 1990, 76). Collin Brooks, a financial journalist, noted that there were "two bodies of opinion, a small minority, no longer very vocal, who deprecated, whatever the emergency, any departure from the principles of Insular Free Trade, and a large majority in favour of the use of tariffs" (1931, 221).

In August 1932, at the Ottawa Conference, Britain formally adopted a commercial policy of imperial preferences.[26] In 1931, Neville Chamberlain, with support from the Conservative Party, introduced the Import Duties Bill calling for (1) imposition of a general customs duty of 10 percent on almost all imports, (2) the exemption from the duty of goods from within the empire, pending the Imperial Economic Conference to be held in Ottawa, and (3) the exemption of certain other goods, which were placed on a free list.[27] The Ottawa Conference produced a network of twelve bilateral agreements among the commonwealth countries, granting special trading privileges to British Commonwealth countries. Britain offered imperial preferences in return for concessions by the Dominions for British manufactured goods (the exchange was primarily foodstuffs from the Dominions for British manufactured goods).[28] In addition, the British colonies of Sierra Leone, Nigeria, Gold Coast, and Gambia put tariffs on foreign imported goods while giving preference to British cottons. In 1934, Britain abrogated the Indo-Japanese commercial treaty (1904) in order to stem the flow of Japanese cotton textiles.

COMMERCIAL CONCILIATION

Members of the free-trade faction responded to these external pressures by pushing for economic cooperation with imperial Japan, Italy, and Germany. The City had an interest in restraining the scope of the economic nationalists' trade and financial punishment of these states. Free traders advocated extending credits, loans, and trade concessions rather than tariffs, quotas, and imperial preferences in order to moderate Berlin and Tokyo's foreign policies. Invisible exports, banking, the City, shipping, and insurance recognized that the benefits would accrue to the trading community.

The goal of the free traders was threefold. First, free traders feared that punishing these imperial contenders risked exacerbating Britain's financial difficulties and the contenders'. As Germany had been Britain's best customer before the war, the governor of the Bank of England believed that Britain's economic well-being and the cure to its unemployment and stagnant economy depended on returning Germany to the liberal fold and on restoring German economic health (Coghlan 1972, 208). The City of London and British banks continued to maintain extensive credit lines to provide Germany with foreign exchange to purchase British and Commonwealth goods, the latter experiencing serious debt to London (Forbes 1987, 580). Worse, free traders recognized that Germany's reliance on credit after 1932 had led to a grave foreign exchange crisis that could be resolved by conquest (Parker 1975, 646; Deist 1994, 383). Free-trade supporters proposed extending foreign credits and lower tariffs to Germany so that Hitler could purchase the British goods that Germany needed, quelling the urge to expand (MacDonald 1972; Wendt 1983; Peden 1984; Schmidt 1986b; Forbes 1987; Newton 1991, 1995). In the Far East, to obtain fair treatment for British trade and enterprise in China (and hopefully Manchukuo), London had to keep the goodwill of China without antagonizing Japan (Trotter 1975, 10; Bennett 1992).

Second, the City believed that trade would improve Germany and Japan's political-economic climate by strengthening moderates and domestic free-trade constituents. A strong economic connection existed between the major financial and commercial institutions in London and Berlin. After 1919, British merchant and joint stock banks had raised money for the reconstruction of German cities and financed German transactions. Further developing the Anglo-German financial partnership was encouraged by the Bank of England and its governor to show that commercial and industrial collaboration and not aggression would bring prosperity to Germany (Newton 1991, 183; Cain and Hopkins 1993a, 97–99). Free traders appealed to their moderate German counterparts in charge of economic affairs. The intent was that British penetration would pull Germany away from economic autarky, state subsidies, and currency control, and toward a more open and orthodox economic policy (MacDonald 1972, 106, 117; Wendt 1983, 163–64). Free traders countered that any attempt to block short-term loans to Germany would weaken economic moderates (while a budget crash risked contributing to external expansion for raw materials) (Kennedy 1983, 103). As Chamberlain argued, there are sections in Germany "which are anxious to restore international good relations and thereby alleviate the economic difficulties" facing their country (MacDonald 1972, 109).

In the Far East, the Treasury pushed for strengthening Japanese moderates over naval and military extremists.[29] Cooperation would bolster the "better elements" in Tokyo, strengthening the reformers in the Konoe government (Lee 1973, 141).[30] To advance this agenda, in 1935, the Treasury sent Sir Frederick Leith-Ross to China and Japan (known as the Leith-Ross Mission) with the immediate goal of providing a currency loan to China. Before departing for the Far East, Leith-Ross conducted interviews with bankers, financial interests in the City, and businessmen interested in trade with China.[31] Joint Anglo-Japanese financial cooperation on aid to China might give way to a solution to Manchukuo, save the Washington Naval Conference system, arrive at a working arrangement in regard to occupied China, and lead to Japan's return to the League of Nations (Louis 1983, 366).

Finally, neither the Treasury nor the Bank of England wished to become involved in the considerable rescue operation that would inevitably follow from the termination of financial relations with Germany or Japan (Newton 1991, 185). British international creditors that had issued a large volume of short-term credits to Germany opposed calls for stringent exchange and import control arrangements (183–84). Germany had already issued decrees halting the withdrawal of foreign loans, endangering the City. As the Governor of the Bank of England warned, punishment will result in "a loss or freezing up of £35,000,000 of British money" (186). In 1931, in response to the high levels of capital withdrawals from Germany that escalated into a Europe-wide scramble and at the behest of the City Bankers and the Bank of England, London erected the Anglo-German Standstill Agreement (renewed annually until 1939) (Roberts 1991, 64). The Standstill Agreement froze existing credits while interest payments continued, with the goal of keeping the German banks afloat and, more broadly, liberalizing Anglo-German trade. In conjunction (and in opposition to the FBI), bankers called for the temporary suspension of German reparations until conditions improved.[32] Thus, as one author summarizes, free traders lobbied for "a wide range of measures of co-operation in foreign trade and finance which could be appropriately deployed to keep a foot in the door in Central Europe, to check the general drift towards autarky, to relieve international political tension and thus preserve a basis for the re-establishment in the future of the world economic order with the inclusion of Germany" (Wendt 1983, 165).

In the Far East, the inflation rate in China and the instability of China's currency caused alarm in London's financial circles (Trotter 1977, 43). To put China on sound financial ground, the Bank of England, the commercial banks (Hongkong and Shanghai Bank), insurance and trust companies, businessmen, and the commercial and industrial lobby proposed a joint Anglo-Japanese loan to China in 1935 (and another in 1937, issued in London and guaranteed by Britain and Japan). The joint rescue package, the reconstruction of China, and currency reform would benefit British industry by improving economic stability in China.[33]

By 1937, there was declining support among free traders for accommodating Germany and Japan.[34] For instance, the British Bankers' Association passed a resolution that no new credits should be granted for financing German business that could be financed by means of a Standstill Agreement (Forbes 1987, 584, 586). After the outbreak of the Sino-Japanese War (1937), Britain's policy toward Japan became less conciliatory, with commercial groups clamoring for economic retaliation (Lee 1971, 156–65; Trotter 1977, 44–45; Lowe 1981, 161–62). Stephen Endicott suggests that British loan discussions, support for China's currency reserves, and aid in the building of strategic railroads might have pushed the Japanese military into action in 1937 (1973–74, 494–95).[35] Japan's actions threatened Britain's position in Shanghai, its stake in the Maritime Customs, and its shipping and railway interests, while British economic activity throughout north China suffered heavily.[36] Japan was also engaged in a major campaign to undermine the Chinese currency in the hope that the leader of the Chinese Nationalists, Chiang Kai-shek, would be destroyed and that occupied China would be completely absorbed into a yen bloc. To resist Tokyo's further encroachments in China, the City of London, with the support of the Treasury and the Bank of England, extended loans to strengthen China's Nationalist government (and prevent its collapse), encouraged British firms to negotiate partnerships with Chinese corporations (T. V. Soong's China Development Finance Corporation), fostered British investment and trade through Hong Kong, and constructed the Burma Road to deliver supplies (completed in 1938).[37] In 1938, the cabinet approved a scheme for a British stabilization loan for China's currency (Lee 1971, 163). In 1939, London announced a loan provided by four banks (two Chinese and two British), with the British contribution guaranteed by the Treasury.

THE STERLING AREA: THE TRIUMPH OF ORTHODOXY

Within the empire, beleaguered invisible exports ensured that orthodoxy triumphed in the Sterling Area, reinforcing fiscal conservatism (Longstreth 1979, 172; Tomlinson 1990, 102–3, 113–21). Free traders argued that protection would foster inefficiency within the trading bloc (Tomlinson 1990, 75). First, in the Ottawa Agreements, London granted generous provision for the empire in British markets, to the detriment of British manufacturing, allowing the Dominions to secure a relatively greater share of the British market than London secured in the empire markets. This was not a sign of British weakness or the power of the empire countries, but reflected the residual strength of invisible exports (Cain and Hopkins 1993a, 87, 306). Since the empire countries were borrowers and were dependent on Britain's financial services and shipping, they had heavy bills to meet for invisible items. Colonial debtors needed preferential treatment to obtain sterling to service their debt to the City.

Second, as in the past, the prerequisite for the Sterling Area was a stable pound (many countries' exchange rates were pegged to the pound). Free traders still aspired to maintain a high degree of financial authority within the sterling camp in order to retain the confidence of sterling holders. As Cain and Hopkins note, "If, by 1931, they could no longer manage a world economy, the British still aspired to run an empire" (1993a, 73).[38] This was the price Britain had to pay for a smoothly functioning sterling bloc. Third, the Bank of England pursued central bank cooperation within the empire. This included the development of central banking in the Dominions, which maintained a close liaison with the Bank of England and facilitated monetary cooperation. With the development of Dominion central banks, the responsibility of the Bank of England as the center of the whole system was considerably increased, becoming the central bank of central banks (Stewart 1937, 191–94). Finally, the Treasury extended "Treasury control" or its supervisory role to the colonies. The Treasury placed foreign loans under its strict control, lending capital only to the Sterling Area, especially the Dominions. The purpose was to contribute to the stability of exchange rates in the bloc and to help keep non-Dominion currencies linked to the British pound and stable in relation to sterling (185). One unintended consequence of the ability of colonies and dominions to borrow freely on the London market was the strengthening of ties between the City and the empire (Peden 2000, 258).

REARMAMENT

In 1932, the Cabinet revoked the Ten Year Rule, warning that this did not justify immediate increases in defense spending without considering Britain's economic crisis. The Ten Year Rule assumed "that the British Empire will not be engaged in any great war during the next ten years, and that no Expeditionary Force is required for this purpose" (Gibbs 1976, 3). The combination of the Depression, societal pressures, and Treasury control contributed to the further reduction in military spending. The outcome was that actual military preparedness fell well below the minimum levels dictated under the Ten Year Rule. With the suspension of the Ten Year Rule, the military services began to make new demands for military expenditure. In response, in 1934, the Cabinet created the Defence Requirements Committee (DRC) with the goal of preparing a program for Britain's rearmament "for meeting our worst deficiencies."[39]

The DRC's Three Reports

Between 1934 and 1935, the DRC issued three reports on Britain's rearmament program. Much of the early discussions in the DRC focused on a dispute over Britain's priorities: whether the Continental or Far Eastern theater would receive priority. The navy favored the Far East, while the air force emphasized the dangers of an air threat from Germany, and the army called for the need for a Continental Field Force. The Foreign Office (Sir Robert Vansittart) and the Treasury (Sir Warren Fisher) argued that Germany posed the greatest threat. Maurice Hankey (the secretary to the CID) was convinced that Japan posed the long-term threat to Britain's empire.The compromise reached by Hankey was that Japan posed the immediate threat and Germany the long-term threat.

In the initial stages, the DRC's rearmament program was intended to remedy, by 1939, the worst deficiencies in the defense services that disarmament and the Ten Year Rule had caused, while a longer period would be necessary to remedy all military deficiencies.[40] According to the DRC's First Report, in the Far East, the Navy would play the primary role, while the Army and Air Force would help defend ports and bases.[41] To deal with Japan, the DRC called on Britain to modernize its old capital ships and to replace obsolete ones, and to build up Singapore's defense by 1938 in order to demonstrate Britain's commitment to the region, followed by a new attempt at diplomatic rapprochement with Tokyo.[42] The Navy concurred that the most likely threat came from the capital ships of Japan, and not Germany, since the latter was building pocket battleships to raid British commerce (Peden 1979, 114–15). The Admiralty supported the principle of "showing a tooth" to demonstrate Britain's readiness and capacity to send a sufficient fleet to Singapore to prevent unreasonable Japanese action (Shay 1977, 33; Peden 1979, 110).

The DRC's Third Report (1935) called for revising the navy's existing one-power standard to a two-power standard (referred to as the New Standard). The New Standard would ensure that the Royal Navy would be sufficient in size to send a fleet to Singapore to meet the Japanese threat in the Far East, while maintaining a force in its home waters to defend against Germany and a force to protect its trade routes.[43] In 1937, on the first possible day allowed by treaty, Britain laid down five new battleships. In 1938, two additional battleships were laid down. Modernization of older ships was also important to the capital ship program.

While the DRC viewed Japan as the immediate threat, Germany was seen as the long-range threat to Britain's national security interests. Britain's primary fear was that Germany might launch a preemptive knockout air strike against Britain. In order to deter a German air attack, the DRC recommended the completion of fifty-two bomber squadrons and substantial reinforcements of the Fleet Air Arm. The DRC also called for the creation of air reserves. An Army expeditionary force was to be prepared to put four infantry divisions, one tank brigade, one cavalry division, and two air defense brigades on the Continent within one month of war, with the goal of defending the Low Countries (Gibbs 1976, 110–11).

Free-Trade Opposition

Free-trade constituents were apprehensive about the economic nationalists' program of punishing Germany, Japan, and Italy through rearmament. First, they believed that such an expensive program could not be financed without doing damage to the economy and threatening Britain's promising economic recovery. Second, they feared that another Great War would enhance the role of the state in the regulation and management of the economy, curbing the influence of traditional finance and the City (as World War I had shaken gentlemanly capitalism). Such an outcome would permanently shift the locus of relative political strength to the economic nationalist faction. To save their coalition, the free trader solution was to moderate the extreme policies of the economic nationalists' rearmament program, press for arms limitation agreements with Germany and Japan in order to lower the cost of hegemony, and exchange British credits and loans for arms control arrangements, participation in collective security, and their return to the League of Nations.[44]

Free traders, especially the Labour Party, Treasury, the Board of Trade, and the Bank of England, opposed the DRC's rearmament program for three reasons.[45] First, Britain was already running a trade deficit, and the DRC's rearmament program would increase the size of this deficit. Between 1931 and 1938, Britain ran a balance of trade deficit and a balance of payments deficit in every year except for 1935 (Murray 1994, 403). Britain's dependence on foreign imports for food, raw materials, and engineering products required that England maintain a high level of exports in order to strengthen its balance of payments. Rearmament would require an increase in imports and shift production from exporting industries (it was estimated that as much as 25 to 30 percent of the cost of rearmament would come from imported raw materials) (Shay 1983, 92). As such, Britain would have to increase its exports or run a negative balance of payments, drawing down its foreign currency, gold reserves, overseas investments, and ability to raise credit abroad—the main components of its war chest. The Treasury feared that a long-run balance of payments deficit would reduce international confidence in the stability of the pound, further undermining Britain's financial reserves.[46] This would be reinforced by the loss of foreign confidence in sterling on the part of holders of short-term capital (Parker 1975, 645; Peden 1984, 17).

Second, export trade opposed massive prewar rearmament because it would cause dislocation of both skilled labor and industry from civil trade. The most troublesome bottleneck from the perspective of the armament industries was associated with the shortage of skilled labor and machine tools. After World War I, Britain experienced a rapid demobilization of its war industry. The movement of skilled labor and the conversion of civilian industry to military production would hurt Britain's export trade and balance of trade by diverting labor and factories from the production of foreign-exchange-earning export goods (Thomas 1983, 563–65). Free traders especially opposed calls for industrial mobilization, compulsion of industry for rearmament, and interference in such matters as the level of profit.[47] After 1938, with the weakening of the free-trade coalition, the government asked industry to give priority to rearmament orders.

Third, free traders resisted financing the DRC's rearmament program by large increases in government borrowing or taxation (Peden 1979, 1984). Borrowing was opposed by the Treasury because deficit spending would cause inflation and perhaps a financial crash on the scale of 1931. Inflation would adversely affect trade by increasing the price of Britain's exports, resulting in a rise in imports and a decline in exports. Alternatively, increased taxation was opposed by the Treasury because it would lower consumer demand (hindering Britain's economic recovery) and draw down Britain's ability to mobilize additional resources in the event of prolonged war.[48] The only choice was financial stringency.

The Free Traders' Alternative Rearmament Program

The free traders advanced an alternative rearmament program.[49] Their solution to imperial Germany's military challenge was to build up the RAF

(Peden 1979, 106–50). The RAF was viewed as the most cost-effective "shop window" deterrent against a German air attack. Britain would construct as many frontline bombers as possible, with few air reserves. Initially, the purpose was to discourage Germany from trying to compete with Britain, accepting a permanent inferiority in the air. Later, the goal was to deter Germany from attacking by demonstrating that Berlin could not win a short war with a knockout blow. In the worse-case scenario, once the nation survived, Britain could focus on a more offensive and Continental role. In 1937, with the advent of radar, which would allow fighters to find and confront an enemy's attacking bombers, as well as with advances in fighter planes, the Treasury called for the construction of cheaper fighter planes over more expensive bombers (Smith 1978, 315, 329–34; Peden 1979, 128–34; Greenwood 1994, 30–31).

One debate between the Treasury and the Air Staff centered on the question of reserves. The Air Staff called the Treasury's policy "window dressing" (Shay 1977, 41–44). They demanded that sufficient reserves also be provided in order to maintain Britain's frontline strength despite losses (Peden 1979, 118–20). The Treasury argued that the bulk of the reserves should be provided only after 1939. A second debate, after 1937, centered on the ratio of bombers to fighters (Shay 1977, 172–73). Chamberlain and Fisher favored cheaper fighters, while the Air Staff backed bombers. According to the government, one bomber cost the equivalent of four fighters (Peden 1979, 134).

To curb Japan's naval rearmament and to prevent a prohibitively expensive naval race in the Far East, free traders supported the Washington and London Naval Agreements.[50] For free traders, naval arms limitation with Japan between 1921 and the mid-1930s constituted the most successful aspect of their effort to reduce the military spending of a rival power. The Washington Naval Conference approved three agreements: the Four Power Treaty, the Nine Power Treaty, and a naval construction ratio. First, bowing to American suspicions, Britain replaced the Anglo-Japanese Alliance of 1902 with the Four Power Treaty signed by the United States, Britain, Japan, and France. The four states agreed to common consultation, with disputes to be referred to a conference of the major interested powers. Second, the Nine Power Treaty affirmed China's integrity and sovereignty, preserving the territorial status quo. Third, the Washington Conference called for the immediate cancellation of all existing capital shipbuilding programs, a naval holiday of ten years duration in which no capital ship construction would be allowed, and the scrapping of a number of new and old ships.[51] This ratio just permitted the Admiralty to send a fleet to the Far East while keeping a one-power standard against the next largest European navy (Kennedy 1976, 341).

At the London Naval Conference (1930), the Labour government signed a second naval limitation treaty with Japan. Unresolved at the Washington Conference was the matter of limiting warships displacing less than ten thousand tons. While Japan pushed for a 70 percent ratio in heavy cruisers, Britain and the United States advocated to extend the 60 percent ratio for capital ships to all categories of vessels. The compromised agreement was a 10:6 ratio on large cruisers, parity on submarines, and a 10:7 ratio on other categories of auxiliary craft.

To moderate Germany's military buildup, while preventing a repeat of the costly naval race that preceded World War I, free traders supported diplomacy in the form of the Anglo-German Naval Agreement (1935).[52] The Naval Agreement permitted the maintenance of a German navy no larger than 35 percent of the size of Britain's surface fleet in all classes of vessels and 45 percent in submarines. For financial interests that were anxious to limit overall spending on armaments, restricting the German fleet allowed Britain to rearm at the moderate pace dictated by fiscal orthodoxy, while providing for a sufficient force to protect against Japanese aggression in the western Pacific (Howard 1972). There was also the belief that bilateral negotiations might move from naval matters to the urgent question of air power and a multilateral Air Pact directed against surprise aerial bombardment. Between 1934 and 1938, Britain launched several attempts to conclude an air pact with Germany. Britain had added pressure to reach an agreement with Germany, because in 1934, Japan announced that it did not intend to renew the Washington and London Naval Treaties when the latter expired in 1936. Yet, free traders opposed any upward revision of the Navy's one-power standard to a two-power standard since it might trigger competition with Germany and Japan.

Free traders, especially the Treasury, opposed expenditure for a Continental size army in peacetime and during the initial stages of war (see Peden 1979, 113–50, for army, naval, and air policy; Cain and Hopkins 1993a, 96–105). A Continental army was expensive and would cause economic dislocation by diverting manpower from production. Instead, British labor (kept at home) would build the equipment to support the armies of its Continental allies. Eventually, Britain might have to commit an army to the Continent (Murray 1979a). As well, with the advent of long-range aircraft the RAF could simply fly over the Low Countries, reducing their strategic worth and further reducing the Continental role of the army (rejecting a "Continental Commitment" for a doctrine of "Limited Liability"). Finally, the outbreak of civil disturbances in Palestine beginning in 1936 required eighteen battalions of the British army.

Finally, Chamberlain argued that a strong British economy would deter emerging contenders from challenging its regional hegemony (Coghlan 1972, 215; Smith 1978, 330–32; Greenwood 1994, 30). The Treasury's position was that Britain had a financial advantage over its enemies in a long war due to its strong economy and large war chest. Britain's superior war potential would deter a rising challenger because any conflict would become a costly and protracted war, which Britain would win. Consequently, Britain had to safeguard its fiscal strength, for if the emerging challengers detected a strain in Britain's economy, they would no longer be deterred by the prospect of a prolonged war (Peden 1979, 65).

The Treasury's financial concern was not unwarranted. As Britain's peacetime defense spending increased, its gold reserves began to decline. Britain's defense spending jumped from 8.1 percent of GNP in 1938, to 21.4 percent in 1939, to 51.7 percent in 1940 (Dunbabin 1975, 588). Between April 1938 and March 1939, Britain's gold reserves alone declined from 800 million pounds to 300 million pounds (Parker 1975, 643; Peden 1984, 17). By 1939, Britain had already diminished its war chest to pay for the necessary imports (compared to 1914, Britain had less resources and could not borrow from the United States, because the 1934 Johnson Act banned loans to defaulting nations). By 1941, gold stocks had dwindled to almost nothing and Britain was dependent upon American financial and military assistance to defend its empire.

The Collapse of Free-Trade Resistance

By 1936, Britain committed itself to full rearmament, reflecting the weakening of the free-trade coalition and the defection of many of its core supporters to the economic nationalists' side. As Hancock and Gowing note, "after 1935, the initiative passed to the men who were attempting, very often under great pressure, to build up the war sector of the British industry" (1953, 45). In 1936, the cabinet approved the whole of the DRC's new program, except for the proposed expenditure on the Territorial Army. In the same year, the Treasury relaxed the procedure for the annual Estimates, funding individual projects rather than allocating sums annually, speeding the construction period (Peden 1979, 40). By 1937, Sir Thomas Inskip (Minister for the Co-ordination of Defense), who was authorized to review defense spending and supported the Treasury view, called for maximum armaments production between 1938 and 1939.[53] His rationale was that Britain could bargain only from a position of strength (Shay 1977, 189–93, 214–16; Peden 1979, 92–100). Even the Labour Party stopped voting against the military Estimates and passed a resolution stating that "we must confront potential aggressors with an emphatic superiority of armed strength," but they still opposed military conscription (Gordon 1969, 66–77; Lloyd 1970, 197; Shay 1977, 218). The public was also more vocal concerning the conduct of the rearmament program. Indeed, budget rationing barely survived the *Anschluss* (Greenwood 1994, 33). After the Munich Conference, the Treasury recognized that it was "being progressively put out of action" (Peden 1979, 44) and that "Treasury parsimony" would no longer effectively set limits on the production of weapons (Parker 1981, 313).

Between 1933–34 and 1938, defense spending more than doubled, from 103 million pounds to 262 million pounds, and then nearly doubled again by 1939, to 400 million pounds (Thomas 1983, 554, table 1). The most dramatic increase in defense outlays was on the air force, whose plans were increased from the DRC's recommendations in 1934. Naval expansion was restrained by the terms of the Washington and London Naval Treaties until 1937, and after 1937 by limitations in industrial capacity. After 1937, expenditures rose rapidly, as if the full two-power standard was in effect (Bright 1985, 241). The Admiralty was able to lay down nearly all the major fleet units it planned in 1936–39 for the New Standard, especially in terms of capital ships and cruisers (Peden 1979, 165). Until 1934, the Admiralty had enjoyed preeminence among the services, leaving it with fewer shortages than the other branches.[54] In contrast, the army was restrained until 1939 and then drastically expanded by conscription, although this move was opposed by the Labour Party.[55]

Shortages of skilled labor in key industries slowed rearmament. In response, economic nationalists advanced their agenda of state intervention, compulsion, and defense production through the force of law, while free traders resisted calls for government control of wages, prices, profits, and production (Shay 1977, 92–102). In 1938, the Cabinet asked industry to give preference to military work, speeding up the rearmament program, however, only on a voluntary basis that rejected the use of state controls (Barnett 1972, 415; Peden 1979, 128–33). There was also discussion of a scheme to create a "shadow armaments industry" of new factories built through government contracts and managed by existing firms (Dunbabin 1975, 597–98; Peden 1979, 46, 100, 171–72).

DISTRIBUTIONAL CONSEQUENCES

The grand strategy of restrained punishment altered the relative balance of domestic power, ratcheting-up the strength of the supporters of the economic nationalists while weakening the entrenched free traders. Economic nationalists translated these political and economic gains into a successful propaganda campaign leading the general public to depart from the traditions of free trade, fiscal orthodoxy, arms limitations, and collective security to become more defense, protectionist, and empire oriented (Darby 1987, 125–26). The outcome benefited inefficient industry, empire-oriented bureaucrats, and the military services.

As the free traders feared, empowering economic nationalists meant the death of "gentlemanly capitalism," with the state playing an important role in managing the economy and industry. At home, the government led the reorganization of industry. Arguing that British industry was too individualistic and too competitive, the state supported huge industrial consolidation, strengthening monopolistic tendencies and thereby breaching economic liberalism. The government also directly intervened in the economy to promote industrial planning. A Director General of Munitions Production was appointed followed by the creation of a Directorate of Industrial Planning to survey the industrial capacity of the country and its readiness to convert to the production of weapons in time of war. A Ministry of Supply was created to control the distribution of raw material to those industries most vital to the nation's defense.

Abroad, the Federation of British Industries (FBI), the primary business lobby, called for binding agreements with Japan and Germany to protect Britain's market share and to limit competition in manufacturing (Holland 1981, 295–96). In 1937, the FBI invited the Japan Economic Federation to a conference to push for comprehensive cartels, including a managed price-system (contacts ceased once fighting on the mainland intensified) (Newton 1995, 492–94). Next, the FBI called for an Anglo-German cartel of producer alliances covering production, fixing prices, and allocating markets and quotas (Holland 1981, 296–98). In 1938, the FBI initiated conversations with the Reichsgruppe Industrie (RI) on industrial relations, resulting in the Anglo-German Coal Agreement (1939) allocating to Britain and Germany quotas for the total exports of the European coal-exporting countries. The sequel, the Dusseldorf Agreement, was intended to increase the consumption of British and German products through the regulation of production and consumption by market sharing, quotas, fixed prices, and joint development schemes (Francis 1939, 325–28; Newton 1995, 495–96).

CONCLUSION

The shift in Britain's international environment guided London's grand strategy by altering the relative political power of domestic actors and interest groups. In contrast to the decades prior to World War I in which Britain confronted a mix of liberal and imperial contenders, during the interwar period, Britain confronted mostly imperial contenders, especially in regions that were important markets. Specifically, Germany, Japan, Italy, and to a lesser degree France sought to impose a system of economic autarky and commercial self-sufficiency in any region they came to dominate, blocking Britain's future access to its traditional interests in the locale.

Confronting predominantly imperial contenders altered the domestic structure of opportunities within Britain, strengthening economic nationalists, while diminishing the standing of the free traders, especially the City as a financial center. Empowered economic nationalists translated these gains into a program of imperial preferences, tariffs, duties, and embargo on capital issues for non-empire borrowers; rearmament; and retreat from laissez-faire economics through abandonment of the gold standard, producer cartels, state intervention in the economy, and industrial planning.

For reasons of economy and to safeguard their faction's existence, the entrenched free-trade coalition pushed for a self-reinforcing strategy of cooperation with Germany, Japan, and Italy. Their fear was that the economic nationalists' agenda would completely destroy gentlemanly capitalism in Britain. Cooperation had the domestic consequence of moderating the rollback of their faction's relative political power, even though it risked undermining the nation's interests (see chap. 6 for an extended discussion of this point). After 1935, the impact of the free-trade coalition was felt more on their resistance to the economic nationalists' calls for transitioning to wartime government control over the economy than on restricting military Estimates. As one author notes, three changes would have made Britain more prepared for war by 1939: (1) the creation of a Ministry of Supply (to organize the economy by implementing physical controls); (2) securing labor's and industry's cooperation to shift skilled labor into defense industry and training unskilled labor for these tasks; and (3) Chamberlain as prime minister in 1935 rather than 1937 (Shay 1983, 90). The first and second options were resisted by the free traders. Free traders feared that minor state encroachment and partial controls would lead to general controls and would require government intervention further back and forward, destroying their laissez-faire precepts of liberalism and voluntarism.

One lasting consequence of empowering economic nationalists was that it made it difficult to reverse Britain's grand strategy in later periods. The superior strength of the economic nationalists retarded Britain's liberalization, even after other states, such as the United States, reversed their foreign commercial policy. As a result, empowered economic nationalists clashed with the United States, whose goal was to dismantle the British empire and to roll back imperial preferences. Washington used the leverage created by London's dependence on American financial assistance during the war to punish Britain by destroying its imperial economic bloc, dismantling Ottawa, and breaking up the Sterling Area (Kimball 1971). The United States included clauses in the Atlantic Charter and the Lend-Lease Act calling for the elimination of nondiscriminatory trade barriers. Not surprisingly, Winston Churchill called Lend-Lease the "most unsordid act."

CHAPTER 5

Imperial Contenders and Spain's Grand Strategy of Punishment, 1621–1640

In the late sixteenth century, Spain was the preeminent world power, and its wealthy overseas empire was the envy of the emerging European states (G. Williams 1966, 9). In 1580, Madrid's claims became even more all-encompassing when King Philip II of Spain secured the Crown of Portugal and its overseas empire in Brazil, Africa, and the East Indies, adding them to Spain's global empire. Spain found itself in an unrivaled position, dominating the world's trade routes, markets, resources, and strategic lines of communication. The Spanish Crown became the largest handler of bullion and accounted for nearly all of the world's deposits of good quality marine salt, provided the bulk of Europe's sugar, and became Europe's leading emporium of pepper. This great wealth allowed Spain to extract resources and borrow money at short notice and in large amounts to finance extensive fortifications and fortresses, a large standing army, and a big navy for the defense of its Continental and overseas empire.

Spain's imperial wealth and its scattered empire also attracted challengers for regional hegemony. As early as the 1570s, emerging states began to encroach upon Spain's global interests at uneven rates, in disparate regions, and without the expense of imperial defense.[1] On the Continent, Spain confronted England, France, and the United Provinces (Dutch), as well as periodic challenges from the Ottoman Sultan.[2] In the East and West Indies (Asia and America), and in Africa, Spain's empire was challenged by English and Dutch assaults. Attacks by the Barbary pirates and from the Ottoman Empire harassed Spanish shipping and trade in the Mediterranean and North Africa. During the Thirty Years' War, in Germany, Spain supported the Catholics against the Protestants, in France, the Catholic League against the Huguenots, and its Austrian cousins against the Turks. As Paul Kennedy notes, "[Spain's] price of possessing so many territories was the existence of numerous foes" (1987, 48).

Within Spain, opposing economic nationalist and liberal factions competed for control over the declining state's grand strategy. Their preferred grand strategies clashed on important issues such as taxation, *vellón* coinage (Madrid resorted to the coinage of copper to save silver), army and navy construction, royal absolutism, international peace settlements and truces, and Empire Unity. The constituents of the economic nationalists coalition included the military, King Philip IV (1621–65) and his Count-Duke of Olivares, Gaspar de Guzmán (1622–43), the Council of States, the Council of the Indies, the Council of Portugal, and the supporting administrators. The economic nationalists' desired grand strategy called for restoring Spain's power by punishing France, England, and the United Provinces through (1) greater military preparedness and engaging in offensive military operations, (2) creating new exclusive trading companies, and (3) increasing societal resource extraction by expanding the king's fiscal powers and absolutist claims (over the Cortes of Castile) and unifying the kingdoms of the monarchy. In 1621, Olivares and his advisers called for the renewal of the Dutch war because the humiliating Twelve Years' Truce of 1609 had undermined Spain's international reputation (Elliott 1989, 121). Even the president of the Council of Finance argued that the truce was "worse than if the war had gone on," while the cost of maintaining a standing army in peacetime was not much more than in wartime (Elliott 1963, 321). Economic nationalists argued that the failure to extract additional resources to augment the nation's military capability would undermine Spain's national security, leaving it weak and vulnerable to attack by France, England, and the United Provinces. Cooperation was resisted because it risked strengthening the war-making capacity of these challengers, eroding Spain's reputation for predation, undermining Madrid's exclusive trading companies, and, most importantly, strengthening the contending liberal faction who would push for a more accommodative grand strategy.

In opposition, the members of the liberal coalition included the ministers in Philip IV's Council of State, the deputies of the Cortes of Castile (the Cortes existed to vote taxes through the *millones*, a sales tax on basic foodstuffs, that were granted to the Crown), Ambrogio Spínola (commander of the Flanders army and chief proponent for the original 1609 truce with the Dutch), Spain's archduke in Brussels, Seville's business community and merchants, Castile's aristocracy, and industry (textiles, metallurgy, and shipbuilding). Concerned with lowering the cost of hegemony, the liberals' grand strategy called for cooperation by (1) military retrenchment, (2) fiscal restraint in government spending and taxation, and (3) renewal of the Twelve Years' Truce with the United Provinces and diplomatic approaches to France and England. Liberals argued that prolonged and steep resource extraction through *vellón* coinage and the debasement of coinage, attempts to squeeze additional revenue from Castile, government borrowing, confiscated private remittances, and suspension of debt payments would create an unfavorable investment climate and thereby erode the home market, the underpinning for future military spending.

The commercial nature of the rising states swayed Spain's grand strategy toward punishment. Spain only confronted imperial contenders for hegemony; the Dutch, French, and English sought to replace Spain's exclusive spheres with their own mercantilistic order. Their commercial nature pushed the Crown, the governors of the main fortresses in Flanders, different councils, and the military to advance a grand strategy of punishment, often on several fronts simultaneously. Spain punished these states by building and creating new armies, *armadas*, and fortifications, and launching offensive land and sea operations; subsidizing Catholic allies; and creating exclusive trading companies. Punishment required extracting additional men and revenue at home and in the empire. Members of the liberal coalition supported facets of the economic nationalists' policy package, recognizing that the loss of wealthy locales risked strengthening the war-making capacity of these imperial challengers, who would block Spain's exclusive access to its empire. However, liberals lobbied to restrain the economic nationalists' extreme fiscal, political, and military programs for reason of economy and for fear of further strengthening the opposing coalition, who would press for a more belligerent grand strategy.

The domestic distributional consequences of punishment ratcheted-up the economic and political clout of the economic nationalists, while further weakening the liberal coalition. Empowered economic nationalists translated their gains into Royal Absolutism at home and in the monarchy. The two main barriers to the economic nationalists' hard-line grand strategy were the Cortes of Castile (Spain's parliament) and the independence of the provinces outside of Castile. Since the 1590s, the Cortes had experienced a revival in their autonomy over finances. Through a strategy of punishment, the economic nationalists intentionally rolled back the liberal coalition. Total warfare on several fronts pressured the Cortes to approve new and larger *millones*, thereby granting the Crown complete control over public revenue.

The economic nationalists also used the punishment of contenders to unify the empire and to share the burden of war through a program known as the Union of Arms. Much of Spain's empire was a collection of inherited lands that were ruled under different constitutions.[3] The economic nationalists capitalized on the fiscal necessity from the war with France (especially after the French invasion of the Iberian peninsula in 1638) to compel autonomous republics to contribute to the war effort. As discussed in chapter 6, the danger of punishing everywhere is that this strategy undermined Spain's economic capacity for future military security and contributed to revolts throughout the kingdom.

This chapter examines how Spain responded to these multiple challengers. The first section examines the emerging contenders that Spain confronted in disparate parts of its empire. The second section examines the conflicting agendas of the economic nationalist and the liberal coalitions. The last sections discuss the distributional impact of punishment on the domestic balance of political power and on Madrid's grand strategy.

THE EMERGING CONTENDERS FOR REGIONAL LEADERSHIP

The major challenges to Spain's empire came from the French army and the English and Dutch navies. The conventional view that Spain lost its global hegemony to France in 1659 with the signing of the Peace of Pyrenees oversimplifies the dilemma that Spain confronted during this period. Had Spain encountered only an emerging France on the Continent, Madrid could have concentrated its extensive military and naval resources from its global empire, overwhelming France's military capability.[4] Instead, Spain's hegemony was challenged by several protagonists, who rose at uneven rates and threatened Spain's leadership in disparate theaters and corridors of communication.

First, rather than confronting a single emerging contender for global hegemony, Spain confronted the United Provinces, France, and England, as well as other challengers such as the Ottoman Empire and Sweden under Gustavus Adolphus. Beginning in the 1570s, the Dutch challenged Spain's position in the Low Countries (Flanders). By 1600, an emerging United Provinces challenged Madrid's leadership in the Spice Islands in Asia.[5] Two decades later, with the creation of the Dutch West India Company (1621), the United Provinces concentrated on capturing Spain's (Portugal's) sugar plantations in Brazil. Following on the heels of the Dutch assault, England was repelled by both Spain and the Dutch, failing in its initial attempt to gain a foothold in the Far East.[6] Subsequently, the

English concentrated their assault on the Portuguese empire in the Indian subcontinent and Indian Ocean, while financially and militarily supporting the Dutch revolt on the Continent against Spain. Finally, beginning in the late 1620s, no longer preoccupied by religious wars, France under King Louis VIII and his foreign minister, Cardinal Richelieu, challenged Spain's European empire. This challenge occurred in Italy, Germany, and even Flanders. In the 1650s, France assaulted Spain's overseas empire.

Second, rather than being challenged in a single instance, uneven rates of industrialization meant contenders for regional hegemony encroached on and in some instances surpassed Spain's industrial lead, with some challengers rising earlier and faster than others. The major sectors of industrialization in the seventeenth century included textiles, metallurgy, and shipbuilding (Lynch 1992, 219). The Dutch were the first to surpass Spain in a number of key industrial sectors such as shipbuilding. In addition, as the leading commercial power, the Dutch were able to convert their financial and industrial strength into military power, building and maintaining the largest navy in the world, in addition to a powerful army. England was the second power to encroach on Spain's lead, especially in central industries such as textiles and metallurgy. With the end of the religious wars in France, Paris began to encroach on Spain in metallurgy, which was an essential component for creating a modern military.

NETHERLANDS: UNITED PROVINCES, ENGLAND, FRANCE

The Dutch republic was a loose confederation of seven provinces (known as the United Provinces) that had successfully rebelled against Spain beginning in the 1570s (the ten southern provinces remained loyal to Spain, or were suppressed by Spain, and were called the Spanish Netherlands). This rebellion (the Eighty Years' War) lasted until Spain formally recognized the Dutch Republic in the Treaty of Munster in 1648.

In 1609, after years of fighting, Spain and the United Provinces agreed to the Twelve Years' Truce (Truce of Antwerp). In this humiliating truce, the Crown unofficially recognized Dutch sovereignty. In 1621, upon the expiration of the truce and with the renewal of its war on the Spanish Netherlands (including the North Sea and the Atlantic approaches), the United Provinces was the first contender to challenge Spain. Since the Low Countries were characterized by a dense network of forts, strongholds, fortified towns, and dikes, the war quickly became a costly land war of attrition for both sides. Beginning in 1626 (and lasting for the next eight years), the Dutch launched a series of offensives against the Spanish Netherlands. In 1628, the Dutch position in Europe was strengthened by three events that occurred in disparate parts of Spain's empire: (1) the onset of the Mantuan Succession crisis in Italy between France and Spain, opening another front, (2) the loss of the annual Spanish treasure fleet to the Dutch off the coast of Cuba (New Spain silver fleet), and (3) the fall of the Huguenot stronghold at La Rochelle to Louis XIII's army, freeing the French army for war against Spain.

Preparing for the Dutch assault on the Spanish Netherlands, the Dutch army ballooned to 128,000 men, including West India Company troops, nearly four times the size of the Spanish army of Flanders (Israel 1982, 176–77). In 1632, the Dutch forces continued to pressure Spain in the Netherlands, threatening Antwerp and capturing Maastricht, one of the most serious defeats suffered by Spain during the war. In 1635, opening a second front in the Netherlands, France declared war on Madrid, threatening Spain's strategic lines of communication and military highway, known as the Spanish Road, which connected the wealthy and strategic areas of northern Italy (Milan) and the Spanish Netherlands. Control over the Spanish Road allowed Spain to shift resources between the fronts in Italy and the Netherlands.[7] Advancing north with 30,000 troops through Luxemburg and meeting up with 30,000 Dutch troops, France penetrated the Spanish Netherlands south to Antwerp, before being repelled by Spain's army of Flanders.

ITALY: FRANCE, OTTOMANS

In Italy, Spain controlled almost half of the peninsula, including the states of Lombardy, Naples, Sicily, and Sardinia. The initial threat to Spain's leadership in Italy came from the Ottoman Empire. By the mid-1570s, the Ottoman threat had receded because Istanbul was preoccupied with Persia, only to be replaced by the French onslaught on Spain's European hegemony. During 1625, the French invaded the strategic Valtelline Pass in North Italy and blockaded Genoa, threatening to cut the Spanish Road (in the same year, the English fleet launched a raid on Cadiz; now Spain was at war with France, the United Provinces, and England simultaneously).[8] In 1629, opening another front and further stretching Spain's resources, Cardinal Richelieu led the French invasion of Spanish Italy (resulting in the War of Mantua) in an attempt to assert France's preeminence in Europe and to capture the wealth of northern Italy (it was widely recognized that the Netherlands and Italy were the foundations of Spain's domination over the world at large). In the aftermath of the War of Mantua, France continued to harass Spain's empire in Italy.

GERMANY: SWEDEN, GERMANY, FRANCE

In 1618, the Protestant estates in Bohemia revolted against their new Catholic ruler, Archduke Ferdinand II, initiating the Thirty Years' War.[9] Spain's concern was that a successful revolt by Bohemia would be followed by the spread of subversion throughout the empire. In the early 1630s, the Swedish king, Gustavus Adolphus, moved into Germany, inflicting one defeat after another on the Habsburg forces. During 1632, France entered the fray against Spain, taking Lorraine and in 1633 blocking the Spanish Road. From 1632 through 1634, the French also subsidized the anti-Habsburg states.

EAST AND WEST INDIES: HOLLAND, ENGLAND, FRANCE

Europe was only one of several theaters to which Spain had to devote its economic, military, and political resources. In 1580, Spain acquired Portugal and its extensive empire in Brazil and the East Indies. In the Far East, the rising sea power of the United Provinces, and later England, challenged Spain's hegemony from the Cape of Good Hope to the Spice Islands. Dutch encroachment on Spain's Far Eastern empire began in earnest in 1602, with the creation of the mercantilist long-distance trading company, the Dutch East India Company (the Vereenigde Oost-Indische Compagnie, or VOC). By 1619, the VOC had made substantial inroads in the Indies, establishing its principal Far Eastern base at Batavia (Jakarta).

After the Dutch-Spanish Twelve Years' Truce (1621), VOC forces launched a new wave of offensives against Spain's eastern empire (the VOC was aided by a temporary truce in its conflict with the English East India Company, lasting until 1624).[10] The Dutch target was Spain's empire in Malaysia and the Spice Islands. The VOC sought to capture Spain's profitable traffic in pepper and spices (cloves, nutmeg, cinnamon, mace) and replace it with the VOC's own spice monopoly.[11] The Dutch also challenged Spain's possession of Manila (which linked China, Japan, and the New World), China's foreign trade, and Taiwan. By 1623, the Dutch had ninety ships, four large garrisons, and twenty forts in the region (Israel 1982, 117).

Following in Dutch footsteps, England sought to carve out its own exclusive sphere in Spain's East Indies. However, the English East India Company (EIC, established in 1600) was repelled from the region by both Spanish and VOC counterpressure in the 1620s. While the English did make some headway in the region (in Indonesia), the EIC concentrated its assault on Portugal's empire in the Indian Ocean, particularly in India. Beginning with Surat (India), and extending to Basra and Hormuz (Oman) in the Persian Gulf, to the Red Sea, and even to the coast of East Africa, England's expansion forced Spain to divert resources from the other fronts to the Indian subcontinent.[12]

A similar pattern of encroachment unfolded in Spain's empire in the West Indies. During the Twelve Years' Truce, the Dutch were the first to challenge Spain's hegemony in the West Indies. In 1621, with the expiration of the truce, the Dutch created the West India Company (WIC), based on the successful VOC, with the goal of predatory territorial acquisition in the Americas (Appleby 1987). The WIC's first major assault was a large-scale attack on the sugar-producing province of Pernambuco (Brazil) and Puerto Rico. In 1628, ships from the Dutch WIC captured Spain's entire Mexican silver fleet at Matanzas Bay in Cuba (10 million ducats, or equal to two-thirds of the annual cost of the Dutch army), dealing a blow to Madrid in the midst of its costly confrontation with France over Mantua. By 1630, the Dutch had secured a foothold in Brazil (in the province of Pernambuco), and by 1632–33, the Dutch were on the verge of capturing the region's wealthy sugar plantations.

Elsewhere in the Americas, operating from sparsely populated islands, the French and English used small ships to harass Spanish trade in the Caribbean (the English force was centered in Jamaica and the French in St. Dominique). French and English buccaneers crossed the Isthmus, attacking the Spanish Pacific trade as well. Farther north, Dutch, French, and English expansion centered on North America, well out of Spanish reach. The English established colonies in Virginia (1607), Plymouth (1620), and Massachusetts (1630).

Spain's rate of decline was far from simultaneous, rapid, or uniform in nature across its vast empire. While Madrid had the revenue, armies, and resources to defeat any single rising challenger, Spain confronted an emerging France, England, and the United Provinces, as well as the Ottoman Empire and Sweden. Oversimplifying this onslaught makes it difficult to understand the hurdle that Madrid confronted in restoring the balance between its material resources and global commitments while protecting its productive strength and its national security.

IMPERIAL SPAIN

Spain acquired an empire with the primary goal of achieving economic self-sufficiency. Mercantilism was a system designed to increase the economic wealth and the military power of the state (G. Williams 1966, 9, 11). It was widely believed that a favorable balance of trade would bring in gold and silver, thereby increasing the nation's wealth and ultimately its military power. For Spain, overseas colonies guaranteed the use of metropolitan shipping and exclusive access to markets and raw materials, while shutting out foreign commercial competition. In addition, colonies were a source of direct revenue for the Crown not subject to domestic constraints. In the case of Spain, the revenue was outside of the control of Castile's Cortes.

Beginning in 1503, to protect its monopoly on its overseas trade from foreign penetration and domestic competition, Madrid created exclusive trading companies. In the Americas, participation in colonial trade was limited to a single Spanish trading company, the Casa de la Contratación, based in Seville, with a branch in Cádiz (Parry 1966, 66; G. Williams 1966, 10). The Casa de la Contratación checked, taxed, and regulated the entire commerce between Spain and the Americas. As specified by the Casa de la Contratación, each year two large convoys under heavily armed escort sailed from Spain, one to Portobelo and the other to Veracruz. No ships were allowed to sail except in the convoys, no ports could be used for transatlantic trade except the designated few, and no foreigners were allowed to engage in the trade.

Based on the Casa de la Contratación, Madrid established additional monopoly trading companies, including in 1624 the Seville Admiralty Board or Almirantazgo de los paises septentrionales, assigning it jurisdiction and control over all trade with northern Europe and later extending exclusive rights to the whole of the Iberian Peninsula (Israel 1986, 524, 1990, 17–18, 213–45; Lynch 1992, 223–24). The purposes of this mercantilist trading company were to replace the Dutch as the main trading partners of the Hansa towns of north Germany and to check Flemish, German, Danish-Norwegian, French, and English commerce in the region (Israel 1986, 517). By weakening the mercantilist system of the competing states, and especially undermining Dutch economic power, Madrid hoped that

Amsterdam would return to the bargaining table and sue for a truce on Spanish terms.

The Almirantazgo had two roles: (1) organize an armed convoy system (like the Americas' transatlantic convoy system) between Flanders and Spain (stationed on Germany's Baltic coast) and (2) head a system of customs to control trade between all Andalusian ports and northern Europe with the ultimate goal of interlocking the Almirantazgo with a global network of monopoly trading companies in the Levant and India. While the Almirantazgo failed in creating a convoy system, it succeeded in injuring the Dutch by excluding their goods from ports in Flanders, the Iberian Peninsula, Italy, and Spain's overseas empire.[13] Madrid also had the right to check and certify that cargoes for the Iberian and Italian Peninsulas were non-Dutch (cargoes lacking certificates were confiscated). The Almirantazgo halted Dutch shipping, denied the Dutch access to the salt pans in Spain, blocked Dutch goods from entry into Spain, and excluded spices from the Dutch East Indies (Israel 1990, 19). The success of the Almirantazgo forced the Dutch to seek commodities at their source, in the Spanish Indies.

THE IMPERIAL CONTENDERS

The commercial policies of imperial France, England, and the United Provinces were directed at carving out their own exclusive economic spheres and barring foreign access to the region. Each state sought to replace Spain's preferential monopoly with their own mercantilist order, blocking Spain's future access to its markets, investments, and resources in the respective locales. The trading companies of England, the United Provinces, and France tied up much of their resources in military enterprises including armed ships and escorts, troops, fortresses, and fortified settlements. As such, commercial enterprise and armed forces went together (Brightwell 1974, 281–82). Some of these monopoly companies included the Dutch East Indies Company (1602) and the West Indies Company (1621); the English Muscovy Company (1555), the Levant Company (1605), the Massachusetts Bay Company (1628), and the East India Company (1601); the French Compagnie des iles d'Amerique (1627); as well as the Swedish African Company, the Spanish Company (1577), the East India Company (1601), and the Virginia Company (1606).[14] Consequently, Spain viewed all of these emerging contenders for regional hegemony as adversaries and future rivals.

THE UNITED PROVINCES

The Dutch used the years of the Spanish-Dutch Truce (1609–21) to consolidate and extend their gains in the East and West Indies at the expense of Spain's Portuguese empire.[15] Relentless Dutch assaults to carve out its own mercantilist spheres of influence in the Indies undermined Spain's imperial wealth in two ways. First, in capturing the wealthy sugar plantations in Brazil, the treasure fleets in the Americas, and the spice trade in the east Indies, the Dutch trading companies blocked Spain's access to its valuable markets, resources, and investments in the region, which Madrid needed to finance the defense of its empire. Second, with fewer resources coming in from Spain's empire, the Dutch challenge pressured Madrid to increase its internal rate of extraction for the defense of its empire and to divert resources from domestic investment.

In 1602, the States-General of the United Provinces merged the competing trading companies in the East into one great national entity, the United Netherlands Chartered East India Company or VOC (Parry 1966, 110–14). The charter granted the VOC exclusive rights for twenty-one years for the trade between the Cape of Good Hope and the Magellan Straits (Furber 1976, 32–33). With close links to the government, the States-General granted the governing body (or court) of seventeen directors significant autonomy, including the rights to conclude treaties of alliance, wage defensive wars, build fortresses and strongholds in the region, seize foreign ships, establish colonies, and coin money. The VOC could also enlist civilian, naval, and military personnel who would take an oath of loyalty to the Company and to the States-General (Scammell 1989, 101–3). The Dutch state provided the VOC with soldiers and artillery, and even lent the company ships. In exchange, the state claimed the prospective territories, 20 percent of all profits, and payment upon the renewal of the charter. Thus, the VOC was virtually a state within a state, one that was backed, financed, and sustained by the wealth of Holland (Boxer 1965, 23–24).

The aim of the VOC was to capture Portugal's lucrative spice trade in the East Indies, establish a monopoly on the purchase of spices, expel Spain, and exclude England.[16] Local producers were compelled by armed force to supply their produce only to the Dutch, and infringement brought a violent response by the Dutch.[17] When the English EIC tried to break into the spice trade, the Dutch responded with the same naval and military ferocity used against Spain and Portugal. The monopolization of the lucrative spice trade with Europe meant the Dutch could increase their economic strength (and convert it into military power) by determining prices while simultaneously eroding Spain's fiscal power and military strength.

Following a similar pattern, in the Americas, the Dutch created two state-chartered monopoly companies during the Twelve Year Truce with Spain, the New Netherlands Company and the Northern Company, to challenge the Spanish monopoly in the West Indies. Both companies were designed to exclude Spanish and English traders from the region. In 1621, the New Netherlands Company was absorbed into the West India Company (WIC), modeled after the VOC.[18] Like the VOC, the WIC was given a monopoly on all Dutch trade and navigation with America and West Africa, as well as the authority to make war and peace with the indigenous powers, maintain naval and military forces, and exercise judicial and administrative functions in those regions. The WIC's role in the war against Spain's Atlantic empire was emphasized from the start. One author calls the WIC "an offensive weapon for striking against the roots of Iberian power in the New World" (Boxer 1965, 49).[19] According to another, the objective of the WIC was "as much war and piracy as trade" (Howat 1974, 65). As a purchaser of weapons, munitions, foodstuffs, and cloth, the WIC came second only to the state itself.

Spain's empire was the West India Company's main target. This included Spain's lucrative sugar-producing areas in northeast Brazil, the annual Spanish treasure (bullion) fleet, and the salt pans in Punta de Araya (after 1621 the Dutch were excluded from the salt pans in Spain). The WIC's intention was to dominate Brazil's sugar production and to monopolize the trade between the Americas and Europe, excluding Spain from its traditional markets in the region.

IMPERIAL ENGLAND

As an imperial contender, in 1600, England's Queen Elizabeth I issued the charter granting the English East India Company a monopoly on the country's trade with Asia, primarily with India (Lloyd 1984, 20). Further strengthening the monopoly, in 1609, the Stuart government prohibited the importation of pepper by any trader except the East India Company. By contrast to the Dutch companies, the EIC lacked government support, and its powers were less extensive, being instead a chartered monopoly encouraging private enterprise.

By the late 1620s, driven out of south China and Asia after open war with Spain, and from the Indonesian Archipelago by the VOC, the English EIC struggled to survive before establishing itself in the Portuguese-dominated Indian Ocean, where there was less Dutch activity. Like the Dutch, the EIC's commerce between Asia and Europe was conducted in Company ships, and the English came to monopolize various ports. The EIC challenged Portugal in Surat, paving the way for English expansion into Persia and the stronghold of Hormuz (1622), as well as interport trade with Southeast Asia. Laying the foundation of England's domination over the subcontinent, Surat became England's center for trade in the northern sphere of India, Persia, Bengal, and Calcutta. Alarmed by English inroads into the Persian Gulf, Portugal attempted to clear the Gulf of foreign ships.

In the West Indies, well out of Spain's sphere, the English moved into North America. By the time of the death of King James I in 1625, the English had established exclusive colonies in Virginia, New England, and some of the small West Indian islands that the Spaniards had not considered worth settling. For instance, the New Netherlands Company was given a three-year trading monopoly over the area between New France and Virginia. During the reign of Charles I there was a great flood of emigrants to North America and the West Indies. Some of these southern settlements were founded with the intention of establishing bases to attack the Spanish treasure fleets (Scammell 1989, 40).

IMPERIAL FRANCE

France under Cardinal Richelieu concentrated on conquest in Europe (Spanish Netherlands, Germany, Italy). Following the conclusion of the religious wars between the Catholics and the Huguenots, Richelieu established a number of monopoly companies in order to compete with Spain and the ascending European powers with the goal of making France a major maritime and naval power (G. Williams 1966, 22–24). Richelieu treated economics as a weapon to undermine Spanish power. He established the Compagnie des iles d'Amerique (1627), or the Company of the American Islands, in the Leeward Islands and extended it to Martinique and Guadeloupe in 1635 (the various French possessions in the West Indies were also turned over to the Company of the American Islands). Richelieu established the Company of New France (1628) to administer the North American (Canada) settlements, granting it a permanent monopoly of the fur trade stretching from Florida to the Arctic Circle and from Newfoundland to the Great Lakes. By formally linking trade with colonization, the government hoped that the profits from the one would cover the expense of the other.[20]

Spain viewed all contenders, including France, England, and the United Provinces, as challengers to its national security and commercial interests. Each imperial competitor intended to replace the existing mercantilist order with its own preferential system.

SPAIN'S GRAND STRATEGY

Within Spain, the members of the economic nationalist and liberal coalitions competed to advance their desired grand strategy and to capture the associated distributional gains. They differed on the issues of army, navy, and imperial defense spending, taxation, silver confiscation, *vellón* coinage, international truces and embargoes, the Royal prerogative, and retreat from the empire. Economic nationalists favored restoring Spanish hegemony, which concomitantly would have the domestic effect of enhancing their power. Empowered economic nationalists would push Madrid to expand its offensive military and naval operations, to punish all challengers in both the core and the periphery, and to wrest control over finances from the Cortes of Castile and the autonomous provinces. The liberals' grand strategy called for lowering the cost of hegemony, which would have the internal consequence of empowering themselves. Enhanced liberals would push Spain to reach an accommodation with the imperial contenders in order to reduce international tensions, and to improve the investment and trade climate within Castile by lowering taxation, ending *vellón* coinage, and halting the expropriation of the gold and silver remittances.

MEMBERSHIP OF THE LIBERAL COALITION

The membership of the liberal faction included the deputies of the Cortes of Castile, the Council of Castile (judicial tribunal), Castile's aristocracy, Ambrogio Spínola, Archduke Albert (the nominal ruler of the Spanish Netherlands) and his wife Isabella, the productive and outward-oriented sectors of society (shipping, textiles, metallurgy), financial ministers, and Genoese bankers (weary of being fobbed off with *juros* or bonds, instead of cash).[21] Their policy package called for lowering the political and economic costs associated with hegemony through (1) financial discipline by reducing government spending, lowering taxation, and ending abuses such as the confiscation of private remittances, compensation with relative valueless state bonds, and the debasement of coinage; (2) retreat from empire or at least cutting Spain's losses in the core and the periphery;

and (3) diplomatic approaches to some or all of the contenders. The members of the liberal coalition were hostile to increased taxation and especially to the resumption of the costly war in the Netherlands, because it caused inflation and depression in the living standards. Financial ministers resisted any move that might increase public expenditure, while the member towns of the Cortes of Castile opposed the increase in taxation to pay for the Crown's costly grand strategy of total warfare. Castile's aristocracy feared for the financial collapse of Castile due to the Thirty Years' War. Finally, the merchant class contested the confiscation of private remittances, *vellón* coinage and the debasement of coinage, and the suspension of debt payments that created recessionary economic conditions and an unfavorable investment climate in the home market (Elliott 1961, 70–72). The liberal coalitions' solution to Spain's dilemma was accommodation or diplomatic approaches to the United Provinces, England, and/or France. With the United Provinces, they proposed extending the Twelve Years' Truce that was due to expire in 1621, ending the costly war in Flanders (Brightwell 1974, 184–87).

Castilian aristocrats favored accommodation because they suffered heavily from the high cost of war. The aristocrats were victims of the forced reduction of interest payments on *censos* (mortgage rents) and *juros*. In 1626, they were compelled to make substantial "voluntary" donations to the royal treasury, culminating in their total financial collapse (Jago 1979, 66, 82). These included levying troops at their own expense, guarding the frontiers, and accompanying the king to battle, in addition to lending or donating large sums to the king's treasury.

One of the primary opponents of the financial practices of the economic nationalist bloc was the Cortes of Castile. The Cortes of Castile, or parliament, existed to vote taxes, which could not be imposed without the consent of the deputies of the Cortes. By granting the Cortes "power of the purse," the Crown was deprived of fiscal autonomy. Since the beginning of the fourteenth century, the Crown could not impose new taxes without the prior consent of the Cortes.[22] According to one author, the Cortes deprived the Crown of fiscal autonomy by determining "what would be taxed, how, and at what rates" (Thompson 1982, 36). To raise new taxes and to renew existing subsidies, the Crown required the approval of a majority of the eighteen towns represented in the Cortes. The Cortes depended for their assembly on royal summons. While they came with mandates from the cities represented by the Cortes, the Crown pressured for representatives with full powers to commit the cities.[23] The deputies of the Cortes would then agree on an amount to be raised, and they imposed as a condition of the grant that it be applied to the expenditure for which it was requested.

Until the seventeenth century, the Crown had little reason to request increases in the rate of taxation. During most of the fifteenth and sixteenth centuries, ordinary sources of revenue were sufficient for the king to pay his way without going frequently to the Cortes for additional revenue. These sources of revenue included the *alcabala*, a 10 percent tax on sales, paid by the localities to the Crown, revenues from ecclesiastical sources, and the "royal fifth" or 20 to 30 percent of the registered bullion that crossed the Atlantic (both gold and silver). These remittances assured the Crown of a regular supply of silver, which was necessary for large-scale borrowing (Elliott 1989, 237). Since the Spanish monarchy operated on credit (or deficit finance), the annual silver receipts were the most negotiable security for its loans (Stradling 1981, 40–41).

Beginning in 1590, with the increasing cost of hegemony due to the Dutch, French, and English assaults, the Crown required increases in the rate of societal resource extraction for military spending. In 1597, rebuffed in his attempts to gain an annual subsidy from the Cortes, King Philip III struck an accord with them. The *millones*, a new sales tax on basic foodstuffs such as meat, vinegar, wine, and oil, could only be used to meet the expenses for which it had been approved (the Castilian Cortes had granted Philip II the first *millones*) (Thompson 1982, 33–36). This agreement empowered the Cortes by granting them supervisory powers. The *millones* took the form of a fixed grant by the Castilian Cortes to the Crown, with each town in Castile responsible for raising a certain levy.

In 1619, with the resurgence in their autonomy, the Cortes encroached further on the royal prerogative, requiring the Crown to apply for the appropriation of funds and to consult with them about the expenditure of the funds (Jago 1981, 310, 316). Viewing taxation as public revenue, the Cortes sought to ensure the proper usage for the public good through administrative control over the new taxes. With the resumption of war in 1621, the deputies opposed the Crown's request for additional funding because it imposed burdens on the already overtaxed cities (whose returns from the Indies were also sequestered by the Crown).

MEMBERSHIP OF THE ECONOMIC NATIONALIST COALITION

In opposition, the constituents of the economic nationalist coalition included King Philip IV and his assistant, Olivares, the Council of the

Indies, the Council of Portugal, the Councils of War, the Council of State, the Council of Finances, and the governors of the main fortresses in Flanders (Israel 1990, 169). Their preferred grand strategy called for reasserting Spanish power through increased defense spending for the army and navy, establishing new *armadas*, the defense and construction of fortresses and fortifications, and offensive military operations on land and at sea; the triumph of royal absolutism in order to control finances; and the unification of the empire by reducing the autonomous rights of the regions through the Union of Arms and reconquest (especially the northern Dutch provinces). Navalists argued that the preservation of an empire as scattered as that of the Spanish Monarchy required the possession of a first-class fleet, supporting the resumption of global war with the Dutch. The Council of State, the Flanders army, various councils, and other administrative agencies called for military offensives to push the United Provinces back to the negotiation table, to invade France and Italy, and to recover losses in the Indies. The Council of Portugal emphasized the harm of Dutch expansion into Castile's trade in Portugal's overseas possessions. For the Council of States, "everything should be defended to the last breath" since the successful use of force in one theater would discourage challengers in other locales (Elliott 1989, 130).

Within the Spanish government, the Council of State had jurisdiction over foreign policy (Lynch 1992, 23–32, 91–93). Issues of defense, even in the empire, were the responsibility of the Council of State. The Council of State was supported by a number of subcommittees specializing in various regions, such as the Junta de Italia, Junta de Inglaterra, and the Junta de Alemania. Imperialist supporters dominated the Council of State, advocating a hard-line policy in northern Europe, the Netherlands, Italy, and the Indies. Below the Council of State, a number of administrative agencies would also benefit from the reassertion of Spanish power in its empire. These agencies included the Council of Castile, the Council of the Indies, the Council of Aragon, the Council of Inquisition, the Council of Italy, the Council of Flanders, and the Council of Portugal. Within these agencies were subcommittees specializing in military, naval, and financial affairs.

For economic nationalists, any accommodation of protagonists, especially a repeat of the 1609 Twelve Years' Truce with the United Provinces, would undermine Spain's reputation for invincibility.[24] For Philip IV and Olivares, Spain's reputation was an important weapon for deterring states from challenging its global empire. It was widely believed that Spain's reputation could only be sustained through the victorious display of military power, since the successful assertion of power in one locale could deter challenges on other fronts.[25] The reverse was also true—military defeat could damage its international standing. In 1635, Olivares warned that "the first and most fundamental dangers threaten Milan, Flanders, and Germany. Any blow against these would be fatal to this monarchy; and if any one of them were to go, the rest of the monarchy would follow, for Germany would be followed by Italy and Flanders, Flanders by the Indies, and Milan by Naples and Sicily" (Elliott 1991, 97). One of the economic nationalists' foreign policy goals after 1621 was to restore Spain's status by forcing Amsterdam, through a series of quick victories, back to the bargaining table for a better agreement than the truce of 1609 (Stradling 1986, 69–70).

The second goal of the economic nationalists was to impose royal absolutism. The government of Philip IV was contemptuous of the *millones* and unwilling to accept any encroachment by the Cortes on the royal prerogative (Jago 1981; Lynch 1992, 125). Although the Castilian Cortes attempted to assert their independence, the Crown challenged the administration of the *millones* and the need for their consent. Philip IV and Olivares set out to seize control over the Cortes, so as to grant the Crown fiscal autonomy.

The final goal of the economic nationalists was to integrate the empire. Castile was directly ruled and taxed by the Crown, making it easier for Philip IV to extract revenue and manpower for Spain's armies. In the rest of the empire the authority of the Crown was constrained; the Crown had limited authority over territories in the kingdoms that did not belong directly to the king, particularly in Aragon, Catalonia, and Valencia. The privileges of the kingdoms and the strength of their Cortes allowed them to resist previous attempts to introduce a regular system of taxation. Through a scheme known as the Union of Arms, economic nationalists intended to capitalize on the fiscal necessity due to the rising cost of punishment to unify the empire and to share the burden of war.

PUNISHMENT EVERYWHERE

The foreign commercial policy of the rising contenders guided Spain's grand strategy toward punishment everywhere. In facing imperial Holland, France, and England, economic nationalists pushed for renewing the war with the Dutch, defending the Rhineland, Germany, and Milan, invading France, and recovering Brazil (Elliott 1989, 130). Economic nationalists were joined by liberals who argued that the loss of Spain's access to global markets would have a detrimental effect on Castile's wealth and balance of trade, even though this response strengthened the opposition. Liberals were especially threatened by the expansion of Dutch, French, and English mercantilistic trading companies outside of Europe who were subverting Castile's trade and economy. Even a financial minister conceded, "The lack of money is serious, but it is more important to preserve reputation" (Elliott 1989, 124). Yet, liberals resisted the extreme punishment policies of the economic nationalists. To fortify their coalition, members of the liberal faction lobbied for a cost-saving defensive military strategy, ending exclusive trading companies and embargoes, renewing the truce with the Netherlands, rapprochement with France, and cutting Madrid's losses in the periphery.

PUNISHMENT: NETHERLANDS

In the Netherlands, Spain punished the emerging Dutch Republic in a war lasting more than eighty years. The Spanish Netherlands were valuable to Spain for a number of reasons. First at stake in the Low Countries was imperial defense. Engaging the Dutch in a war in the Netherlands would reduce the resources Amsterdam could allocate to the conquest of Spain's empire.[26] Second, Flanders (one of the states in the Spanish Netherlands) was a center of mercantile wealth and capital. Economic nationalists and liberals feared that retrenchment meant either the Dutch or the French would capture the economic means of the region, increasing their potential war-making capacity.[27] The added wealth from Flanders would grant the Dutch East and West India Companies or France additional resources for the war on Spain's remaining empire. Finally, from the Spanish Netherlands, Spain could protect Italy and Spain from invasion by France. With an entrenched army at its rear, close to Paris, France could not shift the bulk of its forces southward for an all-out attempt on either Spain or Italy without being exposed (Parker 1994, 121).

Many liberals called for Madrid to renew the Truce of 1609, ending the costly war in Flanders. They countered, "The war in the Netherlands has been the total ruin of this monarchy" (Parker 1979b, 200). On average, 8,000 men per year were recruited from Castile for eighty years out of a population of 4.5 million. In 1627, as a consequence of this heavy military spending, Madrid decreed bankruptcy.[28] To further reduce the costs of hegemony, liberals pushed for a rapprochement with France (which ultimately failed).

Through a series of quick victories to repair Spain's reputation, the economic nationalists intended to renegotiate the peace treaty with the Dutch from a position of strength and to detach the Dutch from their alliance with France. After 1621, Spain's expenditures on the army of Flanders increased from 1.5 million ducats during the Truce to 3.5 million ducats, while in the best years the treasure fleets were bringing in 1.5 million ducats (Lynch 1969, 83). Another 1 million ducats were allocated to the Atlantic fleet.[29] Between 1566 and 1654, Castile sent the Military Treasury in the Netherlands roughly 218 million ducats, while Castile received only 121 million ducats from the Indies (Parker 1979a, 174; Kennedy 1987, 51; Rasler and Thompson 1989, 53, fig. 2.2). The difference in revenue was made up by ever-greater taxation in Castile, the coinage of *vellón*, and heavy government borrowing.

Beginning in 1621, Spain's army of Flanders went on the offensive, reconquering parts of the Netherlands.[30] In 1634, the Crown again renewed its effort to restore Spanish prestige (especially after the humiliating setbacks by the Dutch in 1629–33), hoping to inflict enough defeats on the Dutch front to produce terms for a satisfactory truce (Israel 1982, 157). In 1635, in the aftermath of France's invasion of the Low Countries (opening a new front and jeopardizing imperial communications), Spain's Cardinal-Infante invaded France, advancing to within eighty miles of Paris before the conflict petered out into a costly war of attrition. During 1637, the Dutch front was once again the center of conflict, while the French were preparing to attack the Basque country of northern Spain. The Spanish land offensives were another attempt to improve Spain's bargaining position with the Dutch. French and Dutch attacks stalled the Spanish offensive, especially with the French closure of the Spanish Road in 1638 (Parker 1972, 80–105).

The final phase of the Dutch-Spanish war was a last Spanish offensive at sea intended to reverse its position in northern Europe and to restore its hegemony in the Atlantic. In 1639, two large *armadas* were dispatched from Spain, one to the English Channel to force military supplies through to Flanders and to challenge the Dutch for supremacy at sea, and the second force to Brazil to recapture Pernambuco and its sugar plantations from the Dutch.[31] The construction of the two large *armadas* was possible by increasing the rate of extraction in Castile and Italy. In the English Channel, both Spain and the Dutch deployed about a hundred ships each, with 20,000 Spanish and Italian troops, while the *armada* sent to reconquer Brazil included a powerful fleet of forty-one ships and 5,000 troops (reinforcement from the region brought the *armada* up to eighty-six ships and 10,000 troops). Unfortunately for Spain, its Continental *armada* was defeated in the Battle of the Downs in the English Channel, and its American *armada* was defeated by the Dutch and by bad weather off of the coast of Brazil.

In 1640, the Spanish Netherlands were invaded by both the French and the Dutch. Spain's response was to strike into France from Flanders so as to limit French support for the revolts in Catalonia and Portugal. Yet, in 1643, the army of Flanders was defeated in Rocroi, with the bulk of the high-grade troops captured or killed. Worse, in 1645, the French captured ten major towns in the Spanish Netherlands.[32]

PUNISHMENT: ITALY

In Italy, Spain punished the Turks and French. Spain's wealthy empire in Italy was vital for Madrid. First, it was the outer perimeter of Spain's defense against the Ottoman Empire. As late as 1600, Turkish successes in Croatia brought Ottoman forces within 90 miles of Trieste. Second, Italy was a wealthy region in which the Spanish king extracted additional resources for the defense of his empire, and its loss (especially the loss of wealthy Milan) would have strengthened the war-making capacity of imperial France. For this reason, in 1623 the Council of Italy was informed of the need to exploit the resources of Naples and Sicily. During the 1620s, Naples's *millones* was 1.2 million ducats annually; reflecting the increasing cost of imperial defense, by the 1630s, the amount rose to 3.5 million ducats annually (Lynch 1969, 43). Finally, Italy was the gateway of the Spanish Road that connected Italy to the Netherlands. Robert Stradling calls this area the "nerve-centre of communications and of the whole war-machine" (1981, 88). Control over strategic passes such as the Valtelline Pass were key in regulating the flow of armies and commerce in Europe.[33]

In 1628, to defend Italy from France, Spain initiated the War of Mantua, forcing Madrid to fight simultaneously in Italy and the Netherlands (Lynch 1969, 76). In a war that was supposed to be quick and easy, Spain invaded Mantua to capture the strategic passes around Casale, making its position in northern Italy impregnable, while its loss risked undermining Spain's reputation. Unfortunately for Spain, the end of the religious wars in France freed the French army to oppose Madrid by aiding the new Duke of Mantua. The ensuing war with France forced Spain to divert valuable resources away from the Netherlands, bringing the campaign to a virtual halt. In 1631, the Peace of Cherasco recognized Nevers's succession (a victory for France), further eroding Spain's reputation and threatening the Spanish Road. In the aftermath of Mantua, the French continued to harass Spanish Italy, launching offensives against Milan (1637–48) and Genoa (1645), and later assaulting Naples (1647).

The war in Mantua placed additional strain on Castile's aristocracy and merchants (at a time of poor harvests and rising food prices) (Elliott 1989, 128–29). Financing of the wars against France in the Netherlands and Italy were achieved by augmenting taxes, when at the same time the loss of the treasure fleet was playing havoc with royal finances. In 1629, the Mantua conflict required 1.8 million ducats, and in 1630, above the 1.8 million from the two treasure fleets, the Crown added a half-million loan to cover the cost of the conflict (Lynch 1992, 106).

PUNISHMENT: NORTHERN EUROPE

In addition to Flanders and Italy, Spain punished challengers in northern Europe. Spain supported the king of Bohemia in his attempt to put down the Protestant revolt. Germany was an important link in Madrid's defense of the Spanish Road. The loss of this locale and its wealth would have undermined Spain's ability to reinforce its position in the Spanish Netherlands and to move men, money, and troops between the Low Countries and Italy as needed (Brightwell 1979, 420).

In 1619 and 1620, a joint Habsburg force crushed the Bohemian revolt, capturing Alsace, which was vital to Spain's communications between Lombardy and the Low Countries, and the Lower Palatinate, important for communications between Italy and the Netherlands. By 1632, to counter the gains of Sweden and France, Olivares renewed his collaboration with Austria, signing a treaty of mutual assistance known as the Catholic League that required additional contributions of men and money, including 350,000 ducats a year (Lynch 1969, 78–79).

PUNISHMENT: AMERICAS

Outside of Europe, Spain punished the Dutch and the English in the wealthy East and West Indies. Madrid could not afford to retreat from the Americas. First, as a source of extreme wealth (silver, gold, sugar, and salt), the Americas' remittances contributed to the Crown's total income. The Spanish Crown received its "royal fifth" of the silver and gold mined in the American empire, while the private returns increased the tax base and wealth that the Crown could extract. By the 1630s, due to the growing burden of empire, the Crown confiscated private shipments of bullion in exchange for *vellón*.

Second, the wealth of the Americas allowed Madrid to borrow money at short notice and in great amounts (Brightwell 1974, 271–72). Madrid's creditworthiness was the real strength of Spain's finances. Spain's creditworthiness was determined by the size and reliability of its forthcoming revenue. For the Crown, the silver bullion of the Americas provided a large and relatively certain source of revenue that Spain could borrow against. Spain often owed several years of bullion to Italian and Portuguese creditors. Therefore, any decline or loss of this remittance would undermine Spain's ability to finance its imperial defense.

Third, Spain's retrenchment from the Americas risked strengthening the war-making capacity of the United Provinces and England. As an imperial challenger, the Dutch would bloc Spain's future access to the Americas by creating its own exclusive sphere in the region. By capturing the wealth of this region, the Dutch would have the resources to continue Holland's assault on Spain's remaining empire and Flanders. The Dutch already had the world's largest navy and the only standing army in Europe comparable in strength to Spain's (Israel 1990, 5–6).

Economic nationalists lobbied the government to build new fortresses, strengthen its garrisons, and station additional troops and ships throughout the region, especially in the silver producing areas of Peru and Mexico. Up until 1621, Spain maintained only a few fixed garrisons in the Americas.[34] After 1621, the Dutch WIC and English penetration could be prevented only if a much more ambitious defense policy was adopted. In 1625, 1630, and 1639, Spain sent large *armadas* to Brazil to retake territory lost to the Dutch. To recapture lost territories in the Caribbean, Spain implemented a scheme to base a permanent naval task force strong enough to expel Dutch fleets.[35] The Crown also built a cordon of strongholds in forward positions across the Caribbean to provide bases for rapid deployment. New militias were established in Cuba and Mexico, and a standing army in Chile.

To pay for Spain's forward policy in the Americas, in addition to resources from Castile, the Council of the Indies was directed to find 500,000 pesos yearly in New Spain for the building, arming, and maintaining of fourteen heavy galleons (Israel 1990, 269). In 1624, the viceroy of Peru spent 200,000 ducats on defense, and by 1643, the amount had risen to 948,000 ducats (Parker 1979b, 190). The same pattern held for Mexico. Following the partial success of the Union of Arms in Europe, Olivares expanded it to the New World, forcing an additional 250,000 ducats from New Spain and a further 350,000 from Peru (Lynch 1969, 99; Israel 1990, 268).

DISTRIBUTIONAL CONSEQUENCES

The supporters of the economic nationalists' bloc captured the distributional gains from punishment, augmenting their balance of political forces. Beneficiaries of this strategy included the Council of States, the Council of the Indies, the Council of Portugal, the Council of Finances, the army of Flanders, and the royal *armada*. The Council of the Indies tightened its grip on Spanish America and Flanders, so as to extract additional resources from the empire. The Council of Portugal preferred war with the Dutch to an improved truce. The Council of Finances expropriated responsibilities from the dissolved Cortes of Castile. The army of Flanders was vastly expanded. Finally, the royal *armada* was enlarged in the Indies, the Caribbean, and the Atlantic to defend trade routes and gold shipments, while new *armadas* were established in Flanders, Galacia, and Gibraltar (Israel 1990, 11). With the death of Archduke Albert, an opponent of renewing the war with the Dutch, the south Netherlands reverted back to the Spanish Crown, further tightening the king's grip on the empire. Empowered economic nationalists used their distributional gains to annex the financial power of the Cortes and to put forth a plan to unify the various kingdoms of the empire.

The losers from punishment included Castile's outward-looking merchants, business community, productive sectors, bankers, aristocracy, and the Cortes. The Crown's fiscal policies and the Crown's attempt to squeeze additional revenue from Castile proved especially defeating when applied to the Castilian merchant community and the productive sectors of society. The coinage of *vellón* and the debasement of coinage were intended to increase the Crown's profits. Between 1621 and 1626, the Crown coined 19.7 million ducats of *vellón*, from which it made a profit of 13 million ducats, stopping only in 1628 due to domestic opposition from the business community.[36] The problem with *vellón* coinage was that it wreaked havoc with the rate of exchange, confusing the monetary system, and its debasement contributed to inflation. In 1628, the nominal value of the *vellón* coinage was reduced by 50 percent, bringing instant relief to the royal treasury, but heavy losses to merchants and businessmen holding *vellón*.[37] Meanwhile, merchants were harmed by the Almirantazgo de Sevilla, whose purpose was to defend the embargo against Dutch, English, and French goods from entering the peninsula. For merchants, the Almirantazgo de Sevilla undermined industry in Castile by driving up the price of imports and re-exported goods. Further, merchants in Seville whose

American silver was confiscated were compensated with relatively worthless *juros*. Finally, the hostile business environment and the diversion of men and resources from industry wrecked the productive sectors of the economy.

THE ANNEXATION OF THE CORTES OF CASTILE

Empowered economic nationalists deprived the Cortes of their fiscal autonomy. In meeting resistance from the embattled members of the liberal faction, political and not financial considerations were the primary determinant of the king's foreign policy. As the cost of hegemony increased, so did the Crown's dependence on the Cortes to wage war, relying on them for over 60 percent of its revenue (up from 25 percent in 1573) (Thompson 1982, 31). The Crown engaged in total warfare on several fronts to pressure the Cortes to appropriate increases in the *millones*, thereby undermining its fiscal, administrative, and distributive powers, while imposing his royal prerogative.

Philip IV turned toward the Cortes on eight occasions for additional revenue for war. While the *millones* was initially set at 2 million ducats a year, in 1626 it was raised to 4 million ducats a year.[38] From 1635, Castile entered a period of total war on multiple fronts, thereby forcing the cessation of any financial planning. The only response for the deputies was to vote for unparalleled increases in the number and scale of the *millones*. For this reason, the Cortes granted most of Philip IV's requests (Lynch 1969, 88–93; 1992, 130; Stradling 1988, 129–50). As one author notes, "with a French invasion and war within the Peninsula, the money just had to be found if Spain were to be defended at all" (Thompson 1982, 36). As royal absolutism triumphed in Castile and the Cortes were subdued, the king snatched the *millones* from municipal control and in 1658 succeeded in annexing the commission of *millones* to his Council of Finance, dissolving the Cortes in 1664.

Philip IV also penetrated the Cortes of Castile to undermine their autonomy (Jago 1981, 310). Philip IV first attempted to bypass the Cortes, going directly to the cities. In 1622 and 1624, his approach was rejected by a majority of the cities. With more success, in 1632, when Philip IV convened the Cortes to request an especially large subsidy due to the rising costs of the war in northern Europe, he insisted that the cities grant their delegates full powers. Such power would allow them to settle agreements directly with the Crown, without the prior consent of the cities (Lynch

1992, 127). Preoccupied by the outbreak of war with imperial France and isolated from the immediate control of their cities, the king used financial inducements to the deputies and the appointment of four senior royal officials to share administrative responsibilities to tip the balance in his favor (Jago 1981, 319–22). The weakened Cortes capitulated to the Crown's demands, granting an extra subsidy in 1632 of 2.5 million ducats every six years.[39]

THE UNIFICATION OF THE EMPIRE AND THE UNION OF ARMS

Outside of Castile, Olivares enacted a series of reforms to unify the empire by advancing the royal prerogative over regional privileges.[40] Through unification, the empire would carry a larger burden of their defense. As the Council of Finance argued, "the greatest benefit from these frontier garrisons accrues to the provinces themselves . . . and Castile should not have to bear the entire burden" (Lynch 1992, 132). The problem for Philip IV was that beyond Castile, Madrid had limited constitutional power to extract revenue and resources. The constitutional structure of the Spanish empire and the diversity of the laws within it prevented the central government from taxing the periphery by executive means; the Spanish monarchy was not a federal system, but a union with independent and partially autonomous provinces. Aragon, Catalonia, and Valencia were governed independently, with their own laws and tax systems, and rejected the Crown's demand in 1626 of a subsidy to maintain 16,000 men. The Catalan Cortes had legislative powers, unlike the Cortes of Castile. In each case, the king was represented by only a viceroy. In Sicily, Naples, and the duchy of Milan, the king of Spain ruled through governors. In the Low Countries, the king governed by archdukes. Portugal was completely autonomous in fiscal matters. As a consequence, the burden of defense of the empire fell primarily on Castile, with some provinces bearing little or no costs of defense. For Olivares, unification or "Castilianization" of the Spanish monarchy was the solution to the rising cost of hegemony. A unified Spain with shared rights and duties would require that provincial laws and liberties be brought into conformity with Castile's, which the provinces were likely to resist.

Short of unification of the king's domains, in 1625, Olivares called for the creation of a burden-sharing arrangement known as the Union of Arms to mobilize resources more effectively for war.[41] Under the existing system, Castile contributed the bulk of revenue for imperial defense, followed by the Italian states, and then the Low Countries, whose defense was subsidized by Castile (Lynch 1992, 132). Navarre, Aragon, and Valencia granted occasional amounts to Castile, while Portugal and Catalonia refused to contribute to imperial defense beyond their frontiers. The Union of Arms (see table 2) scheme assigned each kingdom and province of the monarchy responsibility for the provision of a quota of men for the army. Under the Union of Arms a common reserve of 140,000 men would be supplied and maintained proportionally by all the provinces of the Monarchy, reducing the burden on Castile.

The barrier to Olivares's plan was the autonomous rights of the kingdoms. The Cortes of Aragon and Valencia objected to raising money and troops for use outside of these provinces. In 1626, under pressure, these Cortes agreed to a subsidy to support troops for fifteen years. Better equipped to resist the Crown, the Catalan's Cortes and the Portuguese rejected the Union of Arms. Peru and Mexico were also assigned a financial quota to apply to the naval defense on the transatlantic route.

To compel the other regions to comply, economic nationalists capitalized on the punishment of France, England, and the Netherlands to further unify the empire. To force Catalonia into making a contribution, Olivares made the province a theater of operation in the war with France (which had been under siege by France since 1637). When Olivares planned military operations for 1639, he deliberately chose Catalonia as the front to fight France in order to force Catalonia to contribute to the Crown. In a similar fashion, Spain attempted to integrate Portugal into the Union of Arms.[42] Portugal supplied no regular revenue to the central treasury, and its Iberian defenses were subsidized by Castile, which was also expected to come to the defense of Brazil. Olivares used the second front

TABLE 2. The Union of Arms

Region	Men (thousands)	Region	Men (thousands)
Castile	44	Aragon	10
Catalonia	16	Milan	8
Portugal	16	Valencia	6
Naples	16	Sicily	6
Flanders	12	The Islands	6

Source: Elliott 1963, 330.

on the peninsula opened by the war with France to draw Portugal into the war and offered improved status and opportunities to Lisbon in exchange for contributing troops and money.

CONCLUSION

The foreign commercial policy of the rising contenders pushed Spain's response toward punishment. Both liberals and economic nationalists within Spain identified imperial France, Holland, and England as foes. Members of the liberal bloc supported aspects of the economic nationalists' agenda of punishment, even though the domestic result was the ratcheting-up of the strength of the opposing coalition. The main barrier to the economic nationalists' hard-line grand strategy were members of the liberal faction such as the Cortes of Castile, Castile's aristocracy, bankers, and merchants who called for lowering the cost of hegemony through fiscal discipline, defensive military operations, ending the exclusive trading companies and embargoes, retreating from empire, and approaches to the contenders. Through a strategy of punishment, the economic nationalists set out to weaken the liberal coalition's resistance and circumvent the Cortes of Castile, thereby granting the Crown fiscal autonomy and complete control over public revenue. By pressuring the Cortes to grant *millones* for war, the Crown steadily undermined the Cortes' administrative and distributive powers. In addition, the Crown sought to use the outbreak of war to unify the disparate monarchies of the empire.

The crushing weight of punishment everywhere fell almost exclusively on Castile's population and liberal constituency. Increases in the *millones* and the *alcabala* deprived Castile of capital for domestic investment and forced the peasants into subsistence farming, undermining Castile's home market and contributing to prolonged famines in the 1620s and 1640s. High prices left peasants with little for consumption, while heavy taxes, increased rents, and depressed living standards meant that there was no reason to remain on the land, contributing to Castile's massive depopulation (Elliott 1961, 57–68; Parker 1979a, 147, table 6; Lynch 1992, 112, 392). Deurbanization and the loss of skilled labor further undermined the likelihood of Castile's economic revival.

Punishment proved fatal to Castile's economy. Confiscation of remittances resulted in the decay of Castile's profitable trade system between Seville and America, and the decline in the Sevillian credit structure (Elliott 1961, 71; Jago 1979, 60). Castile's fledgling economy meant that Spain increasingly carried foreign goods (instead of its own products) to

Spanish colonies in the Americas (Elliott 1989, 235). The colonies, especially Mexico and Peru, developed their own indigenous industries and agriculture, growing less dependent on Spain. Further, despite economic embargoes, Spain lost a large share of its domestic market to foreign goods. For this reason, Spain became increasingly dependent upon England, France, and the United Provinces for industrial and agricultural imports, undermining its ability to make an economic recovery and exacerbating its relative industrial and technological decline.

By the seventeenth century, virtually every sector of Spain's industry was depressed, and Spain was growing increasingly backward in the key growth industries of textiles, metallurgy, and shipbuilding (Elliott 1989, 233; Lynch 1992, 211–20). In the textile industry, technical inferiority and inflation meant Spain lost its market share to competition from English cloth. In one major textile city the number of textile looms declined from 600 in 1580 to 300 during Philip IV's reign and to a low of 159 in 1691 (Lynch 1992, 212). In the sixteenth century, Spain possessed a small but active metallurgical industry, which was an essential component for creating a modern arms industry. By 1619, the metallurgical industry could no longer meet domestic demands. Spain became heavily dependent upon foreign-based iron production for the supply of military parts, particularly France and England, and by the 1650s, its factories had nearly ceased production (Stradling 1981, 63). In the area of shipbuilding, Spain failed to keep pace with the new techniques of the north European dockyards. As John Lynch notes, Spanish shipyards produced "huge and ponderous galleons, floating castles which were years behind the vessels of northern Europe in manoeuvrability and adaptability" (1992, 218).[43] As Madrid began to lag behind in productive investment in new products, its traditional wares—silk, textiles, leather, wood, wool, and iron—were priced out of their customary markets in Europe.

The import of the collapse of Castile's economy, as discussed in chapter 6, is that Castile could no longer finance a modern army and navy to defend Spain's global commitments. In desperation, the king sought resources outside of Castile, where he had limited constitutional power, contributing to revolts in Portugal and Catalonia in 1640, and eventually to the dissolution of the Spanish monarchy.[44]

CHAPTER 6

Great Power Tenure

THE DOMESTIC CONSEQUENCE OF INTERNATIONAL POLITICS

In integrating systemic and domestic politics, this book makes a second image reversed plus a second image argument to explain a declining state's grand strategy. I argue that the nature of and shifts in the international environment will affect the constellation of political power within the declining hegemon and thereby guide its grand strategy. If the hegemon confronts predominantly liberal contenders, this will empower the constituents of the free-trade coalition who will lobby for a cooperative grand strategy, while if it encounters predominantly imperial states, this will enable the supporters of the economic nationalist faction who will press for a belligerent grand strategy. The empowered coalition will use the political and economic distributional gains to advance its preferred policy package. In certain instances, these external pressures will push the coalition that is in threat of being rolled back to advance a grand strategy that will enhance its relative coalitional power, even though it threatens to undermine the nation's economic capacity or to erode its military security. Any reversals in the commercial orientation of the rising states will roll back the gains of the empowered coalition and will once again alter the domestic balance of political power, the distributional gains and losses, and ultimately the orientation of the hegemon's grand strategy.

The two key components of this argument are the contenders' foreign commercial orientation and the hegemon's domestic coalitional competition. Foreign commercial policy reflects the commercial order that a state will impose on its overseas formal and/or informal empire and any regions that it comes to dominate. A liberal strategy entails creating and maintaining an open door commercial order in any sphere that the state controls. An imperial strategy means imposing an exclusive economic order in any locale that the state controls, favoring a commercial policy of economic autarky, imperial preferences, or self-sufficiency. An imperial contender will impose such an order whether the existing trading arrangement is open or closed.

The second component of this argument is the domestic coalitional competition between the members of the free-trade and the economic nationalist factions. Within the hegemon, two broad and logrolled coalitions will compete to advance their preferred program for the declining state's grand strategy and to capture the associated distributional gains (while avoiding the losses). The membership of the free-trade coalition includes financial conservatives, capital-intensive export-oriented firms, large banking and financial services, skilled labor, and finance-oriented government bureaucracies. The free-trade coalition favors lowering the cost of hegemony through retrenching from empire, especially in regions with emerging liberal states; ensuring efficient industry has access to foreign capital, markets, and resources; implementing fiscal and monetary orthodoxy; and participation in collective security arrangements, disarmament, and arms limitation agreements. In opposition, supporters of the economic nationalist coalition include public sector workers, the military services, settler pressure groups, unskilled labor, inefficient industry, agriculture and landowners, import-substituting manufacturing, labor-intensive industry, colonial and empire-oriented state bureaucrats, pro-empire lobby groups, small businesses that compete with imports, and trading companies. The policy preference of the economic nationalist coalition is protecting inefficient industry from foreign competition; greater military preparedness and engaging in offensive military operations; and strengthening economic and military ties to the empire.

COOPERATION AND EMPOWERED FREE TRADERS

In encountering new and old competitors on disparate fronts, free traders will respond to these external pressures by pushing the government to cooperate with liberal contenders and perhaps even imperial contenders. The domestic outcome of cooperation will ratchet-up the strength of efficient industry, the financial sector, consumers, and fiscal conservatives. Cooperation entails reduced protectionism, elimination of exchange controls, participation in NGOs and IGOs, territorial concessions, membership in collective security arrangements, and the negotiation of arms limitation agreements. Economy-minded free traders will favor aiding in the rise of liberal contenders, thereby expediting the hegemon's cost-saving retreat from the locale. In doing so, the hegemon will retain access to its traditional interests in the locale without bearing any of the economic, political, or military costs associated with regional hegemony. Free traders will resist punishing states, even imperial competitors, because that will bolster the political clout of economic nationalists who will push for a more hard-line grand strategy. Punishing liberal contenders (even in a vital or strategic locale) will create the false illusion of incompatibility that can intensify into a self-defeating hostility spiral that disrupts trade, results in protectionism and beggar-thy-neighbor economic policies, and contributes to an arms race.

In confronting a mix of liberal and imperial contenders, ruling free traders in Britain (1889–1912) pushed for a moderate grand strategy that further entrenched their political power. Britain cooperated with liberal Japan, the United States, and France, devolving leadership, extending loans, reducing protectionism, and assisting in their naval ascent (France turned toward a liberal foreign commercial policy by 1904). Cooperation enhanced the relative power of the free traders by lowering the economic and military cost of hegemony, while increasing trade activity, foreign lending, and export performance. The beneficiaries included finance, efficient industry, the Liberal Party, the City of London and invisible exports, and fiscal conservatives. Empowered free traders lobbied the government to block proposals for economic and military punishment of these liberal contenders. Free traders joined economic nationalists in favor of punishing imperial Russia, France (before 1904), and Germany. For reasons of economy and for fear of empowering the opposing economic nationalist coalition, the free traders moderated the extreme economic and military policies of the economic nationalists, even advocating a policy of accommodating imperial Russia in Central Asia. The free-trade faction used the economic and political gains from cooperation to further broaden and strengthen its domestic coalition by enacting a number of popular social and economic reform schemes.

PUNISHMENT AND EMPOWERED ECONOMIC NATIONALISTS

Economic nationalists will respond to liberal and imperial competitors by lobbying to punish them (even liberal states, where cooperation is possible). The internal effect of punishment will ratchet-up the strength of inefficient industry, the military and the military-industrial complex, and settler- and empire-oriented organizations and bureaucrats. Punishment entails protectionism and extraction of resources for military spending. Concomitantly, the heightened tension from punishment has the added benefit of checking moves by free-trade supporters to collaborate with their counterparts in liberal and imperial states. Economic nationalists will resist cooperating with contenders because it will bolster the opposing free traders who will push for a more accommodative policy, such as retreat from empire, liberalization of trade, reduction in the state apparatus, and fiscal orthodoxy. As discussed later, the danger of punishing contenders is that excessive and prolonged peacetime military spending will divert resources from domestic investment, limit future economic growth, and undermine the financial basis of the declining hegemon.

Spain confronted imperial France, England, and the United Provinces (Netherlands). Economic nationalists favored punishing the contenders by increasing the size of the army and navy, building new fortifications, engaging in offensive land and sea military operations, and forming new exclusive trading companies. Many liberal supporters, including Castile's Cortes, merchants, business community, and outward-oriented industry, called for diplomacy toward the United Provinces, England, and France in order to lower the cost of hegemony. Disapproving of the Cortes' autonomy and unwilling to accept their inroads on the royal prerogative, economic nationalists set out to weaken them. By punishing the Dutch Republic in the Netherlands, and France in Italy during the War of Mantua; defending its position in northern Europe against Sweden, Germany, and France; and fighting the Dutch, English, and French in the wealthy East and West Indies, economic nationalists undermined the liberal coalition and the Cortes, and thereby granted the Crown fiscal autonomy and wrested control over public revenue.

SELF-REINFORCING STRATEGIES AND ENTRENCHED FREE TRADERS OR ECONOMIC NATIONALISTS

A dilemma occurs when economic nationalists confront liberal contenders and free traders confront imperial contenders. In both instances, the external pressure will push the faction to advance its coalitional interests (ratcheting-up its own relative power) over the national interest (restoring the balance between capabilities and commitments without eroding the state's economic base or undermining its security). The members of such a coalition are threatened by the domestic distributional consequences from ratchets, reversals, and rollbacks. They will often adopt a self-reinforcing strategy that will boost their own faction's power by capturing the distributional gains, even though they risk undermining the nation's productive strength or eroding its military security. When coalitions advance their factional interest but harm the nation's interest, they chance shortening the hegemon's great power tenure.

For economic nationalists that confront liberal contenders, the external pressure is to advance their own coalitional interests through punishment, but the national interest calls for cooperation. Cooperation with a liberal contender will lower the cost of hegemony, safeguarding the nation's economic capacity. Cooperation is possible because the ascending liberal state's concern for economy will curb it from using the gains to initiate an arms race. Yet, the constituents of the economic nationalist coalition will lobby against cooperation since they will bear the burden from deregulation, greater foreign access to their markets, budget cuts, and the dismantlement of state-owned enterprises and monopolies. Such liberalization will enhance the economic and political status of the opposing free-trade coalition who will push for a more accommodative grand strategy.

In confronting imperial contenders, the external pressure for free traders is to advance their coalitional interests through cooperation, but the national interests call for punishment. Punishment of an imperial contender will protect the hegemon's national security by ensuring that the state has sufficient military capability to defend its global commitments. However, free-trade supporters will oppose punishment because increased defense spending and preferential trading arrangements will augment the relative power of the competing economic nationalist coalition who will urge the state to adopt a more hard-line grand strategy. In such instances, free traders will push to co-opt imperial contenders through military (arms reduction agreements), economic (loans, reduced protectionism), and/or territorial concessions.

By the 1930s, Britain confronted imperial Germany, Italy, and Japan, and a liberal United States. This reversal in the nature of the foreign commercial policy of the rising contenders, from a mix of liberal and imperial contenders prior to World War I to mostly imperial contenders prior to World War II, ratcheted-up the strength of the economic nationalist coalition while weakening the entrenched free traders. Empowered economic nationalists lobbied the government to punish the contenders by abandoning the gold standard, adopting imperial preferences, enacting colonial quotas, and increasing defense spending. Concerned about the cost of punishment and their faction's survival, the free-trade coalition pushed for a self-reinforcing strategy of cooperation, including limited military rearmament (emphasizing a less costly air deterrent over a large standing army or a two-power naval standard), economic concessions, arms limitation agreements, and territorial compromises. The outcome was the delay in Britain's rearmament necessary to defend its global commitments. By the late 1930s, the free traders' and especially the Treasury's influence over rearmament had collapsed, and the economic nationalists pressed for their agenda of rearmament, state intervention and government controls, producer cartels, and protectionism, thereby further enhancing their power.

In each of these instances, the empowered coalition used the gains from cooperation or punishment to further enlarge its domestic political constituency while the loser was weakened politically and economically. This process involved access to new sources of funds, generating additional supporters and greater public attention for their cause, and establishing or expanding political parties and peak lobbying organizations. Each faction had its distinct advantage in organizing supporters. Economic nationalists used the rents from protection and imperial preferences to reward supporters, while free traders created more wealth for social and economic redistribution.

SUCCESS AND FAILURE IN MANAGING DECLINE: DILEMMAS OF STRATEGY AND FINANCE

Why are some states more successful in managing their decline than others? The nature of the hegemon's international environment can enhance or undermine a state's great power tenure. A waning hegemon's grand strategy involves restoring the balance between its capabilities and global obligations while simultaneously safeguarding its productive capacity and military security. A hegemon that chooses a security strategy that neglects either fiscal or security interests will have insufficient economic or military means to protect its global interests. Such a state will fall from the ranks of the great powers, relying on the goodwill of the remaining great powers to protect its global interests. To prolong its tenure in the great power game, the hegemon must select a security strategy that simultaneously acknowledges the limits on its fiscal resources and the importance of its national security interests.

There is a hierarchy among nations in the international system. Hierarchy connotes influence over the behavior of the other states in the international system, allowing the great powers to establish the rules of the game which advance or favor their national interests over the other states'. For Jack Levy (1983, 16–17), great powers play a major role in international politics and possess a high level of military capability, think of their interests as global, defend their interests more aggressively, are treated with greater respect by other states, and are included in major international organizations and treaties. By managing its decline successfully, the hegemon will remain a leader among the great powers; it will prolong its ability to influence global politics and to protect its commercial and security interests. In failing to manage its decline, the hegemon will accelerate its fall from the ranks of the great powers. As a second-rank power, its influence will be regional or local in scope. With limited influence, a second-rank power will depend on the goodwill of the existing great powers to protect its interests.

MANAGING DECLINE

Managing hegemonic decline involves retarding the rate of decline. In the short term, success means selecting the security strategy that will lengthen the hegemon's tenure as a great power over its alternative options. That is, the strategy that will allow the hegemon to remain in the ranks of the great powers longer than the alternatives to that state. A hegemon can undermine its national interests in two ways. First, if the ruling free traders or economic nationalists lobby to cooperate with an imperial contender, they will accelerate the state's immediate rate of decline over the alternative foreign policy option of punishment. By cooperating, the hegemon risks emboldening imperial contenders to redouble their challenge, and it risks strengthening the war-making capacity of a rival, thereby eroding the hegemon's own immediate commercial and security interests. Second, if free traders push to punish a liberal contender, they risk creating the false illusion of incompatibility, which can translate into a costly and unnecessary hostility spiral, and losing an opportunity to lower the costs of hegemony without strengthening an adversary.

A hegemon can also extend its immediate great power tenure. First, ruling free traders and economic nationalists should lobby to punish an imperial contender, thereby ensuring that the hegemon has adequate military capability to defend its global commitments. Second, free traders should press to cooperate with a liberal contender, safeguarding its economic capacity. More ambiguous is whether economic nationalists should support punishing a liberal contender. Cooperation has the benefit of lowering the cost of hegemony, and an economy-minded liberal contender is unlikely to use gains from collaboration to initiate an arms race. However, a liberal state will seek to alter the regional status quo by imposing a liberal trading order on any sphere that it comes to dominate, allowing unrestricted access to the hegemon's exclusive sphere. Such an outcome will undermine the erstwhile leader's fiscal strength.

The failure of a declining hegemon to recognize the dilemma of balancing capabilities and commitments can be fatal. Napoleonic France and the Soviet Union responded to challenges and restored the balance by increasing their military capacity. Both states increased their rate of domestic resource extraction to prepare and to fight preventive wars against several contenders for regional hegemony simultaneously. However, excessive and sustained increases in the rate of military spending exhausted France's and the Soviet Union's economic bases of power and ultimately their ability to construct and maintain a modern military force. Rome also failed to heed the dilemma. Exhausted and facing competitors on several fronts, Rome appeased the Visigoths in 382 to lower the costs of governance. Rome allowed the Visigoths to settle as allies in northern Thrace along the Danube. The Visigoths proved to be revisionist challengers, however, using the settlement to strengthen their war-making capacity without fearing a preventive strike from Rome. From 406 to 410, the Visigoths swept through Rome's possessions in the Balkans, Gaul, and Spain, finally sacking Rome in 410. Likewise, John Elliott argues that to moderate the erosion of Spain's primacy, Madrid could have "cut its coat according to its cloth" (1989, 133). But this strategy ignores the strategic ramification of losing wealthy Flanders, Italy, or the Americas to imperial France, England, or the Dutch. The United States' experience proves no exception. The Pentagon's 1992 Defense Planning Guidance for 1994–99 calls on the United States to maintain its primacy or the current unipolar moment by "discourag[ing] . . . advanced industrial nations from challenging our leadership or . . . even aspiring to a larger regional or global role."[1] However, in dissuading all contenders, including Japan and Germany (or the European Union) from playing a greater role in bearing the burden of regional hegemony, the United States risks eroding its economic staying power.

EXTENDING GREAT POWER TENURE

In the long run, a hegemon can modify its rate of decline. Successful management involves, among other factors, selecting the foreign commercial policy that will decelerate its rate of decline over its alternative foreign commercial policy. Due to its international environment, hegemons in which free traders (that confront at least some liberal contenders) are the dominant coalition can remain a key player in the great power game longer than where economic nationalists rule; for economic nationalists, even if aware of what is happening, will fail to manage their decline because they can only select from a range of grand strategies that will erode either the state's economic strength or its military security. A strategy of punishment risks eroding the hegemon's long term fiscal strength. In allocating too many resources to defense, the hegemon will have insufficient economic capacity to finance a modern military. A strategy of cooperation to lower the cost of leadership risks undermining the hegemon's security. In accommodating contenders and by allocating too few resources to defense, the hegemon will have insufficient military capability to protect its global commitments. As the hegemon falls from the ranks of the great powers, its influence will become local in scope. In lacking sufficient military and economic resources, the hegemon will come to depend on the altruism of the remaining great powers to protect its global interests.

Ruling free traders that confront some liberal contenders can prolong their great power tenure. They will push for a foreign policy strategy that will safeguard both the hegemon's economic strength and its security objectives, ensuring the state has sufficient capability to defend its global interests. Devolution of regional governance to liberal contenders will lower the cost of hegemony. By centralizing these freed-up resources in its remaining commitments, the hegemon will augment its military capability. The erstwhile hegemon will continue to influence the rules of the game by remaining in the ranks of the great powers. By discriminating among challengers, such hegemons are less likely to suffer from overcommitment and "imperial overstretch" (Kennedy 1987; Brawley 1999). Once more, in contrast to the work on the domestic sources of grand strategy that stresses that domestic politics may lead to the adoption of suboptimal grand strategies, this book highlights that the international environment and domestic political constraints can enable policymakers to pursue strategies that are close to ideal (Friedberg 1988; Snyder 1991; Rosecrance and Stein 1993; Kupchan 1994).

A foreign policy of devolution contradicts the geopolitical neorealist prescription. Retrenching in regions with liberal contenders and standing firm in regions with imperial challengers will mean that the hegemon is likely to retreat from some highly strategic spheres. By contrast, according to the realist strategy of disengagement or selective engagement, as a hegemon declines, it will punish all challengers in the core while disengaging in the periphery. This assumes: (1) "loss" of a valuable locale can tip the delicate balance of global power against the hegemon and ultimately threaten its survival, and (2) retrenchment from less vital regions will have little if any impact on the global balance. For such realists, irrespective of the commercial nature of the contender or the military cost of punishment, the hegemon should punish everywhere except in peripheral regions.

The role of grand strategy in safeguarding a hegemon's financial well-being is often ignored.[2] While neorealists differentiate across regions and among challengers, and they recognize the significance of industrial capacity as a component of potential military capability, they discount the fiscal consequence of substantial and sustained levels of defense spending. Failure to devolve leadership to a liberal contender, even in a strategic locale, means that the hegemon risks jeopardizing its economic staying power by prolonging excessive defense expenditures unnecessarily. The erosion of the hegemon's fiscal strength will undermine its productive capacity and ultimately its future military security, thereby reducing its influence over the international system.

The liberal peace literature also neglects the import of finance in power shifts among liberal states. For instance, Randall Schweller concludes that a declining liberal hegemon will accommodate a liberal challenger, but does not discuss the ramifications of accommodation on the leader's grand strategy (1992, 250–51). Specifically, he ignores the distributional benefits from cooperation in lowering the military, economic, and political costs associated with regional hegemony.

SPAIN: UNDERMINING ECONOMIC CAPACITY

Of the cases discussed in this book, only Britain (1889–1912) could remain in the ranks of the great powers as long as possible. Economic nationalists in Spain could only choose from a range of strategies that either undermined the state's military security (cooperation) or eroded its economic strength (punishment). Favoring Spain's security over its economy had the domestic result of eroding Castile's agriculture (prolonged famines in the 1590s, 1620s, and 1640s), industrial underpinnings, and ultimately its ability to marshal a modern military force.

By 1648, the shortfalls in economic and military resources meant that the Spanish monarchy was dependent on its erstwhile enemy, the Dutch, to protect its global interests. First, sustained military spending diverted economic resources from domestic investment, limiting the scope of Spain's future economic growth. Second, the Crown's fiscal policy, the erosion of the home market, foreign encroachment on Spain's colonial trade, and the Crown's attempt to squeeze additional revenue from Castile all contributed to an unfavorable investment climate. Third, the diversion of resources from domestic investment to military spending (and discouragement of domestic investment) caused Spain's economy to suffer severe dislocation, lagging behind France, England, and the United Provinces in key growth industries of the period. Finally, deindustrialization and depopulation undermined Spain's capacity to finance and field a modern army and navy in defense of its global commitments.

The year 1640 marks the beginning of the dissolution of Spain's empire and the erosion of its European primacy. Madrid fell technically behind the emerging challengers in naval construction and was unable to recruit or finance an adequate number of troops or supply its infantry. On repeated occasions, financial exhaustion forced Spain to seek a cessation in its military activities. In the Netherlands, no military campaigns were prepared between October 1628 and May 1629, because no money arrived from Madrid (Parker 1972, 256). After 1629, provisions sent to the Netherlands were limited because money was needed to fight the French in Mantua and the Dutch in the Americas. Reductions in the army's budget meant Madrid could no longer afford a modern military. The Spanish defeats at the battles of Rocroi (1643) and Lens (1648) were a direct result of a drastic reduction in the army's budget (Parker 1979b, 40). The absence of a cavalry contributed to Spain's defeat at the battle of Rocroi; the army of Flanders went into battle against the French with inadequate cavalry because horses were too expensive (Stradling 1984, 213–14; Lynch 1992, 165). This defeat further eroded the reputation of the army of Flanders and is often seen as the end of Spain's military power.

Decline in the revenue from the Atlantic trade and silver supplies, growing debt, the collapse of Spanish shipping, and Castile's inability to meet the demands for manpower and money forced Philip IV either to look elsewhere in the kingdom for additional resources where he had limited constitutional power or to abandon his military buildup for the defense of the empire. Desperate for additional revenue, the Union of Arms scheme was designed to create an army recruited and paid in appropriate proportions by the various provinces of the kingdom. While opponents to this scheme in Valencia and Aragon eventually conceded, the

Catalans and the Portuguese refused to cooperate. For Olivares, this open opposition to Madrid was a public trial for the Union of Arms, affecting the compliance of the other provinces (Lynch 1992, 145). To force Catalonia to contribute money and troops to the Crown, Olivares made the province a theater of operation in the war with France.[3] In May 1640, Catalonia rebelled. As Geoffrey Parker notes, "there are few clearer examples than the revolt of Catalonia of the role of war in turning a tense political situation into open rebellion" (1979a, 257). In the aftermath, Catalonia formed an alliance with France, forcing Spain to divert reserves to Catalonia. To incorporate Portugal into the Union of Arms, Olivares offered improved status and opportunities. In 1640, Portugal declared its independence from Spain.[4] Again, Richelieu extended French assistance, opening a second front on the peninsula. With troops in the Catalian front, Italy, Germany, and the Low countries, and Spanish naval losses in Brazil and at the Battle of The Downs, Spain had few troops to resist Lisbon.

As the decade progressed, Spain was on the defensive, reliant on the goodwill of the remaining great powers to protect its global interests. Lacking resources to continue fighting on several fronts simultaneously, in 1644, Philip IV released a decree informing his ministers that he sought peace on all fronts.[5] In 1648, in the Treaty of Munster, Spain recognized Dutch independence and gave the Dutch all the territory they occupied in the Americas, promising not to trade with Spanish domains.[6] In return, the Dutch came to Spain's aid against the French assault on the Spanish Netherlands.[7] Concerned about the growing power of France, the Dutch preferred a weak Spanish buffer between itself and France. In the Treaty of Pyrenees (1659), Spain ceded territory in the Netherlands and parts of northern Catalonia to the French. During 1667, Louis XIV attacked the Spanish Netherlands (the War of Devolution). Only the intervention of the maritime powers fearful of French Continental hegemony prevented Spain's loss. At the subsequent Conference of Aix-la-Chapelle, Spain was hardly consulted when deciding which gains France should retain (Stradling 1979, 182). The treaty required that Spain make payments to the Swedish army (i.e., Protestant mercenaries) for the defense of the Netherlands against France. The process of dissolution continued with the independence of Portugal (1668) and the loss of Flanders and Italy at the Peace of Utrecht (1713). With the loss of Portugal (1668), Spain ceded most of its wealthy overseas empire, especially Brazil.

BRITAIN (1932–1939): ERODING MILITARY SECURITY

Unlike Spain, Britain chose a grand strategy of restrained punishment in the 1930s, undermining its military security. Until the mid-1930s, concerns about economy and worries that punishment would roll back their postwar gains meant that the entrenched free-trade coalition backed a grand strategy of cooperation, restraining Britain's rearmament and the associated physical and administrative infrastructure. Both the Anglo-German Naval Agreements and the Washington and London Naval Conferences were intended to impede Germany's and Japan's naval ascent and to prevent a costly naval arms race, ensuring that a one-power standard would suffice. In addition, territorial concessions instead of punishment to moderate German and Italian demands meant that Britain would not need to divert manpower from industrial production for a costly British Expeditionary Force for the Continent. Finally, conciliation meant that in peacetime Britain did not need to depart from laissez-faire practices by creating shadow arms industries, state planning boards and ministries, unbalanced budgets, trade deficits, increased taxation, or inflation.

Free-trade restraint (even after 1936, although greatly diminished in strength) on Britain's strategy of punishment shortchanged the nation's security interests. Since Germany, Japan, and Italy preferred an alternative commercial arrangement, and concessions were unlikely to achieve their final objective, these states were not willing to accept a permanent junior position in their respective locales. For Britain this meant that the arms control and arms limitation agreements and territorial concessions negotiated by London were not renewed or that the challengers defected on the accords.[8] The consequence was that Japan and Germany rearmed without the fear of a British preventive strike. Meanwhile, after the collapse of free-trade opposition, as war approached, empowered economic nationalists made it difficult for Britain to cooperate with a liberal United States.

In the Far East, the Washington and London Naval Conferences granted Japan local naval hegemony. To gain Japan's consent to the naval tonnage limitations set at the London and Washington Naval Agreements, Britain and the United States agreed not to fortify any of their island possessions in the Pacific and neither upgrade nor build any new naval bases in the region (Lee 1973, 2; Kennedy 1976, 324–25, 335; Nish 1977). The United States could not improve existing naval facilities in the Philippines (there were no limitations on Hawaii). Britain could build up Singapore, but not Hong Kong, into a first class naval base (McKercher 1993). However, Singapore was far from complete due to free-trade opposition. Thus, neither Britain nor the United States had a base within striking distance of Japan (Trotter 1975, 12–13).

In 1934, unwilling to accept permanent naval inferiority, Japan denounced the Washington and London Naval Agreements. As expected, at the Second London Naval Conference (1936), Japan demanded a common upper limit, seeking parity with the fleet strengths of Britain and the United States. In response to Japan's invasion of China (1937), London rejected a naval show of force to punish Japan, instead choosing to provide a loan to China for its defense and military supplies via Hong Kong and the new Burma Road. As war approached, the combination of Britain's one-power standard, the Anglo-German Naval Agreement, and the growing conflict with Italy in the Mediterranean meant that Britain could spare few ships and would not dispatch the main fleet to Singapore to defend the Dominions or British interests in the Far East.[9]

Like the Washington and London Naval Agreements, the Anglo-German Naval Agreement allowed Berlin to construct the Imperial Navy without the fear of a British preventive strike (Hall 1976, 483). Chamberlain's cost-saving Limited Liability strategy meant that Britain could only moderate Germany and Italy's expansion through territorial concessions. There was belief that concessions could form the basis of a comprehensive settlement. The Munich Agreement, intended to defuse the immediate danger of war, strengthened Germany's immediate war-making capacity by granting Berlin foreign exchange, strategic raw materials, industrial power (especially the Skoda armament works), and equipment to arm Germany for war.[10] In March 1939, with little fear of retribution, the German army invaded the rump of Czechoslovakia. In April, unwilling to accept an everlasting position of naval inferiority, Hitler rejected the 1935 Anglo-German Naval Agreement, calling for a massive naval construction program (Z-Plan) (Deist 1994, 377–78). Similarly, in 1938, Britain recognized Rome's position in Abyssinia only to have Italy violate this understanding by invading Albania in 1939. The settlement conceded to Italy large segments of Abyssinian territory currently occupied by Italian troops and made frontier adjustments between Abyssinia and Italian Somaliland in favor of Italy.

In confronting primarily imperial contenders, Britain had few good options. As Paul Kennedy notes, Britain "could have a balanced economy but with inadequate forces to protect itself and its overseas interests against those threats; or it could have much larger armaments and a bankrupt economy. It could not have both" (1981, 235). Britain could have devolved hegemony over the Middle East and the Far East to a liberal United States and consolidated these freed-up resources against Germany and Japan (the question remains whether the United States was willing to play a leadership role outside of the Americas). Beginning in 1938, there were limited discussions between Britain and the United States on this issue in the Far East.[11] Yet, empowered economic nationalists and their desire to preserve Britain's imperial preference system against the United States' promise to dismantle it explains in part why London resisted devolution of regional hegemony to Washington.[12] By 1941, Churchill was willing to defer to the United States "in the matters concerning the Pacific theater of war" (Lowe 1977, 191–93).

BRITAIN (1889–1912): SAFEGUARDING ECONOMIC STRENGTH AND MILITARY SECURITY

For Britain at the turn of the century, devolution of regional hegemony safeguarded London's economic capacity and its military security, lengthening its great power tenure.[13] The nature of the foreign commercial policy of the rising states contributed to Britain's successful adjustment. In confronting liberal contenders, Britain devolved leadership over the Americas to the United States, the northeast Pacific to Japan, and the eastern Mediterranean to France. Devolution meant that London no longer bore any of the political, economic, and military costs of regional hegemony. Furthermore, Britain directly and indirectly accelerated the naval ascent of the United States and Japan, ensuring each could assume the responsibilities associated with regional hegemony. Had London been unwilling to retrench from strategic locales, Britain would have risked undermining its economic strength by prolonging its defense spending.

The consequence of devolution of regional hegemony to the United States, Japan, and France was drastic naval and military savings. The allocation of these freed-up military resources to Britain's remaining commitments strengthened London's immediate military preparedness in these locales, safeguarding its national security. Beginning in 1904, London concentrated the freed-up naval and military resources from the Americas and Far East in its home waters and the Mediterranean against Germany. The Fisher Reforms abolished the Pacific, the South Atlantic, and the North

America and West Indies squadrons. The Cape squadron was to take over the two latter stations and the West Coast of Africa. The Eastern fleet, with its center at Singapore, was to consist of the amalgamated squadrons of the Australian, China, and East Indies stations. The Home fleet was renamed the Channel fleet, centered at Dover and increased to twelve battleships; the old Channel fleet was renamed the Atlantic fleet, based at Gibraltar and remained at eight battleships; and the Mediterranean fleet based in Malta was reduced from twelve to eight battleships. The Atlantic fleet could reinforce either the Channel or the Mediterranean fleet. As a result of the Fisher naval reforms of 1904–5, Britain matched Germany's military buildup while reducing its naval Estimates every year from 1904–5 to 1909–10. By gathering resources and appropriating new funds for naval construction programs, Britain punished France, Germany, and Russia (except in Central Asia) until they capitulated in their naval challenges. Thus a strategy of devolution ensured that London had ample economic capacity and military capability to be a leading player in the great power game. Alternatively, had London adopted the imperial preference system advocated by Joseph Chamberlain between 1903 and 1906, Britain would have risked hastening its fall from the ranks of the great powers.

THEORETICAL IMPLICATIONS

The theoretical implications of this second image reversed plus a second image argument are several-fold. In contrast to long cycle, power transition, and deterrence theorists, hegemonic decline is not always associated with great power war. All three arguments contend that a hegemon in the decline phase will select punishment strategies against rising or emerging challengers. Yet, ruling free-trade coalitions in rising and declining states will both advocate a grand strategy of cooperation toward the other, benefiting their domestic constituents and capturing the associated distributional gains. In the case of Britain (1889–1912), free traders in London pushed the government to respond to a rising liberal United States and Japan by a policy of commercial and military conciliation. Changes in France's foreign commercial policy after 1904, and not its military capability, account for its differential treatment by British free traders, while free traders continued to take a hard stance against imperial Russia (except in Central Asia).

Second, in contrast to hegemonic stability theory, declining hegemony is not necessarily associated with rising levels of protectionism. According to hegemonic stability theory, a state's relative position across the international system will affect its foreign commercial policy (Kindleberger 1973; Krasner 1976; Gilpin 1981; Keohane 1984). As the hegemon declines relatively, it will no longer provide the public good of free trade, explaining the leader's and the contenders' turn toward protectionism. An alternative version contends that to gain liberal followers the hegemon must grant economic and commercial concessions (Stein 1984; Lake 1988; Brawley 1993). As the hegemon becomes too weak to entice or cajole the followers, the leader and the contenders will adopt protectionism.

Based on the differentiated framework developed in this book, a hegemon's descent is far from global, rapid, or uniform. Instead, a hegemon is likely to confront different protagonists who rise at uneven rates and who challenge the hegemon's leadership in disparate parts of its empire. This differentiated framework suggests that all else being equal, a declining state will remain more hegemonic and hence more free-trade-oriented in some locales than others. Combined with the argument developed in chapter 2, where the leader confronts liberal contenders, it can devolve regional leadership. By aiding in their ascent, the hegemon can entice liberal states to assume the mantle of leadership and to bear the associated economic, political, and military costs. Elsewhere, the leader can concentrate its freed-up resources, augmenting its relative power and cajoling states to gain liberal followers. Free traders in Britain (1889–1912) lobbied the government to accelerate the naval ascent of the United States and Japan to assure that they could assume greater responsibility in managing regional affairs, to the dismay of the economic nationalists.

Third, changes in military power may not provoke counterbalancing behavior. Free traders will lobby against punishing liberal contenders in order to prevent a hostility spiral that will be "financially disastrous to both sides" (Kennedy 1976, 250). Ruling free traders in Britain did not identify a rising United States as a threat to its open door commercial interests. Even though America's potential naval power was widely recognized as early as the mid-1890s, economy-minded free traders lobbied for the United States to be excluded from the two-power naval standard.

POLICY IMPLICATIONS FOR THE UNITED STATES

Similar issues for how Spain and Britain identified friends and foes and how they rank-ordered overseas commitments are at the center of a number of American policy debates.[14] Should the United States encourage Germany (or the European Union) and Japan to assume greater regional leadership in their respective locales?[15] Should the United States discourage both states from developing independent military capabilities by expanding NATO into central and eastern Europe, encouraging European defense arrangements (so long as they are subordinate to NATO), and renewing its security treaty with Japan? Should the United States intervene in peripheral regions to demonstrate to potential challengers its credibility and resolve to defend its core interests? Thus, how should the United States manage its future decline?

Some scholars and policymakers call for the United States to maintain the current unipolar moment by discouraging all potential contenders such as Germany (or the European Union), Japan, China, and Russia from assuming greater regional economic, political, and military leadership everywhere.[16] A more circumscribed version of primacy calls for a policy of selective engagement (Walt 1989; Posen and Ross 1996–97). According to this strategy, the United States should discourage any potential contender in the Eurasian land mass and the Persian Gulf, while retrenching from most of the Third World. The assumption is that losses in Eurasia or the Persian Gulf could strengthen an aspiring hegemon, upsetting the global balance of power, while even significant conquest in the periphery will have little effect. Both primacy and selective engagement will at the very least seek to preserve America's preponderance and will discourage many of the same contenders from assuming hegemony. Both also assume that the United States must bear the increased government expenditure needed to raise the military budget, or else America's national security will be undermined.

For the United States, preserving its preponderance will require deep engagement. The rationale is that the United States will need to maintain its preponderance in order to discourage its allies from building independent military capabilities. As long as its allies lack sufficient military capability to defend themselves, the United States will also need to continue to defend their territories and protect their regional interests, resulting in American involvement in local conflicts in which it has no strategic interests. Finally, the United States might intervene in peripheral regions in order to demonstrate to potential challengers its credibility and resolve to defend its core interests, drifting from a strategy of selective engagement to primacy.

In Europe, primacy means expanding NATO into central and eastern Europe and encouraging European defense arrangements so long as they are subordinate to NATO. In this context, NATO's purpose is to manage both Germany and Russia. In the Far East, the United States will discourage Tokyo from militarizing by continuing to extend its nuclear umbrella and security treaty to Japan, and by the forward deployment of U.S. forces to counter North Korea, China, and Russia. In the Persian Gulf, the Middle East, and southwest Asia, the United States will maintain a military presence in order to ensure regional stability and discourage the emergence of a regional hegemon. Finally, in South Asia, the United States will discourage India's hegemonic ambitions.

The danger for the United States of the strategy of punishing everywhere (or almost everywhere according to selective engagement) is that it will affect America's allocation of national resources, undermining its long-term economic capacity. First, in punishing liberal contenders like Japan and Germany (or the European Union) the United States will create the false illusion of incompatibility that can result in a self-defeating and costly hostility spiral. Second, punishing Japan and Germany means that the United States will miss an opportunity to reduce the costs of hegemony without strengthening the war-making capacity of a rival. The danger for the United States is that prolonged peacetime military expenditure will divert resources from domestic investment, thereby limiting America's future economic growth.[17]

The United States should assist Germany (or the European Union) and Japan, accelerating their rate of ascent.[18] As Germany and Japan assume a greater political, economic, and military role in their respective spheres, the United States can retrench, retaining access to its traditional interests without bearing the costs of regional hegemony. Devolving hegemony to different liberal contenders also reduces many neorealists' concern that a single power will dominate the Eurasian landmass, commanding greater industrial capacity than the United States and thus tipping the balance of global power against America. Where there are no liberal successors, the United States should stand firm and hasten emerging liberal followers, even in the Third World. The United States can invest this "peace dividend" and concentrate the freed-up military resources in its remaining commitments, safeguarding its economic strength without eroding its security.

Appendix

By administrative custom, the Treasury is responsible for ensuring that government revenues and expenditures are balanced.[1] The Treasury controls government expenditure through a process known as "Treasury control." According to this historical precedent, the Exchequer must approve any changes or increases in a department's expenditure for the ensuing year (known as Votes). No piece of legislation calling for increased expenditure can proceed to Parliament until a Treasury Minister has consented. The intention of this oversight is to ensure that a department's estimate is both economical and sufficient.

By December, every department prepares detailed Estimates of proposed expenditure for the following year. The Estimates fall into four categories: Navy, Army and Ordinance, Civil Service, and Revenue Department (Customs and Excise, Inland Revenue, and Post Office; later Air Force Estimates were added). A department's Estimates are divided into Votes, representing different aspects of its budget. For instance, in the Admiralty's Vote 1 covered wages, Vote 2 covered clothing. New expenditure and variations in the scope of existing services leading to increased expenditure must be submitted separately to the Treasury for approval. Subsequent increases in the original Estimates are submitted by means of Supplementary Estimates, which must also be approved by the Treasury.

Intense argument and consultation often occurs between the Treasury and the Departments over Estimates. It is not uncommon for the Treasury to modify the Estimates either by addition or by reduction. The Chancellor can criticize a department's proposal either on the ground that finance was not available or on the merits of the proposals themselves. While Treasury control could be used by the Exchequer to hinder individual items, lacking a technical knowledge (especially for military matters), the preferred method of exercising control is to set overall financial limits, allowing individual departments to prioritize their programs. In the event the Chancellor and the minister responsible for a department are unable to agree to a limit to that department's expenditure, the matter is referred to the Cabinet for arbitration.

Once Estimates are approved by the Treasury, they are sent to the House of Commons. Estimates are discussed in the Committee of Supply and agreed to by the entire House. Each Vote can be discussed at length in the Supply Committee, and any item in the Vote can be rejected or reduced, but the House of Commons cannot add to the Vote. As one author notes, "Defence expenditure always required Cabinet approval in principle, and Treasury approval in detail" (Peden 1979, 15). Since all proposals included in the Estimates cannot be reviewed before the Estimates were submitted to the Supply Committee, the Treasury reserves the right for further consideration, and if the Treasury later finds that it cannot approve these proposals, the money allocated to cover them cannot be spent. Savings on Votes can be transferred to meet excesses on another vote only with the approval of the Treasury (know as *virement*). Finally, to exceed its Estimates for the current year (new commitments not approved in time for inclusion in the original Estimates or increases in costs that have arisen since the original Estimates were accepted), a department must submit to the Treasury a Supplementary Estimate which is then submitted to Parliament for approval.

There are slight differences between the Civil Estimates and the Service Estimates (Navy, Army and Ordinance, Air Force), which grant the latter certain advantages.[2] First, the Admiralty and the War Office have large financial departments of their own. Lacking technical knowledge of the development and production of new weapons, when the approximate total figures of expenditure are agreed for each service, the Board of Admiralty and the Army Council settle their detailed programs accordingly. In practice, the Treasury departmental examination is less scrutinizing than in the case of Civil Estimates. Second, the Estimates by Civil and Revenue Departments are presented to the House of Commons by the Treasury, while Estimates of the Services are presented to the House of Commons by the Admiralty and War Office.

Notes

CHAPTER 1

1. On the relationship between grand strategy, trade, and domestic politics, Skålnes (2000) argues that states in need of allies will pursue favorable discriminatory foreign economic policies to strengthen domestic support for alliance in the target country. Papayoanou (1999) contends that economic ties generate domestic economic interests that influence a leader's ability to mobilize resources against threatening powers.

2. I would like to thank a reviewer for the term *second image reversed plus a second image*, which emphasizes that this argument goes beyond examining the effect of international politics on domestic politics, by adding that the empowered coalition will affect the state's foreign policy. On second image reversed politics, see Gourevitch 1977, 1978, 1986; Katzenstein 1978; Skocpol 1979; Kahler 1984; Weir and Skocpol 1985; James and Lake 1989; Rogowski 1989; Frieden 1991; Deudney and Ikenberry 1991–92; Berger and Dore 1996; Keohane and Milner 1996.

3. On integrating international and domestic politics, see Putnam 1988; Evans, Jacobson, and Putnam 1993; Müller and Risse-Kappen 1993; Risse-Kappen 1995. On domestic winners and losers, see Frieden 1991; Freeman 1995; Keohane and Milner 1996; Kapstein 2000.

4. On other international factors affecting domestic coalitional politics and domestic institutional development, see Lane 1958; Bean 1973; Tilly 1975, 1990; Stein 1978; Skocpol 1979; Frieden 1988; and Campbell 1995.

5. On definitions of grand strategy, see Barnett 1976, 11–15; Posen 1984, 6; Walt 1989, 6; Kennedy 1991, 1–7; Leffler 1992, ix–x; Rosecrance and Stein 1993, 4–5; Kupchan 1994, 3, fn 4.

6. For a distinction between resource mobilization (wealth creation) and extraction (consumption of wealth), see the discussion in Mastanduno, Lake, and Ikenberry 1989, 462–64.

7. Hegemonic stability theory makes the same assumption about decline. On

power transition and long cycle arguments, see Organski 1968; Organski and Kugler 1980; Gilpin 1981; Kennedy 1987; Modelski 1987; Goldstein 1988; and Rasler and Thompson 1994.

8. Gilpin (1981) and Kennedy (1987) strengthen Organski's original model by explaining why a hegemon cannot indefinitely sustain its dominant position. Although the hegemon reaps the benefits from preponderance, domestic and international costs of governing the international system will contribute to the hegemon's relative decline. The issue of balancing protection, investment, and consumption to arrest decline is complicated because a reduction in protection will result in external weakness, a reduction in consumption will contribute to internal social tension, and a reduction in investment will reduce the capacity of the hegemon to sustain its level of consumption and investment. Friedberg (1989a, 399–400) contends that the hegemon can maintain its existing rate of military spending by reducing public and especially private consumption. There is extensive literature on the prescriptions for great power resurgence; see Calleo 1987; Huntington 1987–88, 1988; Rosecrance 1990.

9. In contrast, as part of his argument, Kupchan argues that highly vulnerable declining powers will pursue overly cooperative policies in the core (1994, 17, table 2). Goldstein (1988) offers a slight twist to the power transition argument. He holds that more severe wars are likely to occur during the upswing phase instead of during the phase of hegemonic decline. His assumption is that economic expansion triggers competition among the great powers for scarce resources, and war becomes one means to secure them.

10. Kennan 1954; Waltz 1979; Walt 1989; Grieco 1990; Mearsheimer 1990, 2001; Van Evera 1990; Huntington 1993. Vital interests are ranked according to the size of territory, population, industrial capacity, military capability, and natural resources.

11. Writing shortly after World War II and in response to an emerging Soviet Union, Walter Lippmann (1943) and George Kennan (1954) argued that not all regions of the world were equally vital to American security. According to Kennan, only five centers of industrial and military power in the world (the United States, Great Britain, Germany and central Europe, the Soviet Union, and Japan) were central to American national security. Since just one region was in hostile hands, Kennan's policy of selective containment was intended to ensure that none of the other regions came under Soviet control. Kennan's assessment was that only by conquering some or all of these vital power centers could the Soviet Union (or any other emerging contender, including America's allies) tip the balance of power in its favor by commanding greater industrial power than the United States. Kennan objected to the argument that the United States had to resist communism wherever it appeared. There was no need to contain the Soviets in the Third World because even substantial Soviet conquest would have little impact on the global balance of power. Instead, the Third World offered little strategic value for

the great powers and diverted scarce national resources from the main theaters of operation.

Stephen Walt (1989) and Stephen Van Evera (1990) assert that America's vital interests have not substantially changed over the last five decades. The Persian Gulf has been added to the list of strategic regions, to preserve Western access to oil. According to Walt's calculation, Western Europe is the largest "prize," producing roughly 22 percent of the gross world product, and the Far East the second largest, producing 12.5 percent. The entire Third World produces less than 20 percent of the gross world product, scattered over more than 100 countries; all of Africa has an aggregate GNP lower than Britain (Walt 1989, 19). Samuel Huntington (1993) adds that even in the post–Cold War era, the United States can not allow any single state to dominate either Europe or Asia since the threat of the Soviet Union merely masked the conflicting interests among Western democratic states. To ensure no single state dominates the Eurasian land mass, Huntington recommends that the United States limit German power in the new Europe, restrain Japan by continuing the U.S.-Japanese military alliance, maintain its military posture in East Asia, and secure the Persian Gulf and Central American regions.

12. The hegemon's predicament of how to respond to challenges is analogous to the chain store paradox (Selten 1978; Rosenthal 1981; Milgrom and Roberts 1982; Von Hohenbalken and West 1986; Fudenberg and Kreps 1987; Fudenberg and Tirole 1991). According to the chain store paradox, a chain store has branches located in different cities and faces sequential potential entrants into each market. By backward induction, the game-theoretic strategy for the chain store is to pursue a strategy of cooperation in the face of potential entrants. In the last round of the game, the chain store has no incentive to punish the contender in order to establish a reputation for harsh retaliation since there are no future entrants to deter (punishing through a price war is costly for the chain store). By backward induction to the first round, the chain store will always select to cooperate, and the challenger will always enter the market. By forward induction, the chain store will pursue a strategy of deterrence. The chain store will punish any competitor that attempts to enter its market in order to establish a reputation for standing firm. For a hegemon, one solution to this paradox is to distinguish among contenders, accommodating friends and punishing rivals (Lobell 2001).

13. One problem with these arguments, such as Kupchan's (1994), is that they ignore the political cost in failing to adjust to international change. Failure of an overextended state to retreat from its empire due to strategic myths means that the metropole will be even more unprepared for conflict in the core. The general public is likely to punish the government for this poor state of affairs.

14. Friedberg (1988) suggests that with improved analytical tools, Britain would have adjusted better to its changing international environment by increasing military spending, boosting government intervention in the economy, and

maintaining its global empire. However, higher military spending might have prompted higher spending by the Central Powers, lower French military spending, or a more aggressive Franco-Russian foreign policy (McKeown 1991, 270). In Britain, many Liberals and Radicals opposed heightened defense spending for fear it would only provoke other powers to do likewise (Morris 1971, 369).

15. See Cortrell and Peterson (1999) who examine the effects of domestic and international events to account for institutional transformation.

16. For an application of this perspective, see Stein and Lobell 1997. We argue that the end of the Cold War will not have a uniform effect on the post–Cold War era. In regions that were isolated from the Cold War and regions on the periphery of this rivalry, there will be little change. However, in regions that were highly penetrated by the superpowers, future regional relations will depend upon whether superpower intervention in regional affairs increased or decreased regional conflict and whether or not this involvement left a lasting impression on the region.

17. On the literature on subsystems, see Binder 1958; Brecher 1963; Zartman 1967; Cantori and Spiegel 1969; Brown 1984; Noble 1984; Doran 1989. For different definitions of the concept of a region, see Lake and Morgan 1997.

18. For a discussion on spheres of influence, see Kaufman 1976; Keal 1983; Triska 1986.

19. Japan played an active role in Latin America's debt management (Katada 1994).

20. For a counterargument, see Wohlstetter 1968.

21. I term this coalition *liberal* rather than *free trade*. While the former faction called for many of the same economic policies as the latter, such as lowering the cost of hegemony to reduce taxation and spending, and a concern for creating a positive environment for domestic investment, they did not call for free trade (however, they did oppose Madrid's exclusive trading companies and the embargoes against Dutch and English goods).

22. A hegemon can affect the environment that it faces through the policies that it chooses to adopt. For a good example of the effect of the hegemon's commercial policy in changing the contenders' commercial policy (or the "second face of hegemony"), see James and Lake 1989.

23. For instance, Olson (1982) argues that vested interest groups or "distributional coalitions" reduce economic efficiency and constrain economic growth. Ibn Khaldun (1967) and Gilpin (1981) emphasize the corrupting influence of economic prosperity (especially rising public consumption). On the negative effect of Britain's rigid social structure, see Barnett 1972. On Rome's economic decline, see Bernardi 1970; on its moral decay, see MacMullen 1988; on the moral weakening of the ruling classes, see Eisenstadt 1963.

24. See the organizational literature on industrial decline and adaptation to changes in the market: Whetten 1980, 1987; Zammuto and Cameron 1985; Weitzel and Jonsson 1989. External shocks encourage sameness and duplication

(i.e., follow-the-leader) among the great powers. Since states are competing with each other, if one state introduces a change that will give it an advantage or make it stronger than the rest, the others must duplicate it in order to keep pace. Any state that fails to do so will fall behind the states that do adapt; see Stein 1990, 115–16.

25. Latecomers might have an advantage because they can adopt newer technological innovations while earlier investors must wait to recoup initial investment; see Chase-Dunn 1982, 83.

26. Keohane notes that powerful "countries can postpone adjustment; and the stronger they are, the longer it can be postponed . . . but . . . it merely postpones the inevitable, making it more difficult to deal with in the future" (1982, 70).

CHAPTER 2

1. Having a competitive economy does not guarantee the hegemon will pursue a liberal foreign economic policy. In the 1930s, Germany was economically advanced but pursued an imperial foreign economic policy. For a discussion of advanced and backward economies, see Krasner 1976; Lake 1988; Rogowski 1989; Brawley 1993.

2. Kindleberger 1973; Krasner 1976; Keohane 1984. However, a country's international position does not sufficiently explain its foreign economic policy (Lobell 1999).

3. Evans 1992, 143–44; Brawley 1993, 12.

4. A simple signaling game can explain how, in a world of incomplete information, a declining leader can identify whether a rising contender is a supporter or a challenger. If a declining leader has perfect or full information about each rising contender, it can readily determine a rising state's type (type refers to any information that is not common knowledge to all players). Under this condition there is little doubt about how to identify whether an emerging state is a friend or foe.

In the real world it is necessary to relax the assumption of complete information (Jervis 1970; Stein 1983, 1990; Bueno de Mesquita and Lalman 1992). A declining power will look at a trait of the rising states in order to assess their type (just as an individual who prefers to fight a wimp instead of a bully can observe what others have for breakfast to gain insight into their type—wimp if he/she eats quiche and bully if he/she has beer; Kreps 1990, 463–64). The central trait that I focus on is a rising state's foreign commercial policy. For an application to international relations theory, see Powell 1987; Alt, Calvert, and Humes 1988; Morrow 1989; Stein 1990.

5. On the concept of the Manchester Liberals, see Grampp 1960; Blainey 1988, 18–32.

6. On the competition between coalitions for control over domestic and foreign economic policy, see Katzenstein 1978; Gourevitch 1986; Friedberg 1988; Frieden 1988, 1991; Milner 1988, 1997; Nelson 1989, 1990; Rogowski 1989; Sny-

der 1991; Vasquez 1993; Perthes 1994; Keohane and Milner 1996; Lawson 1996; Solingen 1997, 1998; Schamis 1999. While most of this literature explains foreign economic policy, a good example of the effect of coalitional competition in the security realm is John Lewis Gaddis's *Strategies of Containment*. According to Gaddis (1982, 352–57), during the Cold War a debate over America's capabilities and its global commitments raged between the defenders of the "asymmetrical" approach or soft-line realists (fiscal orthodoxy, limitation of resources, and distinction between vital and peripheral commitments) and the supporters of the "symmetrical" approach or hard-line realists (high military spending, deficit spending, and defense of the core and the periphery). The dominance of the former coalition explains the Truman administration's initial restraint in the periphery, the Eisenhower administration's New Look and thrifty massive retaliation policies, and the Nixon administration's cost-saving Nixon Doctrine and Détente. The predominance of the latter coalition explains the U.S. decision after the Korean War to punish emerging contenders in both the core and the periphery (the shift from strong-point to perimeter containment, and from economic to military containment) and the Kennedy/Johnson administration's ambitious and costly policy of Flexible Response, funded by the Keynesian revolution.

7. See the literature on the politics of structural and economic adjustment, which discusses the domestic political consequences of economic liberalization, such as Haggard and Kaufman 1989, 1992; Evans 1992; Kienle 1994; Sahn, Dorosh, and Younger 1997.

8. In contrast, according to Conybeare (1987, 23–28, 271–73) optimal tariffs are the preferred tactic for a hegemon to exploit small states.

9. For free traders, the proper role for the state in any alliance is to act as the quartermaster or the economic powerhouse of the alliance, providing loans and military equipment to their allies (instead of dispatching troops). See French 1986.

10. On the inverse relationship between levels of trade and conflict, see Polachek 1980; Gasiorowski and Polachek 1982; Mansfield 1994.

11. Among others, see Hobson 1938; Lebovics 1967; Fischer 1975; Kehr 1977; Gourevitch 1986; Waterbury 1989; Snyder 1991; Zakaria 1992; Rotte 1997. The timing of development can play a crucial role in differential domestic arrangements. Hirschman (1958) and Gerschenkron (1962) discuss the differences between early, late, and late-late industrializers, which can also affect the relative strength of the free traders and the economic nationalists, since in the former the state is less interventionist (granting free traders more autonomy) and in the latter the state plays a leading role in development (insulating economic nationalists).

12. The military will favor expanding (or retreating) from indefensible positions (Galbraith 1960; Thompson and Zuk 1986).

13. Friedberg 2000. Schumpeter (1955) argues that export monopolists push for imperialist expansion as a way to enlarge their closed markets.

14. Rent-seeking behavior is common for interventionist and regulatory states.

15. For a discussion of *Innenpolitik* and *Aussenpolitik*, see Zakaria 1992, 179–81.

16. See Higgs 1987, 57–74; Porter 1994, 14; and Friedberg 2000, 30–32, for a discussion on the role of ratchets and rollbacks in strengthening and weakening domestic actors and interest groups. For a discussion and example of degrees of coalitional strength, see Solingen 1998, 64, fig. 2.

17. Snyder (1991, 31) labels these power assets: material resources, organizational strength, and information.

18. Among others, see Alt and Gilligan 1994; Alt, Frieden, Gilligan, Rodrik, and Rogowski 1996.

19. Evans 1992, 144. Also, a smaller win-set means that economic nationalists need to satisfy only a powerful few (Brawley 1993).

20. Miller (1995, 15–17) distinguishes between two types of great power collaboration: spontaneous and deliberate cooperation.

21. On the special relationship among commercially liberal states, see Kant 1972 [1795]; Rock 1989; Brawley 1993. On trading states, see Rosecrance 1986. On complex interdependence, see Keohane and Nye 1977, and for alternative views on the correlation between economic interdependence and international cooperation, see Stein 1993b.

22. Such as job retraining for workers in inefficient industry; see Waterbury 1989, 41.

23. Stephen Rock (1989, 13–15) and Mark Brawley (1993, 19–20) challenge the assumption of a peaceful commercial transition among certain liberal dyads. According to Rock, peace is most likely to "break out" among states that are heterogeneous in their economic activity, and tension is most likely to escalate among states that are homogeneous in their economic activity. Rivalry is likely among homogeneous states, even if they are liberal states, because they will compete with one another in home and overseas markets. Similarly, according to Brawley, a capital-abundant declining liberal leader and a capital-abundant liberal challenger are natural economic rivals because they will produce and/or export similar goods and services.

24. For a review of the literature on appeasement, see Schroeder 1976b; Watt 1976; Kennedy 1983, 15–39; Richardson 1988.

25. According to Gowa (1994), rivals are unlikely to trade for fear that economic gains will be converted into military power.

26. I would like to thank Arthur Stein for this term. According to David (1991, 243) and Ayoob (1998), ruling elites in the Third World balance against internal threats to their regime's survival as well as against more traditional exter-

nal threats to the state. Such elites will advance the regime's interests, even if it overrides the state's.

27. A state does have a number of alternative means to increase its rate of resource extraction. Additional domestic resources can be extracted through taxation and borrowing. Other strategies to acquire additional resources include extracting revenue from other states in the empire (i.e., burden-sharing) and territorial conquest to grab or steal wealthy regions.

Domestic reforms can be implemented to create greater efficiency in the means of extracting or using existing resources. In the first century B.C.E., Rome nearly collapsed due to the fighting among governors seeking to enrich themselves. Emperor Augustus implemented a number of administrative reforms that recentralized the bureaucracy, giving it greater control over both money and arms (the wealthy province of Egypt became a possession of the emperor; Starr 1982). Further, to stem the European onrush, a declining Ottoman Empire adopted a series of domestic reforms, borrowing Europe's military technology and seeking to consolidate power in Istanbul (this era of reform is known as the *Tanzimat*).

The state can strike a bargain with society, exchanging greater resource extraction for more social rights and benefits (Levi 1988; Lamborn 1991). Such a bargain can defuse societal opposition to increased resource extraction. The 1905–10 pension and welfare reforms in Britain were intended to offset the massive increases in extraction during the Boer War (Lamborn 1983, 130). Leaders have also extended suffrage to increase the rate of extraction for defense. To increase its capabilities in the long term, the state might be able to generate additional resources, especially if the immediate military threat is not too great. The state can promote greater industrial productivity or industrial revitalization through macroeconomic tools, which will raise societal wealth and increase the base from which the state can extract resources. At the extreme, through state-led development, the government can encourage industrial growth and restructure the economy (Trimberger 1978). This strategy of resource mobilization is highlighted by the Meiji Restoration in Japan and Stalin's five-year plans in the Soviet Union.

28. On the danger of budget deficits, see Thurow 1985; on the trade-off between guns versus butter, see Mintz and Huang 1991.

29. For a critical assessment of the link between military burdens and economic growth, see Rasler and Thompson 1988, 1991; Friedberg 1989a; Kupchan 1989.

30. On the distributional effects, see Frieden and Rogowski 1996, 45–46.

31. A challenger might not rush into war with a more powerful hegemon, but wait until its power exceeds the erstwhile leader's.

32. Rising liberal contenders will find it easier to cooperate in concert against a hegemon pursuing an imperial foreign economic policy. More than a temporary marriage of convenience, liberal contenders will mutually benefit under a liberal commercial arrangement. Imperial challengers will have difficulty creating stable

alliances. An imperial ally is a potential threat since it will seek exclusive control over any locale that it comes to dominate.

CHAPTER 3

1. The Conservative Party was referred to as the Unionist because of its commitment to the union with Ireland.

2. On the ascendance of members of the free-trade coalition (merchant bankers), see Lisle-Williams 1984.

3. As Porter notes of Britain's predicament during this period, "It was a kind of catch-22 situation. Fail to fortify the citadel and it would be stormed from without. Fortify, and it would collapse from within" (1983, 56–57).

4. See Kennedy 1987, 200–202, tables 15, 16, 17, 18.

5. LaFeber 1997, 151–52. According to Brawley, the changing nature of American tariffs from the McKinley Tariff of 1890, to the Wilson-Gorman Tariff of 1894, to the Payne-Aldrich Tariff of 1909, and finally to the Underwood Tariff of 1913 meant that "the emphasis of protection went from industry in the 1880s, to industry and agriculture in the 1890s and 1900s, to agriculture only, to little protection for any sectors in 1913" (1993, 126–27).

6. Russia rebuffed part of the agreement on uniform railroad rates in China because it intended to use differential rates to pay for railroad construction.

7. Despite the rapid industrialization experienced under the Meiji era in Japan (1868–1912), a large percentage of the population remained in agriculture.

8. Japan's expansion in the Pacific during this period is characterized as primarily defensive in nature. In the case of Korea, due to its geographic proximity, the Army General Staff deemed control over the Korean peninsula as essential to the defense of Japan (Crowley 1974, 18). Japan's goal was to deny control over Korea by any other power, since Korea was "a dagger pointed at the heart of Japan" (Crowley 1974, 13). Gillard argues, "As rulers of an island power off the Asian mainland, Japanese leaders felt about Korea much what the British felt about Belgium" (1977, 162). Outside of Korea, Japan was anxious to gain control over the sea approaches to Japan, especially the Straits of Tsushima, and Taiwan and the Pescadores Islands to protect its southern flanks (Duus 1976, 129).

9. The Méline Tariff was also highly selective, and duties were even reduced on some imports (Smith 1992, 235).

10. Geiss 1976, 84–95; Calleo 1978, 9–25, 43–48. The chief architects of Germany's *Weltpolitik* were Chancellor von Bülow, Naval Secretary Alfred von Tirpitz, Minister of Finance Johannes Miquel, and Kaiser Wilhelm II.

11. Kehr (1977) emphasizes the domestic element of *Weltpolitik*. He attributes it to three forces: agrarians, commercial and industrial bourgeoisie, and the industrial working class.

12. Schultz 1989, 322–25. During World War I, *Mitteleuropa* was expanded into the broader concept of *Ostraum*, with Germany extending through the

Ukraine to the Caucasus and Georgia (Fischer 1975, 33–34, 46; Calleo 1978, 48; Hillgruber 1981, 38, 45).

13. The Mendeleyev Tariff of 1891 placed heavy duties on imported manufactured goods and on exported raw materials, allowing free entry to only fourteen products; Sontag 1968; Geyer 1987.

14. One attempt to gain the support of labor for protection was the Trade Union Tariff Reform Association.

15. Kennedy 1980, 331–60. The Liberal Party rapidly declined in strength after the war.

16. Longstreth 1979, 160–63; Ingham 1984, 96–102, 113–16; Cain and Hopkins 1993b, 125–31. Daunton (1989, 149) divides the City into four primary groupings: bankers, financiers and stockbrockers; shipping interests; middlemen and importers; and colonial houses. On other characteristics of the members of the City, see Davis and Huttenback 1986, 162–82.

17. The Treasury interpreted its role as balancing the budget, while the Bank of England was responsible for monetary policy. According to Cain and Hopkins, "The logic of free trade was precisely that debtors had to be given access to other markets so that they could acquire the foreign exchange needed to service their debts. If Britain's creditors had bought more British manufactures, they would have been less able to meet their obligations to the City of London" (1993a, 306).

18. Emy 1972, 114–15. According to the Permanent Under-Secretary of the Treasury, E. W. Hamilton, "One of the principal reasons why there are such uneasiness and stagnation in the City is that the Government have been borrowers on so large a scale on account of the war and of the Transvaal after the war. The Money Market is suffering from a surfeit of Government stocks that in fact have never been properly digested. Digestion of these stocks, as also of other stocks of the gilt-edged order, like Municipal and Colonial Loans, must be a slow process; but, slow though the process may be, the difficulty would be surmounted in course of time, were further issues of a considerable amount not to be feared. Unfortunately, the Loan horizon is not clear" (PRO, T. 168/61, "The Financial Outlook vis à vis the City," 10/9/03).

19. Hamilton warned, "I believe it is difficult to overrate the advantages which result from the maintenance of a considerable Sinking Fund. It not only gives great strength to our credit in times of peace, but it is an immense reserve in times of war. Indeed, the Sinking Fund constitutes our War Chest, and a War Chest administered in a much more scientific and much less wasteful manner than that of Germany. Its legitimate suspension in times of real emergency would enable us to raise, without any additions to taxation, over 200 millions. But in normal times to reduce seriously the amount devoted to redeem debt would, I believe, tell sensibly on our credit and on the financial position which we occupy in the eyes of the world; and any proposal which the chancellor of the Exchequer might make in the direction of trenching upon the national Reserve Fund, opposed as such proposal

would be to the best financial authorities, would be most difficult to defend" (PRO, Cab. 37/39/38, 7/24/95).

20. Britain's income tax and high international credit rating meant that it had superior war potential over its Continental neighbors (Emy 1972; Kennedy 1983; D'Lugo and Rogowski 1993; Ferguson 1994). First, Britain's Treasury had the power to levy and increase both direct taxes and indirect taxes, while most European governments could raise revenue only by indirect taxation. In the case of Germany, only state governments (not the Reich) could raise direct taxes. Consequently, much of Germany's spending on the navy during the Anglo-German naval rivalry had to be financed through loans. In France, indirect taxes, stamp taxes, and a high level of borrowing financed public spending, while in Russia, the government relied on revenues from taxes on consumption and railways, and on foreign capital. Second, Britain's management of public debt meant that the government could borrow large sums of money at relatively low interest rates. In contrast, the Continental states tended to borrow on the money markets, even in peacetime, in order to cover the gap between expenditure and revenue. The result was a high national debt and higher interest rates (however, during the interwar period, Britain's chancellor of the Exchequer warned that during peacetime "we could not compete on taxation basis against nations who were acting on a loan basis"; Shay 1977, 74). Thus, while the combined economic resources of Britain's neighbors were greater than its own, Britain's capacity to extract revenue was much greater than the Continental powers.

21. On left-wing opposition to naval armaments, see Weinroth 1971.

22. In 1886, Chamberlain led the Liberal Unionists into alliance with the Conservatives (known officially as the Conservative and Unionist Party after 1912). Colonial secretary since 1895, Chamberlain resigned in 1903 to campaign for imperial preferences. In 1903, his campaign split the Conservative Party between protectionists (Chamberlain), a powerful minority who favored free traders (Duke of Devonshire), and Balfour, the party leader (who wavered between these two positions to hold the party together), contributing to its defeat in the 1906 elections (Lloyd 1970, 4–8).

23. Britain's relative industrial decline is highlighted by its increasing dependence on the export of cotton and coal.

24. Many farmers expressed concern about proposals for imperial preferences especially those based on free admission of colonial grain.

25. As war approached, some economic nationalists called for a national insurance scheme to reimburse ship owners and merchants for the cost of war risk insurance. The fear was that otherwise ship owners would dock their vessels for the duration of the war. Those willing to take the risks would pass on the higher costs to the consumer, raising the cost of scarce imported goods. The Treasury was not convinced that rising prices would have dire results.

26. Tariffs included: in the United States, the McKinley Tariff of 1890, the

Wilson-Gorman Tariff of 1894, and the Dingley Tariff of 1897; in France the Méline Tariff of 1892; in Russia the Mendeleyev Tariff of 1891; and in Germany the Caprivi Treaties of 1879 and 1902 (Ashley 1970; Lake 1988).

27. Chamberlain also created the Tariff Reform Commission to study the issue.

28. Some in the empire opposed this relationship since it meant that Britain would remain the supplier of manufactures and the colonies would specialize in the export of food and raw materials. This did not satisfy the colonies' own aspirations to develop their manufacturing sectors.

29. Dintenfass (1992, 40–45) challenges the argument that foreign lending starved industry and trade at home. For an extended discussion on the debate over whether the British banks failed British industry and the manufacturing base of the economy by ignoring their needs while focusing on international trade, finance, and services during this period, see Pollard 1985; Best and Humphries 1986; Daunton 1989; Collins 1991.

30. Pollard 1989, 240–41, Green 1995, 69–72. After 1906, the Tariff Reformers dominated the Conservative Party, holding two-thirds of the MPs (Cain and Hopkins 1993b, 220).

31. Phillips 1979, 82–110; Williams 1991, 3, 28–30. Members of the diehards called for the removal of Admiral Fisher due to his naval reforms.

32. The aristocrats were also concerned about R. B. Haldane's (secretary of state for war in the Liberal government) proposed reforms of the army. Organizations favoring consolidation of empire included the Imperial Federation League, Colonial Institute, and the Imperial Institute; see Green 1995.

33. Williams 1991, 28; Marder 1940, 372–92. In 1906, William Le Queux published his bestseller, *The Invasion of 1910*.

34. Ingham 1984, 80; Cain and Hopkins 1993b, 144–45. The bimetallic controversy of the 1880s and 1890s foreshadowed the growing strength of the City of London over industry during the coming decades. The slide in silver prices caused a revaluation of the sterling against silver-based currencies making it harder to export to silver standard countries, but easier to buy imports from them. It increased invisible income and harmed those suffering from foreign competition, such as agriculture. One solution, rejected by the City, called for an agreement that would fix a ratio for gold to silver (Cain and Hopkins 1993b, 151–52).

35. Soviet scholars argue that no Russian threat existed to India. But if Britain perceived it as a threat, that was all that mattered; see Yapp 1987, 647.

36. The Naval Defence Act granted Britain an advantage over the Russian and French naval programs by departing from the existing budget process (Sumida 1989, 13–15). Traditionally, a department submitted budget estimates for the following year, and any unused portion was returned to the Treasury. For the navy, which had projects requiring multiple years of funding, it annually requested funding for the same project. The middle years of naval construction were the most

expensive, necessitating an increase in the level of funding. Lack of funds often meant that naval construction was delayed, and interruptions in construction raised the overall cost of a ship. The Naval Defence Act provided a remedy to this problem. First, it provided funding for five years instead of a single year. Second, it allowed for unexpended balances for naval construction from one year to be used in the next year. Thereby, underspending in the early years of construction would be applied to the more expensive middle years of construction, without requiring the Treasury's and Parliament's annual approval.

37. Responding to France and Russia, as well as addressing German naval construction; Sumida 1989, 23; Williams 1991, 72–73.

38. While Selborne supported Chamberlain's call for preferential tariffs (Boyce 1990, 7).

39. France's naval expenditures, which had risen since the 1870s, fell in 1902 and further in 1903.

40. Monger 1963, 136. Significant for Britain was France's respect for British strategic interests in the Mediterranean (Williamson 1969, 8–10, 15). Determined to prevent the fortification of the narrow eight-mile-wide Straits of Gibraltar, Britain (and France) agreed to give weaker Spain control over the sector of the Moroccan coast adjacent to the Straits, not allowing any fortifications to be built.

41. Williams 1966, 371. The liberal opposition parties in Russia opposed the loan because it would strengthen the government of Nicholas II (Crisp 1961, 497).

42. Steiner 1977, 83. Persia was divided into three spheres—Russian (north), British (south), and a neutral zone. Britain also hoped to prevent partition, keeping the constitutional government in power. One consequence for London was that concessions emboldened imperial Russia to make ever-increasing demands on Britain's commercial interests in Central Asia, especially northern Persia (with the loss of the five northern provinces), where Russian forward policy entered a new phase of aggression, extending their power toward the neutral zone (Robbins 1977, 17–18). In 1909, the Russians dispatched troops to Persia and began their military occupation, encroaching on the south.

43. Rock (1988, 345–46) maintains that America's naval threat forced Britain to retreat from the Western Hemisphere. The combination of America's construction of a "risk" fleet and Britain's unwillingness to concentrate its fleet in the Americas (due to its rivalry with France, Russia, and Germany) forced London into making a number of concessions. The problem with Rock's argument is that the timing is wrong. Britain's departure from the Americas (which was already in process by 1901) prompted the United States to increase the size of its fleet. In 1898, the United States had only six modern battleships, including the *Maine*. The Venezuelan crisis of 1902 served as a great impetus for the construction of a larger American navy. No longer able to free ride on protection from the Royal Navy, the United States initiated a naval buildup (the lead time was roughly three

years to build a battleship). Between 1902 and 1905, Congress authorized ten first-class battleships, four armored cruisers, and seventeen other vessels of various classes (Bourne 1967, 338).

44. In 1903, Britain's prime minister, Arthur Balfour, openly proclaimed his support for American regional hegemony, claiming, "The Monroe Doctrine has no enemies in this country that I know of. We welcome any increase of the influence of the United States of America upon the great Western hemisphere" (Bourne 1967, 350).

45. PRO, FO. 46/547, "Memorandum by Francis Bertie," 9/22/01.

46. PRO, ADM. 116/866B15 1/06.

47. British interests accounted for 70 percent of China's trade, which was one-sixth of total English commerce (LaFeber 1963, 316). To allow Britain to draw down the number of battleships stationed in the Far East, the Foreign Secretary inserted into the original treaty terms that called for each partner to maintain (in the Far East) naval forces superior to those of any other power, using the words "as far as possible" (Marder 1940, 429–30; Monger 1963, 57–58).

48. In a telegram to Yokohama (1902), the Baring Brothers reported that the cooperation of the Bank of England was vital in ensuring the success of the 5.5 percent loan (Warner 1991, 54).

49. The alliance was renewed again in 1911 for ten years.

50. By 1905, an unofficial Anglo-American-Japanese accord had been established in the Far East (Monger 1963, 180–83).

51. PRO, Cab. 37/70/61, 4/30/04.

52. Marder 1961, 28–45. During the 1890s, the army and the War Office were guided by the Stanhope memorandum (1891) that defined the army's duties as home defense, supplying replacements for overseas garrisons, and preparing two corps for operations in colonial areas. By 1903, this duty had been revised; the navy could block any invasion threat, leaving the army to defend against a possible Russian invasion of India.

53. Cabinet Memorandum by Lord Selborne, December 6, 1904, "Distribution and Mobilization of the Fleet" (Boyce 1990, 184–90).

54. Sumida 1989, table 3. Between the fiscal years of 1906–7 and 1908–9, Naval Estimates were 15 percent below the level reached in 1904–5 (Williams 1991, 84).

55. Yet, the navy already excluded the United States in its calculations; Gooch 1994, 289.

56. The German, Austrian, and Italian representatives at the Hague Conference refused to discuss disarmament (Williams 1991, 89).

57. Wilmott 1972, 61. According to Williams (1991, 90), two issues were in dispute among free traders and economic nationalists: whether the Germans could fulfill their target of four dreadnoughts a year and how long construction would take.

58. Peden 2000, 51. In 1908 Herbert Henry Asquith replaced Sir Henry Campbell-Bannerman as prime minister, David Lloyd George went to the Exchequer, and Winston Churchill went to the Board of Trade.

59. The building programs of Germany's allies, Austria and Italy, left the government no choice, and the additional ships of the 1909–10 program were later approved by the cabinet.

60. Lambelet 1974, 23. Lambelet contends that Germany got the shorter end of the agreement: (1) Britain breached the accords in 1912, when it laid down an additional battleship; (2) Germany made concessions in the first year, while Britain's were more spread out.

61. Lambelet 1974, 14–17, table 2. Between 1909 and 1912, eighteen dreadnoughts were constructed. During the winter of 1913–14, Churchill threatened to resign if the cabinet agreed to cuts in battleship construction.

62. For France, maintaining sea control in the Mediterranean was essential to ensuring the transport of troops from North Africa. This arrangement granted France local superiority over the combined Italian and Austrian fleets.

63. Yet between 1890 and 1910, the United States surpassed Britain as the world's leading power without provoking a similar reaction.

64. D'Lugo and Rogowski (1993) and Ferguson (1994) argue that during the Anglo-German naval race (1909–12), Britain mobilized a greater share of its societal resources for naval spending than Germany because Great Britain's constitutional system was more flexible. In Britain, the Treasury had the power both to levy direct taxes and to borrow in order to bridge any shortfall in defense spending. In contrast, after German unification in 1871, as dictated by Germany's constitution, much of the power to tax remained in the hands of the states, rather than the federal Reich. Thus, a weak German Treasury was unable to secure a larger share of revenue for bigger defense budgets.

65. For free traders, the greatest concern was a German naval blockade that would cause economic chaos (Howard 1982, 150).

66. This policy was known as the Limited Liability strategy; see Hancock and Gowing 1953, 12–40; French 1982c; Newton and Porter 1988, 31–39. According to French (1986, 101), the free-trade preponderance was even greater than the numbers suggested since they occupied the key ministerial positions.

CHAPTER 4

1. In fact, the services were authorized to buy more planes and the army more equipment than industry could build (Dunbabin 1975, 601; Shay 1977, 80–83; Peden 1979, 151–67; Kennedy 1981, 232). Shay (1977, 83) notes that "it is safe to say that in 1936 money was not an object for the R.A.F."

2. Voluntary industrial cooperation that granted priority to war production was selected over state compulsion.

3. Some exceptions include Pratt 1975; Gibbs 1976; Walker 1980; Kennedy 1981; McKercher 1991; French 1993; Scammel 1997.

4. London's concern was that any state that dominated the Continent could block Britain's commercial access and invade the British Isles.

5. As Japan met resistance to its expansion in China, Tokyo became dependent on imports from the United States for goods such as machine tools and aviation fuel to continue its war effort. Like Germany and Britain, rearmament greatly reduced Japan's stock of foreign currency.

6. In an attempt to sidestep Britain, in the spring of 1935, Japan's Ambassador Saito Hiroshi tried to convince Secretary of State Cordell Hull that the two governments should issue a joint declaration designating the United States as the stabilizing power in the eastern Pacific and Japan as the stabilizing power in the western Pacific.

7. Japan's investment in China, including Manchuria, represented 82.9 percent of its total foreign investment (Trotter 1975, 19).

8. This move was forbidden by the Treaties of Versailles and St. Germain, and the Geneva Protocol of 1922.

9. German rearmament beyond the limits set in the Versailles treaty were well known (Mowat 1968, 539–41).

10. Many conservatives in Germany wanted to pursue colonial interests, refraining from action in Europe.

11. One concern in Congress was that the Lend-Lease Act would help Britain compete with the United States in world markets. There were strict rules to what Britain could re-export, and Lend-Lease was terminated abruptly at the end of the war.

12. French 1982a, b; Milward 1984; Cain and Hopkins 1993a. In mobilizing for war, Britain progressed from "business as usual" to a "nation in arms" to "total war."

13. The crop area in Britain was increased by three million acres. The effects of the German submarine blockade during World War I led the government to use financial incentives and compulsory powers to attempt to reverse the trend of agricultural development over the previous forty years (Milward 1984, 29–30; Ferguson 1998, 252, table 24).

14. The Treasury was required to approve all new share issues on the stock market. Cheap loans encouraged substitution of imports previously supplied by Germany.

15. The Treasury was viewed as a "general staff." In 1936, Sir Thomas Inskip was appointed Minister for the Co-ordination of Defence. This fell well short of a minister of defense because it lacked a department and had no executive powers.

16. The Treasury adamantly opposed any suggestion of government industrial control during peacetime.

17. The limit of borrowing was dictated by the classical economic belief that a

nation could only borrow as much as its citizens saved (Shay 1977, 160–61). Any borrowing in excess of this limit would simply mean printing money that would give way to inflation, damaging Britain's international credit and trade.

18. White Dominion interest in developing their own manufacturing militated against the vision of the empire as an economic unit. Between 1910 and 1935, British exports to its empire rose from 35 percent to 50 percent, while imports from its empire rose from 25 percent to 40 percent (Porter 1983, 94).

19. The FBI was the national organization for manufacturing firms; see Boyce 1974; Capie 1983, 61–76.

20. The COS consisted of the Chief of Naval Staff, the Chief of the Air Staff, and the Chief of Imperial General Staff.

21. There was no limit on auxiliary ships (smaller than battleships), resulting in a race in cruisers, the next largest ship, between Britain and Japan by 1926.

22. Capie 1983, 72–75. As Keith Robbins notes, "it was unfortunate that opposition to Free Trade was so closely linked to enthusiasm for empire" (1983, 139).

23. Parker 1981, 307; Peden 1979, 82; Shay 1983. This argument challenges John Maynard Keynes's, who claimed at the time that Britain needed to simply pursue a strategy of deficit spending to resolve its weak economy. The lack of skilled labor meant that deficit spending would be inflationary. Furthermore, skilled craft unions resisted breaking down jobs so that they could be carried out by less skilled labor.

24. In 1932, the Exchange Equalisation Account (EEA) was established, marking the transfer of control over the exchange rate from the Bank of England to the Treasury.

25. The government's first step toward protection was the Abnormal Importations Act (1931), designed to defend the balance of payments from imports. Parliament gave the Board of Trade powers for six months to impose duties up to 100 percent on a wide range of manufactured goods that were thought to be entering the country in abnormal quantities. The Horticultural Products (Emergency Act), which passed soon after, gave the Minister of Agriculture similar powers to hamper the importation of fresh fruits, flowers, and vegetables.

26. Many of the Dominions were keen on building up their infant industries behind tariffs intended to protect them from more efficient producers, including Britain's (Porter 1994).

27. According to some scholars the tariff was only for international bargaining (i.e., retaliation) and not a turn toward protectionism (Taylor 1965, 331).

28. The result was that Britain's exports to the Dominions received preference, but chiefly by increasing the tariff against foreign goods.

29. Trotter 1974, 71–72; 1975, 214; Louis 1983. On the clash between the Foreign Office and the Treasury over cooperation with Japan, see Lee 1971; Trotter 1975, 41–46, 56–58, 98–104, 165–67; Lowe 1981, 146–47, 149.

30. Moderates in Japan realized that Tokyo would need British cooperation in the economic development of China.

31. The report by Leith-Ross called for taking China off the silver standard and fixing it to sterling, the establishment of a Central Reserve Bank, and a balanced budget to clear the way for new lending (Cain and Hopkins 1993a, 235–62).

32. Holland 1981, 296. Reparations were abolished in 1932 by the Lausanne Treaty.

33. Endicott 1973–74, 486. The fate of the Chinese currency was important to Britain because of British investments in the country and China's close link with the trade and currency of Hong Kong (also on silver).

34. Especially after the seizure of Prague in 1938 (MacDonald 1972, 127).

35. Yet, in 1938, Britain acquiesced in Japan's insistence that the customs revenues at Shanghai and Tientsin be placed in a Japanese bank (Lowe 1981, 159–60). The danger was that Japan might appropriate the international concessions. Shai (1974) contends that British appeasement (a "Far Eastern Munich") in the Far East persisted.

36. Shanghai represented three-quarters of Britain's holdings in China (Trotter 1975, 18). The city was also important to shipping firms, handling much of the extensive inland trade on the Yangtze River.

37. Endicott 1973–74, 495. It was believed that Tokyo's economic plans for the occupied areas would fail because Japan lacked capital, becoming financially exhausted.

38. Also see Skidelsky 1976, 159–60.

39. The DRC consisted of the Chiefs of Staff Sub-Committee (COS) and the secretaries of the Foreign Office and the Treasury.

40. In 1936, the five-year rearmament program approved by the cabinet relaxed the procedure for approving the annual review of Estimates. To increase the speed of rearmament, instead of withholding sanction until the entire vote had been approved by the Cabinet, the Treasury would now sanction items individually. In addition, contracts were placed on a long-term basis to accommodate the ongoing nature of rearmament (Peden 1979, 40).

41. Since 1922, Britain's leaders had agreed that in the event of war in the Far East, the main fleet would sail to Singapore via the Mediterranean, with reserves left behind to defend the home waters.

42. Gibbs 1976, 122–25. The Royal Navy reconfirmed its commitment in 1937 (at the Imperial Conference) and again in 1939 to send the fleet to Singapore.

43. The Sea Lords discounted a German naval challenge to Britain's home waters; Watt 1956, 172; Scammel 1997, 102–3.

44. The rivalry between Neville Chamberlain and Maurice Hankey was nurtured by the fact that Hankey had a naval background and perhaps favored the

navy, while Chamberlain preferred the air force (Greenwood 1994, 19–21).

45. To diffuse the myth that Chamberlain opposed rearmament, Robert Shay (1983) argues that had Chamberlain been prime minister a year earlier (1936 instead of 1937), Britain would have been much better prepared for war by 1939. In 1937, Neville Chamberlain succeeded Stanley Baldwin as prime minister, and John Simon became the new chancellor of the Exchequer.

46. A recession in the United States further lowered the demand for British exports.

47. For this reason they also opposed the re-creation of a Ministry of Supply.

48. Parker 1975, 643–44. Chamberlain also worried about the negative political repercussions of increased taxation for additional defense spending. The government's desire to grant tax reductions and complete the return of the wages of government employees to their pre-austerity budget levels, while at the same time balancing the budget, meant that any increase in defense spending was not welcome.

49. Free traders added that if war never came, Britain would not undermine its economy with unnecessary military spending.

50. The navy had two ongoing debates with the Treasury. The first was over the role of the navy. For the navy, Japan posed a greater threat to Britain's interests than Germany. The First Lord of the Admiralty stressed that the entire empire in the East, from India to New Zealand, was threatened by the possibility of further Japanese expansion. Second, also related to the role of the navy, was the size (and hence funding) of the navy. The navy called for an upward revision of the existing one-power standard (adopted in 1925) to a two-power standard. Not until August 1939 did the cabinet accept a two-power standard of twenty battleships capable of taking on both Japan and a European enemy at the same time.

51. According to the agreement, the Americans would have eighteen capital ships (500,000 tons), the British would have twenty-two (600,000 tons), and the Japanese would have ten (300,000). The Coolidge Conference (Geneva Naval Conference) of 1927 met to discuss the extension of a shipbuilding ratio to vessels under 10,000 tons. Britain argued it needed cruisers to guard imperial communications. The conference ended in failure because the United States and Britain could not solve the issue over the number of cruisers.

52. Hall 1976. With this agreement, Britain unilaterally altered the naval limitation provisions of the Versailles treaty, harming relations with France and Italy. The Admiralty discounted the German naval threat. They recognized that Germany had only a limited shipyard capacity and a shortage of skilled labor, and it lacked a substantial navy (Deist 1994, 378; Scammel 1997, 102). Instead, the German naval threat was primarily seen from the dangers posed by the combination of other naval powers such as Italy and Japan.

53. Greenwood 1994, 27. On becoming prime minister, Chamberlain suspended Britain's rearmament program until it was reviewed in light of the nation's

financial and industrial resources. The review was conducted by Inskip, whose first report called for a policy of "rationing" or restrictions on the aggregate sum for each service in order to force each department to prioritize its individual programs.

54. In fact, Peden (1979, 161–67) argues that the navy had been quite successful in building toward the New Standard, despite Treasury control.

55. Peden (1979, 172) notes that after 1935, even the army was unable to spend its entire allocation because of manufacturing delays.

CHAPTER 5

1. On the debate of when to date the beginning of Spain's decline, see Kamen 1978; Stradling 1979, 179–86.

2. The United Provinces or the Dutch consisted of the seven northern provinces of the Netherlands that rebelled against Spain beginning in the 1570s.

3. Spain's empire was referred to as the Spanish system or the Spanish monarchy.

4. Around 1620, Spain had four field armies (Flanders, Rhineland, central Europe, Italy), each around 20,000, twice as many garrison troops, 50 galleons under construction, and auxiliary naval squadrons. By 1626, Spain had 300,000 men under arms (Stradling 1981, 62).

5. Scammell 1989, 97. The Portuguese under Spain had been the major suppliers of spice to Europe, accounting for 75 percent of Europe's spice imports. They captured the spice trade from Arab traders.

6. In this discussion, Spain includes Portugal and its empire.

7. For a discussion of the Spanish Road, see Parker 1972, 80–105.

8. Overland transport was much cheaper than ocean transport.

9. While England did support the Protestant rebellion in Germany, the deepening constitutional quarrel between Parliament and the Crown contributed to England's growing isolation. Much of the literature that focuses on Spain's grand strategy during this period hardly mentions the Thirty Years' War separately, but discusses these events as part of a larger European war (i.e., the ongoing Eighty Years' War with the United Provinces).

10. The Dutch expansion in the region was assisted by a "cold" truce between the VOC and the English EIC, allowing the Dutch to concentrate their forces against the Spanish. Under this agreement, East Indies trade was to be shared on the ratio of two-thirds for the Dutch and one-third for the English, and a joint fleet organized for protection from the Portuguese (Israel 1989, 106). The Dutch concluded this treaty because its Twelve Years' Truce with Spain was about to end.

11. Spain's spice trade included Malacca (in Malaysia), the Moluccas (islands of Indonesia), Bandas (islands of Indonesia), as well as Macoa (China coast), Goa (India), and Ceylon. In 1605, the Dutch made their first significant breakthrough in the East Indies by capturing Ambonia and the Moluccas from the Portuguese.

Eventually, the Dutch would conquer the bulk of Portugal's empire in the Indies.

12. Parker 1979b, 189–90; Newitt 1986, 19–22. According to Israel (1989, 176), the Ambonia massacre of English troops by the Dutch marked the end of British activity in the East Indies. The effect of the war on the EIC was devastating. It required troops, armed ships, and fortresses, which greatly reduced the profitability of the Company. The EIC would become the power par excellence in the East, replacing the Dutch.

13. To the benefit of the English and French, as long as they remained neutral.

14. According to Williams (1966, 31), in England, trading companies were created as a result of mercantile pressure on the government. In France, trading companies were established as the result of government initiative. The Dutch trading companies were the product of a partnership between the government and merchant classes.

15. The truce talks between Spain and the Dutch nearly broke down over the question of Dutch commercial access to Spain's empire in the East and West Indies. This dispute was resolved by making no mention of the issue of overseas trade in the final truce (Parker 1979b, 54).

16. Furber 1976, 34–38. The Dutch unwillingness to disband the East India Company prevented a full peace in 1607–9.

17. Furber 1976, 45. In both the Bandas and Ambonia, the chiefs that did not make oaths to the Dutch were executed. Sea power allowed the Dutch to restrict the growth and harvesting of cloves to Dutch Ambonia, with trees elsewhere destroyed by the VOC (Furber 1976, 44–48; Scammell 1989, 102).

18. Boxer 1965, 48–50. The formation of the WIC was suggested much earlier but was delayed by the conclusion of the Twelve Years' Truce.

19. Williams (1966, 15) calls it "a plundering rather than an orthodox trading venture."

20. In 1664, the newly created Company of the West Indies was modeled on the pattern of the Dutch trading companies. The plan was to increase French wealth at the expense of the Dutch empire.

21. Ambrogio Spínola, the commander of the army of Flanders, was a key advocate for the renewal of the Dutch truce and a negotiated end to the war (Lynch 1969, 76–77; Stradling 1986, 75).

22. Lynch 1992, 121–130. Up until the 1630s, scholars differ on the influence of the Cortes over the Crown. Stradling (1988, 134–50) views the Cortes as a peripheral institution of little political importance, as opposed to Elliott (1963, 328, 336), Jago (1981, 308–11), and to a greater degree, Thompson (1982). There is consensus that by the mid-1630s, the Cortes had been subjugated by the Crown.

23. Representation in the Cortes had its benefits since such towns were able to favor themselves at the expense of the unrepresented towns.

24. Brightwell 1974, 273; Israel 1982, 12. For Spain, there were three points the Dutch had to agree to for a lasting peace: recognition of Habsburg sovereignty,

freedom of worship for Dutch Catholics, and commercial access to Antwerp through the Scheldt estuary.

25. The importance of preserving Spain's reputation as motivation for Madrid's aggressive foreign policy is discussed by numerous authors. For instance, see Parker 1979b, 23; Stradling 1988, 78; Elliott 1989, 117–34; Parker 1994, 121–22, 126–27.

26. From the Dutch perspective, expansion in Asia at the expense of Portugal and Spain was seen as a way to divert Spanish energies and resources away from the United Provinces.

27. The Eighty Years' War marks the decline of Antwerp as a financial center (part of the Spanish Netherlands), which was undermined by the Dutch blockade of the Scheldt during the war, while the growth of Amsterdam strengthened the United Provinces.

28. Declining returns from the Indies hit a low of 1 million ducats in 1627. According to Rasler and Thompson (1989, 93), bankruptcy was declared because the Crown had no unpledged income or no one was willing to lend additional funds. Elliott (1989, 125) claims that this bankruptcy was more of a ruse to reduce the Crown's dependence on the Genoese bankers and to lower the high rates of interests on the *asientos* (loans) by encouraging competition from Portuguese businessmen. The Crown's dependence meant that it was more difficult to reach a peace settlement with the Dutch on the issue of Brazil. The Portuguese bankers were unwilling to abandon their Brazilian empire to the Dutch.

29. Israel 1990, 37. Between 1635–37, Spain spent 15 million ducats in Flanders.

30. By 1625, Spain captured Breda in the north, virtually surrounding the United Provinces. With the intention of inflicting damage on Dutch trade in the Mediterranean, a Gibraltar *armada* was established, and Gibraltar's harbor was improved and fortified. Additional funds were allocated to the main Spanish fleet.

31. With the closure of the Spanish Road in 1638, Madrid had no choice but to reinforce the Army of Flanders by sea.

32. As the French conquest of Flanders continued, Spain and the United Provinces began to negotiate a separate peace.

33. This linked Spanish and Austrian Habsburgs, and Spain's empire in Italy and the Low Countries.

34. Located in Cartegena, Veracruz, Callao, and Acapulco (Israel 1990, 279).

35. Israel 1982, 280; 1990, 267–70. This task force was the *Armada de Barlovento*, consisting of eight galleons (Lynch 1992, 257). The *armada* was manned and supplied by the Americas.

36. Lynch 1992, 118. Much of the copper used in the process had to be purchased from Sweden through the Dutch.

37. Meanwhile, during the decade of 1610–20, the remittances from the Americas began to decline. Instead of the 2 million of the early 1600s, the amount

fell as low as 800,000 in 1620, recovering in the 1620s, but between 1621 and 1640, 1.5 represented an exceptional year and not more than 1 million could be expected (Elliott 1989, 237). In 1640, no treasure arrived from the Indies and in 1641, the *Tierre Firme* fleet brought the Crown only half a million ducats, followed by an equally small return from the New Spanish fleet. In both cases, the Crown compensated half of the merchants' returns, using *vellón*.

38. By a new tax on paper, salt, and ship anchorage.

39. To be raised from new taxes on sugar, paper, chocolate, fish, and tobacco, and by doubling the regular *millones* subsidy.

40. In the continued search for additional resources, Olivares called for the creation of a national banking system (1623) to be under royal jurisdiction. This would allow Spain to mobilize credit for the defense of the empire at relatively low rates. A chain of banks would assist the Crown in reducing its debts, lowering its dependence on foreign loans (Elliott 1963, 328). The banks were mistrusted, and the idea was abandoned in 1626. Attempts were also made to generate additional wealth by promoting the economic revival of Castile through the creation of trading companies and new industry, and encouraging trade by improving the infrastructure such as roads and the navigation of rivers.

41. The Union of Arms was designed to replace the *millones*.

42. Lynch 1992, 141–42. After incorporation into Spain in 1580, Portugal maintained its administrative and fiscal independence.

43. Also, see Elliott (1989, 233–34) on Spain's increasingly technologically backward shipbuilders.

44. Spain's loss of Portugal's empire in the Americas, and especially in Brazil to the Dutch, put additional pressure on Spain's relationship with the Portuguese, contributing to the revolt in 1640 (Elliott 1989, 129).

CHAPTER 6

1. "Excerpts from Pentagon's Plan: 'Prevent the Re-Emergence of a New Rival,'" *New York Times*, March 8, 1992: A14.

2. Realists such as Gilpin (1981) and Kennedy (1987) readily acknowledge the importance of economy. This highlights the problem of treating realism as a single theory. See Brooks (1997) on the trade-off between economy and security.

3. The region had been under siege by France since 1637.

4. The revolt in Portugal opened new opportunities for a truce with the Dutch since the conflict in the Americas was no longer an issue.

5. Olivares pushed for victory in the Netherlands and an acceptable truce with the Dutch, rather than concentrating on the French front.

6. In the United Provinces, the supporters of war with Spain in Flanders were also losing ground. After 1645, Holland (especially Amsterdam, the Republic's richest city) refused to provide funds for the war, bringing the army to a complete halt.

7. The financing of the Spanish Army of Flanders was undertaken by Amsterdam (Parker 1979a, 279).

8. According to Hall (1976, 487), London was merely hoping to limit the extent of the illegal rearmament of Germany based on the Versailles treaty.

9. According to Peden (1979, 117), by the spring of 1939 a change was taking place in Britain naval policy toward the Far East, although no decision had been made yet to totally abandon the region. In May it was recorded that only four capital ships would be available for the Far East if Britain were at war with Germany and Italy.

10. Francis 1939, 327–28; Cozier 1976; Schroeder 1976b; Craig 1978, 556; Deist 1994, 375. In 1937, Lord Halifax's trip was to induce a *modus vivendi* in exchange for England's willingness to accept changes in central Europe. According to Schwoerer (1970, 366–67), the trip prepared the way for the *Anschluss* and Hitler's demand for self-determination of the Sudeten Germans.

11. Pratt 1971; Lowe 1981, 164–65; French 1993, 184. In April, 1938, at Britain's request, the United States moved its fleet to the Pacific (Lee 1971, 171).

12. In devolving leadership to the United States, Britain no longer needed to send the main fleet to Singapore in the event of a Far Eastern war. Britain concentrated these freed-up resources in the Mediterranean (Alexandria) and its home waters. With the active support of the United States, instead of sending eight capital ships to the Far East, Britain reinforced the China Fleet by only two capital ships (Gibbs 1976, 427).

13. Both Friedberg (1988) and Kupchan (1994) agree Britain marshaled its resources from the periphery to the core prior to World War I. While Kupchan codes Britain's response as an instance of successful adjustment, Friedberg codes it as a case of failure.

14. For instance, on the debate at the end of the Cold War over how to rank America's foreign commitments, compare the contradictory arguments on whether "the Third World or Europe matters" by Johnson (1985–86); David (1989); Walt (1989); Van Evera (1990); and Hudson, Ford, Pack, and Giordano (1991).

15. As early as the 1890s, with the closing of the American frontier, statesmen debated whether America's foreign policy orientation should be toward the Far East or Europe (LaFeber 1963, 407–17). The debate between the Asia Firsters and the Europe Firsters continued during the interwar period and even during the early stages of the Cold War.

16. Huntington 1993; Mastanduno 1997. In contrast, on the issue of primacy, see Jervis 1993.

17. Alternatively, Friedberg (1989a) contends that the United States can maintain a high level of military spending without reducing investment if it can lower its rate of consumption (private and public, especially entitlement programs) and divert these freed-up resources to investment.

18. On Japan, see Gilpin 1989; Rapkin 1990; Bergner 1991; Friedman and Lebard 1991; Taira 1991; Nye 1992–93.

APPENDIX

1. This discussion is based on Heath 1927; Beer 1956; Bridges 1964; Burton 1966; Roseveare 1969; Peden 1979; and French 1982a.

2. Heath 1927. Since there was no overarching Department of Defense (Ministry of Defense), each service minister prepared an annual Estimate of their expenditure (interservice coordination was handled by the Committee of Imperial Defence).

Bibliography

DOCUMENTS

Public Records Office (Kew, England)
Admiralty 1/7550A, 12/31/00.
Admiralty 116/866B15 1/06.
Cabinet 37/39/38, 7/24/95.
Cabinet 37/70/61, 4/30/04.
Foreign Office 46/547, "Memorandum by Francis Bertie," 9/22/01.
Foreign Office 55/392, 1/3/1899.
Treasury 168/61, "The Financial Outlook vis à vis the City," 10/9/03.

Abadi, Jacob. 1982. *Britain's Withdrawal from the Middle East, 1947–1971: The Economic and Strategic Imperatives*. Princeton: Kingston Press.

Akita, Shigeru. 1996. "'Gentlemanly Capitalism,' Inter-Asian Trade and Japanese Industrialisation at the Turn of the Last Century." *Japan Forum* 8:51–65.

Allen, Harry C. 1954. *Great Britain and the United States: A History of Anglo-American Relations (1783–1952)*. London: Odhams Press.

Alt, James E., Randall L. Calvert, and Brian D. Humes. 1988. "Reputation and Hegemonic Stability: A Game-Theoretic Analysis." *American Political Science Review* 82:445–66.

Alt, James E., Jeffry Frieden, Michael J. Gilligan, Dani Rodrick, and Ronald Rogowski. 1996. "The Political Economy of International Trade: Enduring Puzzles and an Agenda for Inquiry." *Comparative Political Studies* 29:689–717.

Alt, James E., and Michael Gilligan. 1994. "The Political Economy of Trading States: Factor Specificity, Collective Action Problems and Domestic Political Institutions." *Journal of Political Philosophy* 2:165–92.

Andrew, Christopher. 1968. *Théophile Delcassé and the Making of the Entente Cordiale: A Reappraisal of French Foreign Policy, 1898–1905*. London: Macmillan.

Appleby, J. C. 1987. "An Association for the West Indies? English Plans for a West India Company, 1621–1629." *Journal of Imperial and Commonwealth History* 15:213–41.

Ashley, Percy. 1970. *Modern Tariff History: Germany–United States–France*. New York: Howard Fertig.

Aymard, Maurice, ed. 1982. *Dutch Capitalism and World Capitalism*. Cambridge: Cambridge University Press.

Ayoob, Mohammad. 1998. "Subaltern Realism: International Relations Theory Meets the Third World." In *International Relations Theory and the Third World*, ed. Stephanie G. Neuman. New York: St. Martin's Press.

Bailer, Seweryn. 1976. *The Soviet Paradox: External Expansion, Internal Decline*. New York: Knopf.

Barnett, Correlli. 1972. *The Collapse of British Power*. London: Eyre Methuen.

Barnett, Correlli. 1976. "Strategy and Society." *Royal United Services Institute for Defense Studies* 121:11–19.

Barnett, Michael N. 1992. *Confronting the Costs of War: Military Powers, State, and Society in Egypt and Israel*. Princeton: Princeton University Press.

Barnett, Michael N., and Jack S. Levy. 1991. "Domestic Sources of Alliances and Alignment: The Case of Egypt, 1962–73." *International Organization* 45:369–95.

Barnhart, Michael A. 1981. "Japan's Economic Security and the Origins of the Pacific War." *Journal of Strategic Studies* 4:105–23.

Bean, Richard. 1973. "War and the Birth of the Nation State." *Journal of Economic History* 33:203–21.

Beasley, William G. 1981. *The Modern History of Japan*. 3d ed. London: Weidenfeld and Nicolson.

Beasley, William G. 1987. *Japanese Imperialism, 1894–1945*. New York: Oxford University Press.

Becker, William H. 1984. "1899–1920: American Adjusts to World Power." In *Economics and World Power: An Assessment of American Diplomacy Since 1789*, ed. William H. Becker and Samuel F. Wells Jr. New York: Columbia University Press.

Beer, Samuel H. 1956. *Treasury Control: The Co-ordination of Financial and Economic Policy in Great Britain*. Oxford: Clarendon Press.

Beloff, Max. 1970. *Imperial Sunset: Britain's Liberal Empire, 1897–1921*. Vol. 1. New York: Knopf.

Beloff, Max. 1989. *Dream of Commonwealth, 1921–42: Imperial Sunset*. London: Macmillan.

Bennett, Gill. 1992. "British Policy in the Far East, 1933–1936: Treasury and Foreign Office." *Modern Asian Studies* 26:545–68.

Berger, Suzanne, and Ronald Dore, eds. 1996. *National Diversity and Global Capitalism*. Ithaca: Cornell University Press.

Bergner, Jeffrey. 1991. *The New Superpowers: Germany, Japan, the United States and the New World Order*. New York: St. Martin's Press.

Bernardi, Aurelio. 1970. "The Economic Problems of the Roman Empire." In *The Economic Decline of Empires*, ed. Carlo M. Cipolla. London: Methuen.

Best, Michael, and Jane Humphries. 1986. "The City and Industrial Decline." In *The Decline of the British Economy*, ed. Bernard Elbaum and William Lazonick. Oxford: Clarendon Press.

Bialer, Uri. 1980. *The Shadow of the Bomber: The Fear of Air Attack and British Politics, 1932–1939*. London: Royal Historical Society.

Binder, Leonard. 1958. "The Middle East as a Subordinate International System." *World Politics* 10:408–29.

Blainey, Geoffrey. 1988. *The Causes of War*. 3d ed. New York: The Free Press.

Bond, Brian. 1980. *British Military Policy between the Two World Wars*. New York: Oxford University Press.

Borrus, Michael, Steve Weber, and John Zysman, with Joseph Willihnganz. 1992. "Mercantilism and Global Security." *National Interest* 29:21–30.

Boulding, Kenneth E. 1963. *Conflict and Defense: A General Theory*. New York: Harper.

Bourette-Knowles, Simon. 1995. "The Global Micawber: Sir Robert Vansittart, the Treasury and the Global Balance of Power, 1933–35." *Diplomacy and Statecraft* 6:91–121.

Bourne, Kenneth. 1967. *Britain and the Balance of Power in North America, 1815–1908*. London: Longmans.

Boxer, Charles R. 1965. *The Dutch Seaborne Empire, 1600–1800*. New York: Knopf.

Boyce, George D., ed. 1990. *The Crisis of British Power: The Imperial and Naval Papers of the Second Earl of Selborne, 1895–1910*. London: Historians' Press.

Boyce, Robert W. D. 1974. "America, Europe, and the Triumph of Imperial Protectionism in Britain, 1929–1930." *Millennium: Journal of International Studies* 3:53–70.

Boyce, Robert W. D. 1987. *British Capitalism at the Crossroads, 1919–1932: A Study in Politics, Economics, and International Relations*. Cambridge: Cambridge University Press.

Brawley, Mark R. 1993. *Liberal Leadership: Great Powers and Their Challengers in Peace and War*. Ithaca: Cornell University Press.

Brawley, Mark R. 1999. *Afterglow or Adjustment? Domestic Institutions and Responses to Overstretch*. New York: Columbia University Press.

Brecher, Michael. 1963. "International Relations and Asian Studies: The Subordinate State System of Southern Asia." *World Politics* 15:213–35.

Bridges, Lord. 1964. *The Treasury*. New York: Oxford University Press.

Bridges, Sir Edward. 1950. *Treasury Control*. London: Athlone Press.

Bright, Charles. 1985. "Class Interest and State Policy in the British Response to Hitler." In *German Nationalism and the European Response, 1890–1945*, ed. Carole Fink, Isabel V. Hull, and MacGregor Knox. Norman: University of Oklahoma Press.

Brightwell, Peter. 1974. "The Spanish System and the Twelve Years' Truce." *English Historical Review* 89:270–92.

Brightwell, Peter. 1979. "The Spanish Origins of the Thirty Years' War." *European Studies Review* 9:409–31.

Brooks, Collin. 1931. *This Tariff Question*. London: Edward Arnold.

Brooks, Stephen G. 1997. "Dueling Realisms (Realism in International Relations)." *International Organization* 51: 445–77.

Brown, Carl L. 1984. *International Politics and the Middle East: Old Rules, Dangerous Game*. Princeton: Princeton University Press.

Bueno de Mesquita, Bruce, and David Lalman. 1992. *War and Reason: Domestic and International Imperatives*. New Haven: Yale University Press.

Burton, Ann M. 1966. "Treasury Control and the Colonial Policy in the Late Nineteenth Century." *Public Administration* 44:169–92.

Cain, Peter J., and Anthony G. Hopkins. 1993a. *British Imperialism: Crisis and Deconstruction, 1914–1990*. London: Longman.

Cain, Peter J., and Anthony G. Hopkins. 1993b. *British Imperialism: Innovation and Expansion, 1688–1914*. New York: Longman.

Calleo, David P. 1978. *The German Problem Reconsidered: Germany and the World Order, 1870 to the Present*. New York: Cambridge University Press.

Calleo, David P. 1984. "Since 1961: American Power in a New World Economy." In *Economics and World Power: An Assessment of American Diplomacy since 1789*, ed. William H. Becker and Samuel F. Wells Jr. New York: Columbia University Press.

Calleo, David P. 1987. *Beyond American Hegemony: The Future of the Western Alliance*. New York: Basic Books.

Campbell, A. E. 1960. *Great Britain and the United States, 1895–1903*. London: Longmans.

Campbell, Ballard C. 1995. *The Growth of American Government*. Bloomington: Indiana University Press.

Campbell, Charles S. 1957. *Anglo-American Understanding, 1898–1903*. Baltimore: Johns Hopkins University Press.

Campbell, Charles S. 1974. *From Revolution to Rapprochement: United States and Great Britain*. New York: John Wiley and Sons.

Campbell, John C. 1960. *Defense of the Middle East: Problems of American Policy*. New York: Praeger.

Cantori, Louis, and Steven Spiegel. 1969. "International Regions: A Comparative Approach to Five Subordinate Systems." *International Studies Quarterly* 13:361–80.

Capie, Forrest. 1983. *Depression and Protectionism: Britain between the Wars*. Boston: George Allen and Unwin.

Carr, Edward Hallet. 1964. *The Twenty Years' Crisis, 1919–1939*. 2d ed. New York: Harper and Row.

Carr, William A. 1969. *A History of Germany, 1815–1990*. London: Edward Arnold.

Carroll, Berenice A. 1968. *Design for Total War: Arms and Economics in the Third Reich*. The Hague: Mouton.

Cassels, Alan. 1983. "Was There a Fascist Foreign Policy? Tradition and Novelty." *International History Review* 2:255–68.

Chan, Steve. 1985. "The Impact of Defense Spending on Economic Performance: A Survey of Evidence and Problems." *Orbis* 29:403–34.

Chase-Dunn, Christopher. 1982. "International Economic Policy in a Declining Core State." In *America in a Changing World Political Economy*, ed. William R. Avery and David P. Rapkin. New York: Longman.

Chaudhuri, K. N. 1965. *The English East India Company: The Study of an Early Joint-Stock Company, 1600–1640*. London: Frank Cass.

Checkland, Sidney. 1983. *British Public Policy, 1776–1939: An Economic, Social and Political Perspective*. New York: Cambridge University Press.

Checkland, Sidney. 1989. "British Public Policy, 1776–1939." In *The Cambridge Economic History of Europe, The Industrial Economies: The Development of Economic and Social Policies*, ed. Peter Mathias and Sidney Pollard. Cambridge: Cambridge University Press.

Cipolla, Carlo M. 1970. *The Economic Decline of Empires*. London: Methuen.

Clough, Shepard B. 1939. *France: A History of National Economies, 1789–1939*. New York: Scribner.

Clymer, Kenton J. 1975. *John Hay: The Gentleman as Diplomat*. Ann Arbor: University of Michigan Press.

Coghlan, Francis. 1972. "Armaments, Economic Policy and Appeasement: Background to British Foreign Policy, 1931–7." *History* 57:205–16.

Cohen, Eliot A. 1994. "The Strategy of Innocence? The United States, 1920–1945." In *The Making of Strategy: Rulers, States, and War*, ed. Williamson Murray, MacGregor Knox, and Alvin Bernstein. Cambridge: Cambridge University Press.

Collins, Michael. 1991. *Banks and Industrial Finance in Britain, 1800–1939*. Cambridge: Cambridge University Press.

Conybeare, John A. C. 1987. *Trade Wars: The Theory and Practice of International Commercial Rivalry*. New York: Columbia University Press.

Copeland, Dale C. 2000. *The Origins of Major War*. Ithaca: Cornell University Press.

Cortrell, Andrew P., and Susan Peterson. 1999. "Altered States: Explaining Domestic Institutional Change." *British Journal of Political Science* 29:177–203.

Cotton, Timothy Y. C. 1986. "War and American Democracy." *Journal of Conflict Resolution* 30:616–35.

Cowling, Maurice. 1975. *The Impact of Hitler: British Politics and British Policy, 1933–1940*. Cambridge: Cambridge University Press.

Cozier, Andrew. 1976. "Prelude to Munich: British Foreign Policy and Germany, 1935–8." *European Studies Review* 6:357–81.

Craig, Gordon A. 1978. *Germany, 1866–1945*. Oxford: Oxford University Press.

Craig, Gordon A., and Felix Gilbert, eds. 1953. *The Diplomats*. Princeton: Princeton University Press.

Crisp, Olga. 1961. "The Russian Liberals and the 1906 Anglo-French Loan to Russia." *Slavonic Review* 39:497–511.

Crone, Donald. 1993. "Does Hegemony Matter? The Reorganization of the Pacific Political Economy." *World Politics* 45:501–25.

Crowley, James. 1966. *Japan's Quest for Autonomy: National Security and Foreign Policy, 1930–1938*. Princeton: Princeton University Press.

Crowley, James. 1974. "Japan's Military Foreign Policies." In *Japan's Foreign Policy, 1868–1941: A Research Guide*, ed. James W. Morley. New York: Columbia University Press.

Darby, Phillip. 1987. *Three Faces of Imperialism: British and American Approaches to Asia and Africa, 1870–1970*. New Haven: Yale University Press.

Daunton, M. J. 1989. "'Gentlemanly Capitalism' and British Industry, 1820–1914." *Past and Present* 122:119–58.

David, Steven R. 1989. "Why the Third World Matters." *International Security* 14:50–84.

David, Steven R. 1991. "Explaining Third World Alignments." *World Politics* 43:50–85.

Davis, Lance E., and Robert A. Huttenback. 1986. *Mammon and the Pursuit of Empire: The Economics of British Imperialism*. New York: Cambridge University Press.

Deist, Wilhelm. 1994. "The Road to Ideological War: Germany, 1918–1945." In *The Making of Strategy: Rulers, States, and War*, ed. Williamson Murray, MacGregor Knox, and Alvin Bernstein. Cambridge: Cambridge University Press.

Deudney, Daniel, and G. John Ikenberry. 1991–92. "The International Sources of Soviet Change." *International Security* 16:74–118.

Devereux, David. 1990. *The Formulation of British Defense Policy towards the Middle East, 1948–56*. New York: St. Martin's Press.

Diaz-Alejandro, Carlos F. 1981. "Open Economy, Closed Polity?" *Millennium: Journal of International Studies* 10:203–19.

Dintenfass, Michael. 1991. "The Politics of Producers' Co-operation: The FBI-TUC-NCEO Talks, 1929–1933." In *Contemporary British History, 1931–61: Politics and the Limits of Policy*, ed. Anthony Gorst, Lewis Johnman, and W. Scott Lucas. New York: Pinter.

Dintenfass, Michael. 1992. *The Decline of Industrial Britain, 1870–1980*. New York: Routledge.

D'Lugo, David, and Ronald Rogowski. 1993. "The Anglo-American Naval Race and Comparative Constitutional 'Fitness.'" In *The Domestic Basis of Grand Strategy*, ed. Richard Rosecrance and Arthur A. Stein. Ithaca: Cornell University Press.

Doran, Charles F. 1989. "Globalist-Regionalist Debate." In *Intervention in the 1980s: US Foreign Policy in the Third World*, ed. Peter J. Schraeder. Boulder: Lynne Rienner.

Doran, Charles F., and Wes Parsons. 1980. "War and the Cycle of Relative Power." *American Political Science Review* 74:947–65.

Doyle, Michael W. 1983. "Kant, Liberal Legacies, and Foreign Affairs, Part I." *Philosophy and Public Affairs* 12:205–35.

Doyle, Michael W. 1986a. *Empires*. Ithaca: Cornell University Press.

Doyle, Michael W. 1986b. "Liberalism and World Politics." *American Political Science Review* 80:1151–69.

Drummond, Ian M. 1981. *The Floating Pound and the Sterling Area, 1931–39*. New York: Cambridge University Press.

Dunbabin, John P. B. 1975. "British Rearmament in the 1930s: A Chronology and Review." *Historical Journal* 18:587–609.

Dunbabin, John P. B. 1983. "The British Military Establishment and the Policy of

Appeasement." In *The Fascist Challenge and the Policy of Appeasement*, ed. Wolfgang J. Mommsen and Lothar Kettenacker. London: George Allen and Unwin.

Dunlop, John K. 1938. *The Development of the British Army, 1899–1914*. London: Methuen.

Duus, Peter. 1976. *The Rise of Modern Japan*. Boston: Houghton Mifflin.

Eisenstadt, Stuart E. 1963. *The Political Systems of Empires: The Rise and Fall of the Historical Bureaucratic Empires*. New York: Free Press.

Elliott, John H. 1961. "The Decline of Spain." *Past and Present* 20:52–75.

Elliott, John H. 1963. *Imperial Spain, 1469–1716*. London: Penguin.

Elliott, John H. 1984. *Richelieu and Olivares*. Cambridge: Cambridge University Press.

Elliott, John H. 1989. *Spain and Its World, 1500–1700: Selected Essays*. New Haven: Yale University Press.

Elliott, John H. 1991. "Managing Decline: Olivares and the Grand Strategy of Imperial Spain." In *Grand Strategies in War and Peace*, ed. Paul M. Kennedy. New Haven: Yale University Press.

Emy, Hugh V. 1972. "The Impact of Financial Policy on English Party Politics before 1914." *Historical Journal* 15:103–31.

Emy, Hugh V. 1973. *Liberals, Radicals and Social Politics: 1892–1914*. Cambridge: Cambridge University Press.

Endicott, Stephen F. 1973–74. "British Financial Diplomacy in China: The Leith-Ross Mission, 1935–1937." *Pacific Affairs* 46:481–501.

Evangelista, Mathew. 1993. "Internal and External Constraints on Grand Strategy: The Soviet Case." In *The Domestic Bases of Grand Strategy*, ed. Richard Rosecrance and Arthur A. Stein. Ithaca: Cornell University Press.

Evans, Peter B. 1992. "The State as Problem and Solution: Predation, Embedded Autonomy, and Structural Changes." In *The Politics of Economic Adjustment: International Constraints, Distributive Conflicts, and the State*, ed. Stephan Haggard and Robert R. Kaufman. Princeton: Princeton University Press.

Evans, Peter D., Harold K. Jacobson, and Robert D. Putnam. 1993. *Double-Edged Diplomacy: International Bargaining and Domestic Politics*. Berkeley and Los Angeles: University of California Press.

Feinstein, Charles. 1996. "Exports and British Economic Growth, 1850–1914." In *The Nature of Industrialization: International Trade and Business Economic Growth from the Eighteenth Century to the Present Day*, ed. Peter Mathias and John A. Davis. Cambridge: Blackwell.

Ferguson, Niall. 1994. "Public Finance and National Security: The Domestic Origins of the First World War Revisited." *Past and Present* 142:141–68.

Ferguson, Niall. 1998. *The Pity of War*. New York: Basic Books.

Ferrill, Arther. 1986. *The Fall of the Roman Empire: The Military Explanation*. London: Thames and Hudson.

Fieldhouse, D. K. 1966. *The Colonial Empires: A Comparative Survey from the Eighteenth Century*. New York: Delacorte Press.

Fischer, Fritz. 1974. *World Power or Decline: The Controversy over Germany's Aims in the*

First World War. Trans. Lancelot L. Farrar, Robert Kimber, and Rita Kimber. New York: W. W. Norton.

Fischer, Fritz. 1975. *War of Illusions: German Policies from 1911 to 1914*. Trans. Marian Jackson. New York: W. W. Norton.

Foerster, Friedrich W. 1931. "Germany and Austria: A European Crisis." *Foreign Affairs* 9:617–23.

Forbes, Neil. 1987. "London Banks, the German Standstill Agreements, and 'Economic Appeasement' in the 1930s." *Economic History Review* 40:571–87.

Fox, Edward W. 1991. *The Emergence of the Modern European World: From the Seventeenth to the Twentieth Century*. Oxford: Blackwell.

Francis, Eric V. 1939. *Britain's Economic Strategy*. London: Jonathan Cape.

Freeman, Richard B. 1995. "Are Your Wages Set in Beijing?" *Journal of Economic Perspectives* 9:15–32.

French, David. 1982a. *British Economic and Strategic Planning, 1905–1915*. London: George Allen and Unwin

French, David. 1982b. "The Edwardian Crisis and the Origins of the First World War." *International History Review* 4:207–21.

French, David. 1982c. "The Rise and Fall of 'Business as Usual.'" In *War and the State*, ed. Kathleen Burk. London: George Allen and Unwin.

French, David. 1986. *British Strategy and War Aims, 1914–1916*. Boston: Allen and Unwin.

French, David. 1993. "'Perfidious Albion' Faces the Powers." *Canadian Journal of History* 28:177–87.

Friedberg, Aaron L. 1988. *The Weary Titan: Britain and the Experience of Relative Decline, 1895–1905*. Princeton: Princeton University Press.

Friedberg, Aaron L. 1989a. "The Political Economy of American Strategy." *World Politics* 41:381–406.

Friedberg, Aaron L. 1989b. "The Strategic Implications of Relative Economic Decline." *Political Studies Quarterly* 104:401–31.

Friedberg, Aaron L. 1991. "The Changing Relationship between Economics and National Security." *Political Science Quarterly* 106:265–76.

Friedberg, Aaron L. 2000. *In the Shadow of the Garrison State: America's Anti-Statism and its Cold War Grand Strategy*. Princeton: Princeton University Press.

Frieden, Jeffry A. 1988. "Sectoral Conflict and U.S. Foreign Economic Policy, 1914–1940." *International Organization* 42:59–90.

Frieden, Jeffry A. 1991. *Debt, Development, and Democracy: Modern Political Economy and Latin America, 1865–1985*. Princeton: Princeton University Press.

Frieden, Jeffry A., and Ronald Rogowski. 1996. "The Impact of the International Economy on National Policies: An Analytical Overview." In *Internationalization and Domestic Politics*, ed. Robert O. Keohane and Helen V. Milner. New York: Cambridge University Press.

Friedman, George, and Meredith Lebard. 1991. *The Coming War with Japan*. New York: St. Martin's Press.

Fudenberg, Drew, and David M. Kreps. 1987. "Reputation in the Simultaneous Play of Multiple Opponents." *Review of Economic Studies* 54:541–69.

Fudenberg, Drew, and Jean Tirole. 1991. *Game Theory*. Cambridge: MIT Press.

Furber, Holden. 1976. *Rival Empires of Trade in the Orient, 1600–1800*. Minneapolis: University of Minnesota Press.

Gaddis, John Lewis. 1982. *Strategies of Containment: A Critical Appraisal of Postwar American National Security Policy*. New York: Oxford University Press.

Gaddis, John Lewis. 1992. *The United States and the End of the Cold War: Implications, Reconsiderations, Provocations*. New York: Oxford University Press.

Galbraith, John S. 1960. "'The Turbulent Frontier' as a Factor in British Expansion." *Comparative Studies in Society and History* 2:150–68.

Gardner, Richard N. 1969. *Sterling-Dollar Diplomacy*. New York: McGraw-Hill.

Gasiorowski, Mark. 1991. *U.S. Foreign Policy and the Shah: Building a Client State in Iran*. Ithaca: Cornell University Press.

Gasiorowski, Mark, and Solomon W. Polachek. 1982. "Conflict and Interdependence: East-West Trade and Linkages in the Era of Détente." *Journal of Conflict Resolution* 26:709–29.

Geddes, Barbara. 1994. "How Politicians Decide Who Bears the Cost of Economic Liberalization: The Latin American, South European, and African Experiences." In *Transition to a Market Economy at the End of the Twentieth Century*, ed. Ivan T. Berend. Munich: Südosteuropa-Gesellschaft.

Geiss, Imanuel. 1976. *German Foreign Policy, 1871–1914*. Boston: Routledge and Kegan Paul.

Gelber, Lionel M. 1938. *The Rise of Anglo-American Friendship: A Study in World Politics, 1898–1906*. London: Oxford University Press.

George, Alexander. 1979. "Case Studies and Theory Development: The Method of Structured, Focused Comparison." In *Diplomacy: New Approaches in History, Theory, and Policy*, ed. Paul Gordon Lauren. New York: Free Press.

Gerschenkron, Alexander. 1962. *Economic Backwardness in Historical Perspective*. Cambridge: Harvard University Press.

Geyer, Dietrich. 1987. *Russian Imperialism: The Interaction of Domestic and Foreign Policy, 1860–1914*. Trans. Bruce Little. New Haven: Yale University Press.

Gibbs, Norman H. 1976. *Grand Strategy*. Vol. 1, *Rearmament Policy*. London: Her Majesty's Stationery Office.

Gilbert, Felix. 1977. "Mitteleuropa—The Final Stage." *Journal of Central European Affairs* 7:58–67.

Gillard, David R. 1967. "Salisbury and the Indian Defence Problem, 1885–1902." In *Studies in International History*, ed. Kenneth Bourne and D. Cameron Watt. London: Longmans, Green.

Gillard, David R. 1977. *The Struggle for Asia, 1828–1914: A Study in British and Russian Imperialism*. London: Methuen.

Gilpin, Robert. 1975. *U.S. Power and the Multinational Corporation: The Political Economy of Foreign Direct Investment*. New York: Basic Books.

Gilpin, Robert. 1981. *War and Change in World Politics*. New York: Cambridge University Press.

Gilpin, Robert. 1987. *The Political Economy of International Relations*. Princeton: Princeton University Press.

Gilpin, Robert. 1989. "Where Does Japan Fit In?" *Millennium: Journal of International Studies* 18:329–42.

Glaser, Charles L. 1992. "Political Consequences of Military Strategy: Expanding and Refining the Spiral and Deterrence Models." *World Politics* 44:497–538.

Glynn, Sean, and Alan Booth. 1996. *Modern Britain: An Economic and Social History*. New York: Routledge.

Goldstein, Joshua S. 1988. *Long Cycles: Prosperity and War in the Modern Age*. New Haven: Yale University Press.

Goldstein, Judith. 1993. *Ideas, Interests, and American Trade Policy*. Ithaca: Cornell University Press.

Gooch, John. 1994. "The Weary Titans: Strategy and Policy in Great Britain, 1890–1918." In *The Making of Strategy: Rules, States, and War*, ed. Williamson Murray, MacGregor Knox, and Alvin Bernstein. New York: Cambridge University Press.

Gordon, Michael R. 1969. *Conflict and Consensus in Labour's Foreign Policy, 1914–1965*. Stanford: Stanford University Press.

Gourevitch, Peter A. 1977. "International Trade, Domestic Coalitions, and Liberty: Comparative Responses to the Crisis of 1873–1896." *Journal of Interdisciplinary History* 8:281–313.

Gourevitch, Peter A. 1978. "The Second Image Reversed: The International Sources of Domestic Politics." *International Organization* 32:881–911.

Gourevitch, Peter A. 1986. *Politics in Hard Times: Comparative Responses to International Economic Crises*. Ithaca: Cornell University Press.

Gowa, Joanne. 1994. *Allies, Adversaries, and International Trade*. Princeton: Princeton University Press.

Graebner, Norman A. 1984. *America as a World Power: A Realist Appraisal from Wilson to Reagan*. Wilmington: Scholarly Resources.

Grampp, William D. 1960. *The Manchester School of Economics*. Stanford: Stanford University Press.

Green, E. H. H. 1995. *The Crisis of Conservatism: The Politics, Economics, and Ideology of the British Conservative Party, 1880–1914*. New York: Routledge.

Greenwood, Sean. 1994. "'Caligula's Horse' Revisited: Sir Thomas Inskip as Minister for the Co-ordination of Defense, 1936–1939." *Journal of Strategic Studies* 17:17–38.

Grenville, J. A. S. 1954. "Lansdowne's Abortive Project of 12 March 1901 for a Secret Agreement with Germany." *Bulletin of the Institute of Historical Research* 17:201–13.

Grenville, J. A. S. 1955. "Great Britain and the Isthmian Canal, 1898–1901." *American Historical Review* 61:48–69.

Grenville, J. A. S. 1964. *Lord Salisbury and Foreign Policy: The Close of the Nineteenth Century*. London: Athlone Press.

Grenville, J. A. S. 1982. "Foreign Policy and the Coming of War." In *Edwardian England*, ed. Donald Read. London: Croom Helm.

Grieco, Joseph M. 1990. *Cooperation among Nations: Europe, America, and Non-Tariff Barriers to Trade*. Ithaca: Cornell University Press.

Haggard, Stephan, and Robert R. Kaufman. 1989. "The Politics of Stabilization and Structural Adjustment." In *Developing Country Debt and Economic Performance: The International Financial System*, ed. Jeffrey Sachs. Chicago: University of Chicago Press.

Haggard, Stephen, and Robert R. Kaufman. 1992. *The Politics of Economic Adjustment: International Constraints, Distributive Conflicts, and the State*. Princeton: Princeton University Press.

Haggie, Paul. 1981. *Britannia at Bay: The Defence of the British Empire against Japan, 1931–1941*. Oxford: Clarendon Press.

Hall, Hines H., III. 1976. "The Foreign Policy-Making Process in Britain, 1934–1935, and the Origins of the Anglo-German Naval Agreement." *Historical Journal* 19:477–99.

Halpern, Paul. 1971. *The Mediterranean Naval Situation, 1908–1914*. Cambridge: Harvard University Press.

Hancock, W. K., and M. M. Gowing. 1953. *British War Economy*. London: Her Majesty's Stationery Office.

Haraszti, Eva H. 1974. *Treaty-Breakers or "Realpolitiker"? The Anglo-German Naval Agreement of June 1935*. Trans. Sándor Simon. Budapest: Harald Boldt.

Hardin, Russell. 1982. *Collective Action*. Baltimore: Johns Hopkins University Press.

Healy, David. 1988. *Drive to Hegemony: The United States in the Caribbean, 1898–1917*. Madison: University of Wisconsin Press.

Healy, Melissa. 1992. "U.S. Troops Authorized to Disarm Somali Bandits." *Los Angeles Times*.

Heath, Sir Thomas H. 1927. *The Treasury*. London: G. P. Putnam's Sons.

Herwig, Holger. 1980. *'Luxury Fleet': The Imperial German Navy, 1888–1918*. Boston: George Allen and Unwin.

Higgs, Henry C. 1914. *The Financial System of the United Kingdom*. London: Macmillan.

Higgs, Robert. 1987. *Crisis and Leviathan: Critical Episodes in the Growth of American Government*. New York: Oxford University Press.

Hildebrand, Klaus. 1970. *The Foreign Policy of the Third Reich*. Trans. Anthony Fothergill. Berkeley and Los Angeles: University of California Press.

Hildebrand, Klaus. 1984. *The Third Reich*. Trans. P. S. Falla. London: George Allen and Unwin.

Hillgruber, Andreas. 1974. "England's Place in Hitler's Plans for World Domination." *Journal of Contemporary History* 9:5–22.

Hillgruber, Andreas. 1981. *Germany and the Two World Wars*. Trans. William C. Kirby. Cambridge: Harvard University Press.

Hinnebusch, Raymond A. 1995. "Syria: The Politics of Peace and Regime Survival." *Middle East Policy* 3:74–87.

Hirschman, Albert O. 1958. *The Strategy of Economic Development*. New Haven: Yale University Press.

Hobsbawm, Eric J. 1987. *The Age of Empire, 1875–1914*. New York: Pantheon Books.

Hobson, John A. 1938. *Imperialism: A Study*. London: G. Allen and Unwin.

Hogan, Michael J. 1987. *The Marshall Plan: America, Britain, and the Reconstruction of Western Europe, 1947–1952*. New York: Cambridge University Press.

Holborn, Hajo. 1969. *A History of Modern Germany, 1840–1945*. Princeton: Princeton University Press.

Holland, R. F. 1981. "The Federation of British Industries and the International Economy, 1929–1939." *Economic History Review* 34:287–300.

Howard, Michael E. 1968. *The Mediterranean Strategy in the Second World War*. London: Weidenfeld and Nicolson.

Howard, Michael E. 1972. *The Continental Commitment: The Dilemma of British Defence Policy in the Era of Two World Wars*. London: Temple Smith.

Howard, Michael E. 1982. "The Edwardian Arms Race." In *Edwardian England*, ed. Donald Read. London: Croom Helm.

Howat, Gerald M. D. 1974. *Stuart and Cromwellian Foreign Policy*. New York: St. Martin's Press.

Hudson, Valerie M., Robert E. Ford, and David Pack, with Eric R. Giordano. 1991. "Why the Third World Matters, Why Europe Probably Won't: The Geoeconomics of Circumscribed Engagement." *Journal of Strategic Studies* 14:255–98.

Hunczak, Taras. 1974. *Russian Imperialism from Ivan the Great to Revolution*. New Brunswick: Rutgers University Press.

Huntington, Samuel P. 1987–88. "Coping with the Lippmann Gap." *Foreign Affairs* 66:453–77.

Huntington, Samuel P. 1988. "The U.S.: Decline or Renewal? " *Foreign Affairs* 67:76–97.

Huntington, Samuel P. 1993. "Why International Primacy Matters." *International Security* 17:68–83.

Hurd, Archibald S., and Henry Castle. 1971. *German Sea-Power: Its Rise, Progress, and Economic Basis*. Westport: Greenwood Press.

Huth, Paul K. 1988. *Extended Deterrence and the Prevention of War*. New Haven: Yale University Press.

Inalcik, Halil. 1978. *The Ottoman Empire: Conquest, Organization and Economy*. London: Variorum Reprints.

Ingham, Geoffrey K. 1984. *Capitalism Divided? The City and Industry in British Social Development*. London: Macmillan.

Iriye, Akira. 1965. *After Imperialism: The Search for a New Order in the Far East, 1921–1931*. Cambridge: Harvard University Press.

Iriye, Akira. 1971. "The Failure of Military Expansion." In *Dilemmas of Growth in Prewar Japan*, ed. James W. Morley. Princeton: Princeton University Press.

Iriye, Akira. 1989. "The United States and Japan in the Postwar World." In *The United States and Japan in the Postwar World*, ed. Akira Iriye and Warren I. Cohen. Lexington: University Press of Kentucky.

Iriye, Akira. 1993. "Japan's Drive to Great-Power Status." In *The Cambridge History of Japan*, ed. Marius B. Jansen. New York: Cambridge University Press.

Israel, Jonathan I. 1982. *The Dutch Republic and the Hispanic World, 1606–1661*. New York: Oxford University Press.

Israel, Jonathan I. 1986. "The Politics of International Trade Rivalry during the Thirty Years War: Gabriel de Roy and Olivares' Mercantilist Projects, 1621–1645." *International History Review* 8:517–688.

Israel, Jonathan I. 1989. *Dutch Primacy in World Trade, 1585–1740*. Oxford: Clarendon Press.

Israel, Jonathan I. 1990. *Empires and Entrepôts: The Dutch, the Spanish Monarchy, and the Jews, 1585–1713*. London: Hambledon Press.

Israel, Jonathan I. 1995. "Olivares, the Cardinal-Infante and Spain's Strategy in the Low Countries (1635–1643): The Road to Rocroi." In *Spain, Europe and the Atlantic World*, ed. Richard L. Kagan and Geoffrey Parker. Cambridge: Cambridge University Press.

Jago, Charles. 1979. "The 'Crisis of the Aristocracy' in Seventeenth Century Castile." *Past and Present* 84:60–90.

Jago, Charles. 1981. "Habsburg Absolutism and the Cortes of Castile." *American Historical Review* 86:307–26.

Jago, Charles. 1995. "Taxation and Political Culture in Castile, 1590–1640." In *Spain, Europe and the Atlantic World: Essays in Honor of John H. Elliott*, ed. Richard L. Kagan and Geoffrey Parker. Cambridge: Cambridge University Press.

James, Scott C., and David A. Lake. 1989. "The Second Face of Hegemony: Britain's Repeal of the Corn Laws and the American Walker Tariff of 1846." *International Organization* 43:1–29.

Jervis, Robert. 1970. *The Logic of Images in International Relations*. Princeton: Princeton University Press.

Jervis, Robert. 1976. *Perception and Misperception in International Politics*. Princeton: Princeton University Press.

Jervis, Robert. 1978. "Cooperation under the Security Dilemma." *World Politics* 30:167–214.

Jervis, Robert. 1991. "Domino Beliefs and Strategic Behavior." In *Dominoes and Bandwagons: Strategic Beliefs and Great Power Competition in the Eurasian Rimland*, ed. Robert Jervis and Jack Snyder. New York: Oxford University Press.

Jervis, Robert. 1993. "International Primacy: Is the Game Worth the Candle?" *International Security* 17:52–67.

Johnson, Robert. 1985–86. "Exaggerating America's Stake in Third World Conflicts." *International Security* 10:32–68.

Kahler, Miles. 1984. *Decolonization in Britain and France: The Domestic Consequences of International Relations*. Princeton: Princeton University Press.

Kaiser, David. 1980. *Economic Diplomacy and the Origins of the Second World War: Germany, Britain, France, and Eastern Europe, 1930–1939*. Princeton: Princeton University Press.

Kaiser, David. 1990. *Politics and War: European Conflict from Philip II to Hitler*. Cambridge: Harvard University Press.

Kallab, Valeriana, and Richard E. Feinberg, eds. 1989. *Fragile Coalitions: The Politics of Economic Adjustment*. New Brunswick: Transaction.

Kamen, Henry. 1978. "The Decline of Spain: A Historical Myth?" *Past and Present* 81:24–50.

Kant, Immanuel. 1972 [1795]. *Perpetual Peace: A Philosophical Essay*. Trans. M. C. Smith. New York: Garland.

Kapstein, Ethan B. 2000. "Winners and Losers in the Global Economy." *International Organization* 54:359–84.

Kasaba, Resat. 1988. *The Ottoman Empire and the World Economy: The Nineteenth Century*. Albany: State University of New York Press.

Katada, Saori. 1994. "U.S.-Japanese Collaboration on Latin America's Debt Management, 1982–91." Paper presented at the Annual Meeting of the American Political Science Association, New York, September 1–4.

Katzenstein, Peter, ed. 1978. *Between Power and Plenty: Foreign Economic Policies of Advanced Industrial Countries*. Madison: University of Wisconsin Press.

Kaufman, Edy. 1976. *The Superpowers and Their Spheres of Influence: The United States and the Soviet Union in Eastern Europe and Latin America*. London: Croom Helm.

Kavanagh, Dennis A. 1973. "Crisis Management and Incremental Adaption in British Politics: The 1931 Crisis of the British Party System." In *Crisis, Choice, and Change: Historical Studies of Political Development*, ed. Gabriel A. Almond, Scott C. Flanagan, and Rober J. Mundt. Boston: Little, Brown.

Kazemzadeh, Firuz. 1968. *Russia and Britain in Persia, 1864–1914: A Study in Imperialism*. New Haven: Yale University Press.

Keal, Paul. 1983. *Unspoken Rules and Superpower Dominance*. New York: St. Martin's Press.

Kehr, Eckart. 1977. *Economic Interests, Militarism and Foreign Policy: Essays on German History*, ed. Gordon A. Craig. Berkeley: University of California Press.

Kennan, George F. 1954. *Realities of American Foreign Policy*. Princeton: Princeton University Press.

Kennedy, Paul M. 1976. *The Rise and Fall of British Naval Mastery*. London: Allen Lane.

Kennedy, Paul M. 1980. *The Rise of the Anglo-German Antagonism, 1860–1914*. Boston: George Allen and Unwin.

Kennedy, Paul M. 1981. *The Realities behind Diplomacy: Background Influences on British External Policy, 1865–1980*. London: Fontana Press.

Kennedy, Paul M. 1983. "Strategy versus Finance in Twentieth-Century Britain." In *Strategy and Diplomacy, 1870–1945*. London: Allen and Unwin.

Kennedy, Paul M. 1984. "Great Britain before 1914." In *Knowing One's Enemies: Intelligence Assessment before the Two World Wars*, ed. Ernest R. May. Princeton: Princeton University Press.

Kennedy, Paul M. 1987. *The Rise and Fall of the Great Powers: Economic Change and Military Conflict from 1500 to 2000*. New York: Random House.

Kennedy, Paul M. 1989. "Debate: The Cost and Benefits of British Imperialism, 1846–1914." *Past and Present* 125:186–92.

Kennedy, Paul M. 1990. "Fin-de-Siècle America." *New York Review of Books*. 37 (June 28): 31–40.

Kennedy, Paul M., ed. 1991. "Grand Strategy in War and Peace: Toward a Broader Definition." In *Grand Strategies in War and Peace*. New Haven: Yale University Press.

Keohane, Robert O. 1982. "Hegemonic Leadership and U.S. Foreign Economic Policy in the 'Long Decade' of the 1950s." In *America in a Changing World Political Economy*, ed. David Rapkin and William Avery. New York: Longman.

Keohane, Robert O. 1984. *After Hegemony: Cooperation and Discord in the World Political Economy*. Princeton: Princeton University Press.

Keohane, Robert. O., and Helen V. Milner, eds. 1996. *Internationalization and Domestic Politics*. New York: Cambridge University Press.

Keohane, Robert O., and Joseph S. Nye. 1977. *Power and Interdependence: World Politics in Transition*. Boston: Little, Brown.

Khaldun, Ibn. 1967. *The Mugaddimah: An Introduction History*. Trans. Franz Rosenthal, ed. N. J. Dawood. Princeton: Princeton University Press.

Kienle, Eberhard, ed. 1994. "Introduction: Liberalization between Cold War and Cold Peace." In *Contemporary Syria: Liberalization between Cold War and Cold Peace*. New York: St. Martin's Press.

Kim, Woosang, and James D. Morrow. 1992. "When Do Power Shifts Lead to War?" *American Journal of Political Science* 36:896–922.

Kimball, Warren F. 1969. *The Most Unsordid Act: Lend-Lease, 1939–1941*. Baltimore: Johns Hopkins University Press.

Kimball, Warren F. 1971. "Lend-Lease and the Open Door: The Temptation of British Opulence, 1937–1942." *Political Science Quarterly* 86:232–59.

Kindleberger, Charles P. 1973. *The World in Depression, 1929–1939*. Berkeley: University of California Press.

Kindleberger, Charles P. 1996. *World Economic Primacy: 1500 to 1990*. New York: Oxford University Press.

King, Gary, Robert O. Keohane, and Sidney Verba. 1994. *Designing Social Inquiry: Scientific Inference in Qualitative Research*. Princeton: Princeton University Press.

Kirshner, Jonathan. 1998. "Political Economy in Security Studies after the Cold War." *Review of International Political Economy* 5:64–91.

Knox, MacGregor. 1982. *Mussolini Unleashed, 1939–1941: Politics and Strategy in Fascist Italy's Last War*. Cambridge: Cambridge University Press.

Knox, MacGregor. 1984. "Conquest, Foreign and Domestic, in Fascist Italy and Nazi Germany." *Journal of Modern History* 56:1–57.

Krasner, Stephen D. 1976. "State Power and the Structure of International Trade." *World Politics* 28:317–47.

Krasner, Stephen D. 1978. *Defending the National Interest: Raw Material Investments and U.S. Foreign Policy*. Princeton: Princeton University Press.

Kreps, David M. 1990. *A Course in Microeconomic Theory*. Princeton: Princeton University Press.

Kubicek, Robert. 1969. *The Administration of Imperialism: Joseph Chamberlain at the Colonial Office*. Durham: Duke University Press.

Kugler, Jacek, and A. F. K. Organski. 1989. "The Power Transition: A Retrospective and Prospective Evaluation." In *The Handbook of War Studies*, ed. Manus I. Midlarsky. Boston: Unwin Hyman.

Kupchan, Charles A. 1989. "Empire, Military Power, and Economic Decline." *International Security* 13: 36–53.

Kupchan, Charles A. 1994. *The Vulnerability of Empire*. Ithaca: Cornell University Press.

Kurth, James R. 1982. "The United States and Central America: Hegemony in Historical and Comparative Perspective." In *Central America: International Dimensions of the Crisis*, ed. Richard Feinberg. New York: Holmes and Meier.

Kynaston, David. 1980. *The Chancellor of the Exchequer*. Lavenham: Terence Dalton.

Kynaston, David. 1995. *The City of London*. Vol. 2, *Golden Years, 1890–1914*. London: Chatto and Windus.

LaFeber, Walter. 1963. *The New Empire: An Interpretation of American Expansion, 1860–1898*. Ithaca: Cornell University Press.

LaFeber, Walter. 1997. *America, Russia, and the Cold War, 1945–1990*. 8th ed. New York: McGraw-Hill.

Lake, David A. 1988. *Power, Protection, and Free Trade: The International Sources of U.S. Commercial Strategy, 1887–1939*. Ithaca: Cornell University Press.

Lake, David A. 1992. "Powerful Pacifists: Democratic States and War." *American Political Science Review* 86:24–37.

Lake, David A., and Patrick M. Morgan, eds. 1997. "The New Regionalism in Security Affairs." In *Regional Orders: Building Security in a New World*. University Park: Pennsylvania State University Press.

Lambelet, John C. 1974. "The Anglo-German Dreadnought Race, 1905–1914." *Papers of the Peace Science Society* 22:1–45.

Lamborn, Alan C. 1983. "Power and the Politics of Extraction." *International Studies Quarterly* 27:125–46.

Lamborn, Alan C. 1991. *The Price of Power: Risk and Foreign Policy in Britain, France and Germany*. Boston: Unwin Hyman.

Lane, Frederic C. 1958. "Economic Consequence of Organized Violence." *Journal of Economic History* 18:401–17.

Langer, William L. 1951. *The Diplomacy of Imperialism, 1890–1902*. New York: Knopf.

Langhorne, R. T. B. 1977. "Great Britain and Germany, 1911–1914." In *British Foreign Policy under Sir Edward Grey*, ed. F. H. Hinsley. New York: Cambridge University Press.

Lawson, Fred H. 1994. "Domestic Pressures and the Peace Process: Fillip or Hindrance?" In *Contemporary Syria: Liberalization between Cold War and Cold Peace*, ed. Eberhard Kienle. New York: St. Martin's Press.

Lawson, Fred H. 1996. *Why Syria Goes to War: Thirty Years of Confrontation*. Ithaca: Cornell University Press.

Lebovics, Herman. 1967. "'Agrarians' versus 'Industrializers': Social Conservative Resistance to Industrialism and Capitalism in Late Nineteenth Century Germany." *International Review of Social History* 12:31–65.

Lebovics, Herman. 1988. *The Alliance of Iron and Wheat in the Third French Republic, 1860–1914: Origins of the New Conservativism*. Baton Rouge: Louisiana State University Press.

Lee, Bradford A. 1973. *Britain and the Sino-Japanese War, 1937–1939: A Study in the Dilemmas of British Decline*. Stanford: Stanford University Press.

Lee, H. I. 1971. "Mediterranean Strategy and Anglo-French Relations, 1908–1912." *Mariner's Mirror* 57:267–85.

Leffler, Melvyn P. 1992. *A Preponderance of Power: National Security, the Truman Administration, and the Cold War*. Stanford: Stanford University Press.

Lenin, V. I. 1939. *Imperialism: The Highest Stage of Capitalism*. New York: International.

Lepgold, Joseph. 1990. *The Declining Hegemon: The United States and European Defense, 1960–1990*. New York: Greenwood Press.

Levi, Margaret. 1988. *Of Rule and Revenue*. Berkeley: University of California Press.

Levy, Jack S. 1983. *War in the Modern Great Power System, 1495–1975*. Kentucky: University of Kentucky Press.

Levy, Jack S. 1985. "Theories of General War." *World Politics* 37:344–74.

Levy, Jack S. 1987. "Declining Power and the Preventive Motivation for War." *World Politics* 40:82–107.

Levy, Jack S. 1989. "The Causes of War: A Review of Theories and Evidence." In *Behavior, Society, and Nuclear War*, ed. Philip E. Tetlock, Jo L. Husbands, Robert Jervis, Paul Stern, and Charles Tilly. Vol. 1. New York: Oxford University Press.

Lippmann, Walter. 1943. *U.S. Foreign Policy: Shield of the Republic*. Boston: Little, Brown.

Lisle-Williams, Michael. 1984. "Merchant Banking Dynasties in the English Class Structure: Ownership, Solidarity and Kinship in the City of London, 1850–1960." *British Journal of Sociology* 35:333–62.

Lloyd, Trevor O. 1970. *Empire to Welfare State: English History, 1906–1967*. London: Oxford University Press.

Lloyd, Trevor O. 1984. *The British Empire, 1558–1983*. Oxford: Oxford University Press.

Lobell, Steven E. 1999. "Second Image Reversed Politics: Britain's Choice of Freer Trade or Imperial Preferences, 1903–1906, 1917–1923, 1930–1932." *International Studies Quarterly* 43:671–94.

Lobell, Steven E. 2000. "The Grand Strategy of Hegemonic Decline: Dilemmas of Strategy and Finance." *Security Studies* 10:92–119.

Lobell, Steven E. 2001. "Britain's Paradox: Cooperation or Punishment prior to World War I." *Review of International Studies* 27:169–86.

Longstreth, Frank. 1979. "The City, Industry, and the State." *State and Economy in Contemporary Capitalism*, ed. Colin Crouch. New York: St. Martin's Press.

Louis, William R. 1971. *British Strategy in the Far East, 1919–1939*. Oxford: Clarendon Press.

Louis, William R. 1983. "The Road to Singapore: British Imperialism in the Far East, 1932–42." In *The Fascist Challenge and the Policy of Appeasement*, ed. Wolfgang J. Mommsen and Lothar Kettenacker. Boston: Geoge Allen and Unwin.

Lowe, Cedric J., and M. L. Dockrill, eds. 1972a. "Anglo-American Relations, 1895–1914." In *The Mirage of Power: British Foreign Policy, 1902–1914*. Vol. 1. Boston: Routledge and Kegan Paul.

Lowe, Cedric J., and M. L. Dockrill, eds. 1972b. "The Far East." In *The Mirage of Power: British Foreign Policy, 1914–22*. Vol. 2. Boston: Routledge and Kegan Paul.

Lowe, Cedric J., and Frank Marzari. 1975. *Italian Foreign Policy, 1870–1940*. Boston: Routledge and Kegan Paul.

Lowe, Peter. 1977. *Great Britain and the Origins of the Pacific War: A Study of British Policy in East Asia, 1937–1941*. Oxford: Clarendon Press.

Lowe, Peter. 1981. *Britain in the Far East: A Survey from 1819 to the Present*. New York: Longman.

Lundestad, Geir, ed. 1993. *The Fall of the Great Powers: Peace, Stability, and Legitimacy*. Oxford: Oxford University Press.

Lusztig, Michael. 1998. "The Limits of Rent Seeking: Why Protectionists Become Free Traders." *Review of International Political Economy* 5:38–63.

Luttwak, Edward. 1976. *The Grand Strategy of the Roman Empire: From the First Century A.D. to the Third*. Baltimore: Johns Hopkins University Press.

Lynch, John. 1969. *Spain under the Habsburgs*. New York: Oxford University Press.

Lynch, John. 1992. *The Hispanic World in Crisis and Change, 1598–1700*. Cambridge: Blackwell.

MacDonald, Callum A. 1972. "Economic Appeasement and the German 'Moderates,' 1937–1939: An Introductory Essay." *Past and Present* 56:105–35.

Mack Smith, Denis. 1976. *Mussolini's Roman Empire*. London: Longman.

Mackay, Ruddock F. 1970. "The Admiralty, the German Navy, and the Redistribution of the British Fleet, 1904–1905." *Mariner's Mirror* 56:341–46.

Mackinder, Halford. 1904. "The Geographical Pivot of History." *Geographical Journal* 23:421–44.

Mackintosh, John P. 1969. "Britain in Europe: Historical Perspective and Contemporary Reality." *International Affairs* 45:246–58.

MacMullen, Ramsay. 1988. *Corruption and the Decline of Rome*. New Haven: Yale University Press.

Mahajan, Sneh. 1982. "The Defence of India and the End of Isolation: A Study in the Foreign Policy of the Conservative Government, 1900–1905." *Journal of Imperial and Commonwealth History* 10:168–93.

Mallet, Bernard. 1913. *British Budgets 1887–88 to 1912–13*. London: Macmillan.

Mansfield, Edward D. 1994. *Power, Trade, and War*. Princeton: Princeton University Press.

Marder, Arthur J. 1940. *The Anatomy of British Sea Power: A History of British Naval Policy in the Pre-Dreadnought Era, 1880–1905*. New York: Knopf.

Marder, Arthur J. 1961. *From the Dreadnought to Scapa Flow: The Royal Navy in the Fisher Era, 1904–1919*. London: Oxford University Press.

Mares, David A. 1988. "Middle Powers under Regional Hegemony: To Challenge or Acquiesce in Hegemonic Enforcement." *International Studies Quarterly* 32:453–71.

Marks, Steven G. 1991. *Road to Power: The Trans-Siberian Railroad and the Colonization of Asian Russia, 1850–1917*. Ithaca: Cornell University Press.

Martel, Gordon. 1991. "The Meaning of Power: Rethinking the Decline and Fall of Great Britain." *International History Review* 13:662–94.

Mastanduno, Michael. 1997. "Preserving the Unipolar Moment: Realist Theories and U.S. Grand Strategy after the Cold War." *International Security* 21:49–88.

Mastanduno, Michael. 1998. "Economics and Security in Statecraft and Scholarship." *International Organization* 42:825–54.

Mastanduno, Michael, David A. Lake, and G. John Ikenberry. 1989. "Toward a Realist Theory of State Action." *International Studies Quarterly* 33:457–74.

Maurer, John H. 1992. "Churchill's Naval Holiday: Arms Control and the Anglo-German Naval Race, 1912–1914." *Journal of Strategic Studies* 15:102–27.

McCormick, Thomas J. 1967. *China Market: America's Quest for Informal Empire, 1893–1901*. Chicago: Quadrangle Books.

McKeown, Timothy J. 1991. "The Foreign Policy of a Declining Power." *International Organization* 45:257–79.

McKercher, B. J. C. 1989. "Diplomatic Equipoise: The Lansdowne Foreign Office, the Russo-Japanese War of 1904–1905, and the Global Balance of Power." *Canadian Journal of History* 24:299–339.

McKercher, B. J. C. 1991. "'Our Most Dangerous Enemy': Great Britain Preeminent in the 1930s." *International History Review* 13:751–83.

McKercher, B. J. C. 1993. "No Eternal Friends or Enemies: British Defence Policy and the Problem of the United States, 1919–1939." *Canadian Journal of History* 28:257–93.

McRae, Hamish, and Frances Cairncross. 1984. *Capital City: London as Financial Centre*. London: Methuen.

Mearsheimer, John J. 1990. "Back to the Future: Instability in Europe after the Cold War." *International Security* 15:5–56.

Mearsheimer, John J. 2001. *The Tragedy of Great Power Politics*. New York: Norton.

Medlicott, W. N. 1968. *British Foreign Policy since Versailles, 1919–1963*. 2d ed. London: Methuen.

Medlicott, W. N. 1969. *Britain and Germany: The Search for Agreement, 1930–1937*. London: Athlone.

Medlicott, W. N. 1981. *Contemporary England, 1914–1964*. London: Longman Group.

Melman, Seymour. 1974. *The Permanent War Economy: American Capitalism in Decline*. New York: Simon and Schuster.

Middlemas, Keith. 1979. *Politics in Industrial Society: The Experience of the British System since 1911*. London: A. Deutsch.

Milgrom, Paul, and John Roberts. 1982. "Predation, Reputation, and Entry Deterrence." *Journal of Economic Theory* 27:280–312.

Miller, Benjamin. 1995. *When Opponents Cooperate: Great Power Conflict and Collaboration in World Politics*. Ann Arbor: University of Michigan Press.

Mills, William. 1993. "The Nyon Conference: Neville Chamberlain, Anthony Eden, and the Appeasement of Italy in 1937." *International History Review* 15:1–22.

Milner, Helen V. 1988. *Resisting Protectionism: Global Industries and the Politics of International Trade*. Princeton: Princeton University Press.

Milner, Helen V. 1997. *Interests, Institutions, and Information: Domestic Politics and International Relations*. Princeton: Princeton University Press.

Milward, Alan S. 1984. *The Economic Effects of the Two World Wars on Britain*. London: Macmillan

Mintz, Alex, and Chi Huang. 1991. "Guns versus Butter: The Indirect Link." *American Journal of Political Science* 35:738–57.

Mitchell, B. R. 1962. *Abstract of British Historical Statistics*. Cambridge: Cambridge University Press.

Modelski, George. 1978. "The Long Cycle of Global Politics and the Nation-State." *Comparative Studies in Society and History* 20:214–38.

Modelski, George. 1987. *Long Cycles in World Politics*. Seattle: University of Washington Press.

Modelski, George. 1989. "Long Cycles and Global War." In *The Handbook of War Studies*, ed. Manus I. Midlarsky. Boston: Unwin Hyman.

Modelski, George, and William R. Thompson. 1988. *Seapower in Global Politics, 1494–1993*. Seattle: University of Washington Press.

Monger, George W. 1963. *The End of Isolation: British Foreign Policy, 1900–1907*. London: Thomas Nelson and Sons.

Morris, A. J. Anthony. 1971. "The English Radicals' Campaign for Disarmament and the Hague Conference of 1907." *Journal of Modern History* 43:367–92.

Morris, A. J. Anthony. 1972. *Radicalism Against War, 1906–1914: The Advocacy of Peace and Retrenchment*. Totowa: Rowman and Littlefield.

Morrow, James D. 1989. "Capabilities, Uncertainty, and Resolve: A Limited Information Model of Crisis Bargaining." *American Journal of Political Science* 33:941–72.

Morrow, James D. 1993. "Arms versus Allies: Trade-offs in the Search for Security." *International Organization* 47:207–33.

Most, Benjamin A., and Harvey Starr. 1984. "International Relations Theory, Foreign Policy Substitutability, and 'Nice' Laws." *World Politics* 36:383–406.

Mowat, Charles L. 1955. *Britain between the Wars: 1918–1940*. London: Methuen.

Mowat, Charles L., ed. 1968. "Diplomatic History, 1900–1912." *The New Cambridge Modern History*. Vol. 12, *The Shifting Balance of World Forces, 1898–1904*. Cambridge: Cambridge University Press.

Müller, Harold, and Thomas Risse-Kappen. 1993. "From the Outside In and from the Inside Out." In *The Limits of State Autonomy: Societal Groups and Foreign Policy Formulation*, ed. David Skidmore and Valier M. Hudson. Boulder: Westview Press.

Murfett, Malcolm H. 1984. *Fool-Proof Relations: The Search for Anglo-American Naval Cooperation during the Chamberlain Years, 1937–1940*. Singapore: Singapore University Press.

Murray, Bruce. 1980. *The People's Budget of 1909/10: Lloyd George and Liberal Politics*. Oxford: Clarendon Press.

Murray, Williamson. 1979a. "Munich, 1938: The Military Confrontation." *Journal of Strategic Studies* 2:282–301.

Murray, Williamson. 1979b. "The Role of Italy in British Strategy, 1938–1939." *Royal United Services Institute for Defence Studies* 124:43–49.

Murray, Williamson. 1984. *The Change in the European Balance of Power, 1938–1939: The Path to Ruin*. Princeton: Princeton University Press.

Murray, Williamson. 1994. "The Collapse of Empire: British Strategy, 1919–1945." In *The Making of Strategy: Rulers, States, and War*, ed. Williamson Murray, MacGregor Knox, and Alvin Bernstein. Cambridge: Cambridge University Press.

Neale, R. G. 1966. *Great Britain and the United States Expansion, 1989–1900*. East Lansing: Michigan State University Press.

Neilson, Keith. 1991. "'Greatly Exaggerated': The Myth of the Decline of Great Britain before 1914." *International History Review* 13:695–725.

Nelson, Joan M., ed. 1989. *Fragile Coalitions: The Politics of Economic Adjustment*. New Brunswick: Transaction Books.

Nelson, Joan M., ed. 1990. *Economic Crisis and Policy Choice: The Politics of Adjustment in the Third World*. Princeton: Princeton University Press.

Newitt, M. D. D. 1986. "The East India Company in the Western Indian Ocean in the Early Seventeenth Century." *Journal of Imperial and Commonwealth History* 14:5–33.

Newton, Scott. 1991. "The 'Anglo-German Connection' and the Political Economy of Appeasement." *Diplomacy and Statecraft* 2:178–207.

Newton, Scott. 1995. "Appeasement as an Industrial Strategy, 1938–41." *Contemporary British History* 9:485–506.

Newton, Scott, and Dilwyn Porter. 1988. *Modernization Frustrated: The Politics of Industrial Decline in Britain since 1900*. Boston: Unwin Hyman.

Nish, Ian H. 1966. *The Anglo-Japanese Alliance: The Diplomacy of Two Island Empires, 1894–1907*. London: Athlone Press.

Nish, Ian H. 1974. "Japan's Policies toward Britain." In *Japan's Foreign Policy, 1868–1941: A Research Guide*, ed. James W. Morley. New York: Columbia University Press.

Nish, Ian H. 1977. *Japanese Foreign Policy 1869–1942, Kasumigaseki to Miyakezaka*. London: Routledge and Kegan Paul.

Nish, Ian H. 1985. *The Anglo-Japanese Alliance: The Diplomacy of Two Island Empires, 1894–1907*. London: Athlone Press.

Nish, Ian H., ed. 1982. "Japan in Britain's View of the International System, 1919–1937." In *Anglo-Japanese Alienation, 1919–1952: Papers of the Anglo-Japanese Conference on the History of the Second World War*. Cambridge: Cambridge University Press.

Noble, Paul. 1984. "The Arab State System: Opportunities, Constraints, and Pressures." In *The Foreign Policies of Arab States*, ed. Bahgat Korany and Ali E. Hillal Dessouki. Boulder: Westview Press.

North, Douglass C. 1981. *Structure and Change in Economic History*. New York: Norton.

Nye, Joseph S. 1990. *Bound to Lead: The Changing Nature of American Power*. New York: Basic Books.

Nye, Joseph S. 1995. "The Case for Deep Engagement." *Foreign Affairs* 74:90–114.

Offer, Avner. 1989. *The First World War: An Agrarian Interpretation*. New York: Oxford University Press.

Olson, Mancur C. 1982. *The Rise and Decline of Nations: Economic Growth, Stagflation, and Social Rigidities*. New Haven: Yale University Press.

Organski, A. F. K. 1968. *World Politics*. 2d ed. New York: Knopf.

Organski, A. F. K. 1990. *The $36 Billion Bargain: Strategy and Politics in U.S. Assistance to Israel*. New York: Columbia University Press.

Organski, A. F. K., and Jacek Kugler. 1980. *The War Ledger*. Chicago: University of Chicago Press.

Orme, John D. 1992. *Deterrence, Reputation and Cold-War Cycles*. London: Macmillan Press.

Osgood, Robert E., ed. 1973. "Introduction: The Nixon Doctrine and Strategy." In *Retreat from Empire? The First Nixon Administration*. Baltimore: Johns Hopkins University Press.

Overy, R. J. 1994. *War and Economy in the Third Reich*. Oxford: Clarendon Press.

Palmer, Alan. 1993. *The Decline and Fall of the Ottoman Empire*. London: John Murray.

Papayoanou, Paul A. 1999. *Power Ties: Economic Interdependence, Balancing, and War*. Ann Arbor: University of Michigan Press.

Parker, Geoffrey. 1977. *The Dutch Revolt*. Ithaca: Cornell University Press.

Parker, Geoffrey. 1979a. *Europe in Crisis, 1598–1648*. Ithaca: Cornell University Press.

Parker, Geoffrey. 1979b. *Spain and the Netherlands, 1559–1659: Ten Studies*. London: Collins.

Parker, Geoffrey. 1994. "The Making of Strategy in Habsburg Spain: Philip II's 'Bid for Mastery,' 1556–1598." In *The Making of Strategy: Rulers, States, and War*, ed. Williamson Murray, MacGregor Knox, and Alvin Bernstein. Cambridge: Cambridge University Press.

Parker, Geoffrey, ed. 1972. "The Army of Flanders and the Spanish Road: 1567–1659, The Logistics of Spanish Victory and Defeat." In *The Low Countries' Wars*. Cambridge: Cambridge University Press.

Parker, Geoffrey, and Lesley M. Smith, eds. 1978. *The General Crisis of the Seventeenth Century*. Boston: Routledge and Kegan Paul.

Parker, Robert A. C. 1975. "Economics, Rearmament and Foreign Policy: The United Kingdom before 1939—A Preliminary Study." *Journal of Contemporary History* 10:637–47.

Parker, Robert A. C. 1981. "British Rearmament, 1936–9: Treasury, Trade Unions and Skill Labour." *English Historical Review* 96:306–43.

Parker, Robert A. C. 1993. *Chamberlain and Appeasement: British Policy and the Coming of the Second World War*. Houndmills: Macmillan.

Parry, J. H. 1966. *Europe and a Wider World, 1415–1715*. London: Hutchinson University Library.

Peacock, Alan T., and Jack Wiseman. 1961. *The Growth of Public Expenditure in the United Kingdom*. Princeton: Princeton University Press.

Peden, G. C. 1979. *British Rearmament and the Treasury, 1932–1939*. Edinburgh: Scottish Academic Press.

Peden, G. C. 1983. "The Treasury as the Central Department of Government, 1919–1939." *Public Administration* 61:371–85.

Peden, G. C. 1984. "A Matter of Timing: The Economic Background to British Foreign Policy, 1937–1939." *History* 69:15–28.

Peden, G. C. 1991. *British Economic and Social Policy: Lloyd George to Margaret Thatcher*. New York: Philip Allan.

Peden, G. C. 2000. *The Treasury and British Public Policy, 1906–1959*. Oxford: Oxford University Press.

Pegg, Carl H. 1983. *Evolution of the European Idea, 1914–1932*. Chapel Hill: University of North Carolina Press.

Penson, Lillian M. 1943. "The New Course in British Foreign Policy, 1892–1902." *Transactions of the Royal Historical Society*. London: Offices of the Royal Historical Society.

Perkins, Bradford. 1968. *The Great Rapprochement: England and the United States, 1895–1914*. New York: Atheneum.

Perthes, Volker. 1994. "Stages in Economic and Political Liberalization." In *Contemporary Syria: Liberalization between Cold War and Cold Peace*, ed. Eberhard Kienle. New York: St. Martin's Press.

Peter, Katzenstein J. 1977. "Conclusion: Domestic Structures and Strategies of Foreign Economic Policy." *International Organization* 31:879–919.

Phillips, Gregory D. 1979. *The Diehards: Aristocratic Society and Politics in Edwardian England*. Cambridge: Harvard University Press.

Platt, Desmond C. M. 1968. *Finance Trade and Politics in Britain's Foreign Policy, 1815–1914*. Oxford: Clarendon Press.

Platt, Desmond C. M. 1972. *Latin America and British Trade, 1806–1914*. London: A. and C. Black.

Pletcher, David M. 1981. "Rhetoric and Results: A Pragmatic View of American Economic Expansionism, 1865–98." *Diplomatic History* 5:93–106.

Pletcher, David M. 1984. "1861–1898: Economic Growth and Diplomatic Adjustment." In *Economics and World Power: An Assessment of American Diplomacy since 1789*, ed. William H. Becker and Samuel F. Wells Jr. New York: Columbia University Press.

Poitras, Guy E. 1990. *The Ordeal of Hegemony: The United States and Latin America*. Boulder: Westview Press.

Polachek, Solomon W. 1980. "Conflict and Trade." *Journal of Conflict Resolution* 24:55–78.

Pollard, Sidney. 1969. *The Development of the British Economy, 1914–1967*. 2d ed., rev. London: Edward Arnold.

Pollard, Sidney. 1985. "Capital Exports, 1870–1914: Harmful or Beneficial?" *Economic History Review* 38:489–514.

Pollard, Sidney. 1989. *Britain's Prime and Britain's Decline: The British Economy, 1870–1914*. New York: Edward Arnold.

Porter, Bernard. 1975. *The Lion's Share: A Short History of British Imperialism*. New York: Longman.

Porter, Bernard. 1983. *Britain, Europe, and the World, 1850–1982: Delusions of Grandeur*. Boston: George Allen and Unwin.

Porter, Bernard. 1994. *Britannia's Burden: The Political Evolution of Modern Britain, 1851–1990*. London: Edward Arnold.

Porter, Bruce D. 1994. *War and the Rise of the State: The Military Foundations of Modern Politics*. New York: Free Press.

Posen, Barry R. 1984. *The Sources of Military Doctrine: France, Britain, and Germany between the Wars*. Ithaca: Cornell University Press.

Posen, Barry R., and Andrew L. Ross. 1996–97. "Competing Visions for U.S. Grand Strategy." *International Security* 21:5–53.

Post, Gaines, Jr. 1988. "Mad Dogs and Englishmen: British Rearmament, Deterrence, and Appeasement, 1934–35." *Armed Forces and Society* 14:329–57.

Powell, Robert. 1987. "Crisis Bargaining, Escalation, and MAD." *American Political Science Review* 81:717–35.

Pratt, Lawrence R. 1971. "The Anglo-American Naval Conversations on the Far East in January 1938." *International Affairs* 47:745–63.

Pratt, Lawrence R. 1975. *East of Malta, West of Suez: Britain's Mediterranean Crisis, 1936–1939*. Cambridge: Cambridge University Press.

Putnam, Robert D. 1988. "Diplomacy and Domestic Politics: The Logic of Two-Level Games." *International Organization* 42:427–60.

Ramsden, John. 1978. *The Age of Balfour and Baldwin, 1902–1940*. New York: Longman.

Rapkin, David P., ed. 1990. "Japan and World Leadership?" In *World Leadership and Hegemony*. Boulder: Lynne Rienner.

Rasler, Karen A., and William R. Thompson. 1988. "Defense Burdens, Capital Formation, and Economic Growth: The Systemic Leader Case." *Journal of Conflict Resolution* 32:61–86.

Rasler, Karen A., and William R. Thompson. 1989. *War and State Making: The Shaping of the Global Powers*. Boston: Unwin Hyman.

Rasler, Karen A., and William R. Thompson. 1991. "Relative Decline and the Overconsumption-Underinvestment Hypothesis." *International Studies Quarterly* 35:273–94.

Rasler, Karen A., and William R. Thompson. 1994. *The Great Powers and Global Struggle, 1490–1990*. Lexington: University Press of Kentucky.

Rempel, Richard A. 1972. *Unionist Divided: Arthur Balfour, Joseph Chamberlain, and the Unionist Free Traders*. Hamden, Conn.: Archon Books.

Reynolds, David. 1981. *The Creation of the Anglo-American Alliance, 1937–1941: A Study in Competitive Cooperation*. London: Europa.

Richardson, J. L. 1988. "New Perspectives on Appeasement: Some Implications for International Relations." *World Politics* 40:289–316.

Risse-Kappen, Thomas. 1995. *Bringing Transnational Relations Back In: Non-state Actors, Domestic Structures, and International Institutions*. Cambridge: Cambridge University Press.

Robbins, K. G. 1977. "The Foreign Secretary, the Cabinet, Parliament and Parties." In *British Foreign Policy under Sir Edward Grey*, ed. F. H. Hinsley. New York: Cambridge University Press.

Robbins, Keith. 1983. *The Eclipse of a Great Power: Modern Britain, 1870–1975*. New York: Longman.

Roberts, Richard. 1991. "The City of London as a Financial Centre in the Era of the Depression, the Second World War and Post-war Official Controls." In *Contemporary British History, 1931–61: Politics and the Limits of Policy*, ed. Anthony Gorst, Lewis Johnman, and W. Scott Lucas. New York: Pinter.

Robertson, Alex J. 1990. "Lancashire and the Rise of Japan, 1910–1937." *Business History* 32:87–105.

Robertson, James C. 1974. "The British General Election of 1935." *Journal of Contemporary History* 9:149–64.

Rock, Stephen R. 1988. "Risk Theory Reconsidered: American Success and German Failure in the Coercion of Britain, 1890–1914." *Journal of Strategic Studies* 11:342–64.

Rock, Stephen R. 1989. *Why Peace Breaks Out: Great Power Rapprochement in Historical Perspective*. Chapel Hill: University of North Carolina Press.

Rogowski, Ronald. 1989. *Commerce and Coalitions: How Trade Affects Domestic Political Alignments*. Princeton: Princeton University Press.

Rolo, P. J. V. 1969. *Entente Cordiale: The Origins and Negotiations of the Anglo-French Agreements of 8 April 1904*. London: Macmillan.

Ropp, Theodore. 1962. *War in the Modern World*. London: Collier Macmillan.

Ropp, Theodore. 1987. *The Development of a Modern Navy: French Naval Policy, 1871–1904*. Annapolis: Naval Institute Press.

Rosecrance, Richard. 1986. *The Rise of the Trading State: Commerce and Conquest in the Modern World*. New York: Basic Books.

Rosecrance, Richard. 1990. *America's Economic Resurgence: A Bold New Strategy*. New York: Harper and Row.

Rosecrance, Richard. 1991. "Regionalism and the Post–Cold War Era." *International Journal* 46:373–93.

Rosecrance, Richard, and Arthur A. Stein, eds. 1993. "Beyond Realism: The Study of Grand Strategy." In *The Domestic Bases of Grand Strategy*. Ithaca: Cornell University Press.

Rosecrance, Richard, and Jennifer Taw. 1989. "Japan and the Theory of International Leadership." *World Politics* 42:184–209.

Rosenau, James N., ed. 1969. "Toward the Study of National-International Linkages." In *Linkage Politics: Essays on the Convergence of National and International Systems*. New York: Free Press.

Rosenthal, Robert. 1981. "Games of Perfect Information, Predatory Pricing and the Chain-Store Paradox." *Journal of Economic Theory* 25:92–100.

Roseveare, Henry. 1969. *The Treasury: The Evolution of a British Institution*. London: Allen Lane Penguin Press.

Roskill, Stephen W. 1978. *Naval Policy between the Wars*. London: Trustees of National Maritime Museum.

Rothwell, V. H. 1971. *British War Aims and Peace Diplomacy, 1914–1918*. Oxford: Clarendon Press.

Rotte, Ralph. 1997. "Economics and Peace-Theory on the Eve of World War I." In *Economics of Conflict and Peace*, ed. Jurgen Brauer and William G. Gissy. Aldershot: Avebury.

Rowland, Benjamin M. 1987. *Commercial Conflict and Foreign Policy: A Study in Anglo-American Relations, 1932–1938*. New York: Garland.

Rowland, Benjamin M., ed. 1976. "The Interwar Monetary System." In *Balance of Power or Hegemony: The Interwar Monetary System*. New York: New York University Press.

Russett, Bruce M. 1990. *Controlling the Sword: The Democratic Governance of National Security*. Cambridge: Harvard University Press.

Sachs, Susan. 2000. "Syria's Businessmen Feel Future Won't Wait." *New York Times*, January 27, A1.

Sahn, David E., Paul A. Dorosh, and Stephen D. Younger. 1997. *Structural Adjustment Reconsidered: Economic Policy and Poverty in Africa*. Cambridge: Cambridge University Press.

Sakamoto, Masarhiro. 1989. "Japan's Role in the International System." In *Sharing World Leadership? A New Era for America and Japan*, ed. John H. Makin and Donald C. Hellmann. Washington, D.C.: American Enterprise Institute.

Salerno, Reynolds. 1994. "Multilateral Strategy and Diplomacy: The Anglo-German Naval Agreement and the Mediterranean Crisis, 1935–1936." *Journal of Strategic Studies* 17:39–78.

Scammel, Claire M. 1997. "The Royal Navy and the Strategic Origins of the Anglo-German Naval Agreement of 1935." *Journal of Strategic Studies* 20:92–118.

Scammell, Geoffrey V. 1989. *The First Imperial Age: European Overseas Expansion c. 1400–1715*. London: Unwin Hyman.

Schamis, Hector E. 1999. "Distributional Coalitions and the Politics of Economic Reform in Latin America." *World Politics* 51:236–68.

Schelling, Thomas C. 1966. *Arms and Influence*. New Haven: Yale University Press.

Schmidt, Gustav. 1986a. "Great Britain and Germany in the Age of Imperialism." *War and Society* 4:31–51.

Schmidt, Gustav. 1986b. *The Politics and Economics of Appeasement: British Foreign Policy in the 1930s*. New York: St. Martin's Press.

Schremmer, Eckart. 1989. "Taxation and Public Finance: Britain, France, and Germany." In *The Cambridge Economic History of Europe*. Vol. 3, *The Industrial Economies: The Development of Economic and Social Policies*, ed. Peter Mathias and Sidney Pollard. Cambridge: Cambridge University Press.

Schroeder, Paul W. 1976a. "Alliances, 1815–1945: Weapons of Power and Tools of Management." In *Historical Dimensions of National Security Problems*, ed. Klaus Knorr. Lawrence: University Press of Kansas.

Schroeder, Paul W. 1976b. "Munich and the British Tradition." *Historical Journal* 19:223–43.

Schultz, Hans-Dietrich Schultz. 1989. "Fantasies of 'Mitte': 'Mittellage' and 'Mitteleuropa' in German Geographical Discussion in the Nineteenth and Twentieth Centuries." *Political Geography Quarterly* 8:315–39.

Schumpeter, Joseph A. 1955. *Imperialism and Social Classes*. Trans. Heinz Norden. New York: Meridian Books.

Schweller, Randall L. 1992. "Domestic Structure and Preventive War: Are Democracies More Pacific?" *World Politics* 44:234–69.

Schwoerer, Lois. 1970. "Lord Halifax's Visit to Germany: November 1937." *Historian* 32:353–75.

Selden, Zachary A. 1999. *Economic Sanctions as Instruments of American Foreign Policy*. Westport: Praeger.

Selten, Reinhard. 1978. "The Chain Store Paradox." *Theory and Decision* 9:127–59.

Seton-Watson, Hugh. 1967. *The Russian Empire, 1801–1917*. Oxford: Clarendon Press.

Shai, Aron. 1974. "Was There a Far Eastern Munich?" *Journal of Contemporary History* 9:161–69.

Shay, Robert P., Jr. 1977. *British Rearmament in the Thirties: Politics and Profits*. Princeton: Princeton University Press.

Shay, Robert P., Jr. 1983. "Had Baldwin Resigned in 1936: A Speculative Essay." In *The Fascist Challenge and the Policy of Appeasement*, ed. Wolfgang J. Mommsen and Lothar Kettenacker. London: George Allen and Unwin.

Simmons, Beth E. 1994. *Who Adjusts: Domestic Sources of Foreign Economic Policy during the Interwar Years*. Princeton: Princeton University Press.

Skålnes, Lars S. 2000. *Politics, Markets, and Grand Strategy: Foreign Economic Policies as Strategic Instruments*. Ann Arbor: University of Michigan Press.

Skidelsky, Robert J. A. 1976. "Retreat from Leadership: The Evolution of British Economic Foreign Policy, 1870–1939." In *Balance of Power or Hegemony: The Interwar Monetary System*, ed. Benjamin M. Rowland. New York: New York University Press.

Skocpol, Theda. 1979. *States and Social Revolution*. New York: Cambridge University Press.

Smith, Malcolm S. 1978. "Rearmament and Deterrence in Britain in the 1930s." *Journal of Strategic Studies* 3:313–37.

Smith, Michael S. 1980. *Tariff Reform in France, 1860–1900: The Politics of Economic Interest*. Ithaca: Cornell University Press.

Smith, Michael S. 1992. "The *Méline* Tariff as Social Protection: Rhetoric or Reality?" *International Review of Social History* 37:230–43.

Smith, Steven R. B. 1991. "Public Opinion, the Navy and the City of London: The

Drive for British Naval Expansion in the Late Nineteenth Century." *War and Society* 9:29–50.

Snidal, Duncan. 1985. "The Limits of Hegemonic Stability Theory." *International Organization* 39:579–614.

Snyder, Jack L. 1991. *Myths of Empire: Domestic Politics and International Ambition*. Ithaca: Cornell University Press.

Solingen, Etel. 1994. "The Political Economy of Nuclear Restraint." *International Security* 19:126–69.

Solingen, Etel. 1997. "Economic Liberalization, Political Coalitions, and Emerging Regional Orders." In *Regional Orders: Building Security in a New World*, ed. David A. Lake and Patrick M. Morgan. University Park: Pennsylvania State University Press.

Solingen, Etel. 1998. *Regional Orders at Century's Dawn: Global and Domestic Influences on Grand Strategy*. Princeton: Princeton University Press.

Sontag, John. 1968. "Tsarist Debts and Tsarist Foreign Policy." *Slavic Review* 27:529–41.

Spero, Joan E. 1985. *The Politics of International Economic Relations*. 3d ed. New York: St. Martin's Press.

Spiers, Edward. 1980. "Haldane's Reform of the Regular Army." *British Journal of International Studies* 6:69–81.

Sprout, Harold, and Margaret Sprout. 1944. *The Rise of American Naval Power, 1776–1918*. Princeton: Princeton University Press.

Sprout, Harold, and Margaret Sprout. 1963. "Retreat from World Power: Processes and Consequences of Readjustment." *World Politics* 15:655–88.

Sprout, Harold, and Margaret Sprout. 1968. "The Dilemma of Rising Demands and Insufficient Resources." *World Politics* 20:660–93.

Sprout, Margaret T. 1941. "Mahan: Evangelist of Sea Power." In *Makers of Modern Strategy: Military Thought from Machiavelli to Hitler*, ed. Edward M. Earle. Princeton: Princeton University Press.

Stallings, Barbara. 1992. "International Influence on Economic Policy: Debt, Stabilization, and Structural Reform." In *The Politics of Economic Adjustment: International Constraints, Distributive Conflicts, and the State*, ed. Stephan Haggard and Robert R. Kaufman. Princeton: Princeton University Press.

Stambrook, F. G. 1972. "The German-Austrian Customs Union Project of 1931: A Study of German Methods and Motives." In *European Diplomacy between Two Wars, 1919–1939*, ed. Hans W. Gatzke. Chicago: Quadrangle Books.

Stamp, Albert H. 1957. *Other Nations' Colonies*. Turnbridge Wells: Courier.

Starr, Chester G. 1982. *The Roman Empire, 27 B.C.–A.D. 476: A Study in Survival*. New York: Oxford University Press.

Starr, Harvey. 1992. "Why Don't Democracies Fight Each Other? Evaluating the Theory-Findings Feedback Loop." *Jerusalem Journal of International Relations* 14:41–59.

Stein, Arthur A. 1978. *The Nation at War*. Baltimore: Johns Hopkins University Press.

Stein, Arthur A. 1983. "Coordination and Collaboration: Regimes in an Anarchic World." In *International Regimes*, ed. Stephen D. Krasner. Ithaca: Cornell University Press.

Stein, Arthur A. 1984. "The Hegemon's Dilemma: Great Britain, the United States, and the International Economic Order." *International Organization* 38:355–86.

Stein, Arthur A. 1990. *Why Nations Cooperate: Circumstance and Choice in International Relations*. Ithaca: Cornell University Press.

Stein, Arthur A. 1993a. "Domestic Constraints, Extended Deterrence, and the Incoherence of Grand Strategy: The United States, 1938–1950." In *The Domestic Bases of Grand Strategy*, ed. Richard Rosecrance and Arthur A. Stein. Ithaca: Cornell University Press.

Stein, Arthur A. 1993b. "Governments, Economic Interdependence, and International Cooperation." In *Behavior, Society, and International Conflict*, ed. Philip E. Tetlock, Jo L. Husbands, Robert Jervis, Paul C. Stern, and Charles Tilly. Vol. 3. New York: Oxford University Press.

Stein, Arthur A., and Steven E. Lobell. 1997. "Geostructuralism and International Politics: The End of the Cold War and the Regionalization of International Security." In *Regional Orders: Building Security in a New World*, ed. David A. Lake and Patrick M. Morgan. University Park: Pennsylvania State University Press.

Steiner, Zara S. 1959. "Great Britain and the Creation of the Anglo-Japanese Alliance." *Journal of Modern History* 31:27–36.

Steiner, Zara S. 1963. "The Last Years of the Old Foreign Office, 1898–1905." *Historical Journal* 6:59–90.

Steiner, Zara S. 1977. *Britain and the Origins of the First World War*. New York: St. Martin's Press.

Stewart, R. B. 1937. "Instrument of British Policy in the Sterling Area." *Political Science Quarterly* 52:174–207.

Stradling, Robert A. 1979. "Seventeenth Century Spain: Decline or Survival?" *European Studies Review* 9:157–94.

Stradling, Robert A. 1981. *Europe and the Decline of Spain: A Study of the Spanish System, 1580–1720*. Boston: George Allen and Unwin.

Stradling, Robert A. 1984. "Spain's Military Failure and the Supply of Horses, 1600–1660." *History: The Journal of the Historical Association* 69:208–21.

Stradling, Robert A. 1986. "Olivares and the Origins of the Franco-Spanish War, 1627–1635." *English Historical Review* 101:68–94.

Stradling, Robert A. 1988. *Philip and the Government of Spain, 1621–1665*. Cambridge: Cambridge University Press.

Sumida, Jon T. 1989. *In Defence of Naval Supremacy: Finance, Technology and British Naval Policy, 1889–1914*. Boston: Unwin Hyman.

Sweet, David W. 1977. "Great Britain and Germany." In *British Foreign Policy under Sir Edward Grey*, ed. F. H. Hinsley. New York: Cambridge University Press.

Sweet, David W., and R. T. B Langhorne. 1977. "Great Britain and Russia, 1907–1914." In *British Foreign Policy under Sir Edward Grey*, ed. F. H. Hinsley. New York. Cambridge University Press.

Taira, Koji. 1991. "Japan, an Imminent Hegemon?" *Annals of the American Academy of Political and Social Science* 13:151–63.

Taylor, A. J. P. 1965. *English History, 1914–1945*. Oxford: Oxford University Press.

Taylor, A. J. P. 1971. *The Struggle for Mastery in Europe, 1848–1918*. Oxford: Oxford University Press.

Thomas, Mark. 1983. "Rearmament and Economic Recovery in the Late 1930s." *Economic History Review* 36:552–79.

Thompson, Andrew S. 1997. "The Language of Imperialism and the Meanings of Empire: Imperial Discourse in British Politics, 1895–1914." *Journal of British Studies* 36:147–77.

Thompson, I. A. A. 1982. "Crown and Cortes in Castile, 1590–1665." *Parliaments, Estates and Representatives* 2:29–45.

Thompson, William R. 1990. "Long Waves, Technological Innovation and Relative Decline." *International Organization* 44:249–67.

Thompson, William R., and Gary Zuk. 1986. "World Power and the Strategic Trap of Territorial Commitments." *International Studies Quarterly* 30:249–68.

Thurow, Lester. 1985. "Budget Deficits." In *The Deficits: How Big? How Long? How Dangerous?* ed. Daniel Bell and Lester Thurow. New York: New York University Press.

Tilly, Charles. 1990. *Coercion, Capital, and European States*, AD *990–1990*. Cambridge: Blackwell.

Tilly, Charles, ed. 1975. *The Formation of National States in Western Europe*. Princeton: Princeton University Press.

Tomlinson, Jim. 1990. *Public Policy and the Economy since 1900*. Oxford: Clarendon Press.

Tomlinson, Jim. 1994. *Government and the Enterprise since 1900: The Changing Problem of Efficiency*. Oxford: Clarendon Press.

Tracy, James D. 1990. *The Rise of the Merchant Empires: Long Distance Trade in the Early Modern World, 1350–1750*. New York: Cambridge University Press.

Trimberger, Ellen K. 1978. *Revolution from Above: Military Bureaucrats and Development in Japan, Turkey, and Peru*. New Brunswick: Transaction Books.

Triska, Jan F. 1986. *Dominant Powers and Subordinate States: The United States in Latin America and the Soviet Union in Eastern Europe*. Durham: Duke University Press.

Trotter, Ann. 1974. "Tentative Steps for an Anglo-Japanese Rapprochement in 1934." *Modern Asian Studies* 8:59–83.

Trotter, Ann. 1975. *Britain and East Asia, 1933–1937*. Cambridge: Cambridge University Press.

Trotter, Ann. 1977. "Backstage Diplomacy: Britain and Japan in the 1930s." *Journal of Oriental Studies* 15:37–45.

Turner, John, ed. 1988. "British Politics and the Great War." In *Britain and the First World War*. Boston: Unwin Hyman.

Van Evera, Stephen. 1984. "The Cult of the Offensive and the Origins of the First World War." *International Security* 9:58–107.

Van Evera, Stephen. 1990. "Why Europe Matters, Why the Third World Doesn't: American Grand Strategy after the Cold War." *Journal of Strategic Studies* 13:1–51.

Van Evera, Stephen. 1997. *Guide to Methods for Students of Political Science*. Ithaca: Cornell University Press.

Van Evera, Stephen. 1999. *Causes of War: Power and the Roots of Conflict*. Ithaca: Cornell University Press.

Vasquez, John A. 1993. *The War Puzzle*. Cambridge: Cambridge University Press.

Vives, Jaime V. 1970. "The Decline of Spain in the Seventeenth Century." In *The Economic Decline of Empires*, ed. Carlo M. Cipolla. London: Methuen.

Von Hohenbalken, Balder, and Douglas West. 1986. "Empirical Tests for Predatory Reputation." *Canadian Journal of Economics* 19:160–78.

Walker, Stephen. 1980. "Solving the Appeasement Puzzle: Contending Historical Interpretations of British Diplomacy during the 1930s." *British Journal of International Studies* 6:219–46.

Wallander, Celeste A. 1992. "Opportunity, Incrementalism, and Learning in the Extension and Retraction of Soviet Global Commitments." *Security Studies* 1:514–42.

Wallerstein, Immanuel. 1993. "Foes as Friends?" *Foreign Policy* 90:145–57.

Walt, Stephen M. 1987. *The Origins of Alliances*. Ithaca: Cornell University Press.

Walt, Stephen M. 1989. "The Case for Finite Containment: Analyzing U.S. Grand Strategy." *International Security* 14:5–47.

Waltz, Kenneth N. 1979. *Theory of International Politics*. Reading: Addison-Wesley.

Waltz, Kenneth N. 1993. "The Emerging Structure of International Politics." *International Security* 18:44–79.

Warner, Sir Fred. 1991. *Anglo-Japanese Financial Relations: A Golden Tide*. Oxford: Blackwell.

Warwick, Paul. 1985. "Did Britain Change? An Inquiry into the Causes of National Decline." *Journal of Contemporary History* 20:99–134.

Waterbury, John. 1989. "The Political Management of Economic Adjustment and Reform." In *Fragile Coalitions: The Politics of Economic Adjustment*, ed. Joan M. Nelson. New Brunswick: Transaction Books.

Watt, Donald Cameron. 1956. "The Anglo-German Naval Agreement of 1935: An Interim Judgment." *Journal of Modern History* 28:155–75.

Watt, Donald Cameron. 1965. *Personalities and Policies: Studies in the Formulation of British Foreign Policy in the Twentieth Century*. London: Longmans.

Watt, Donald Cameron. 1975. "Britain, France and the Italian Problem, 1937–1939." In *Les Relations Franco-Britanniques*. Paris: Centre National de la Recherche Scientifique.

Watt, Donald Cameron. 1976. "The Historiography of Appeasement." In *Crisis and Controversy: Essays in Honour of A.J.P. Taylor*, ed. Alan Sked and Chris Cook. New York: St. Martin's Press.

Watt, Donald Cameron. 1984. *Succeeding John Bull: America in Britain's Place, 1900–1975*. Cambridge: Cambridge University Press.

Weinberg, Gerhard L. 1980. *The Foreign Policy of Hitler's Germany: Starting World War II, 1937–1939*. Chicago: University of Chicago Press.

Weinroth, Howard S. 1970. "The British Radicals and the Balance of Power, 1902–1914." *Historical Journal* 13:653–79.

Weinroth, Howard. 1971. "Left-Wing Opposition to Naval Armaments in Britain before 1914." *Contemporary History* 6:93–120.

Weir, Margaret, and Theda Skocpol. 1985. "State Structures and the Possibilities of 'Keynesian' Responses to the Great Depression in Sweden, Britain, and the United States." In *Bringing the State Back In*, ed. Peter B. Evans, Dietrich Rueschemeyer, and Theda Skocpol. Cambridge: Cambridge University Press.

Weitzel, William, and Ellen Jonsson. 1989. "Decline in Organizations: A Literature Integration and Extension." *Administrative Science Quarterly* 34:91–109.

Wells, Samuel F. 1968. "British Strategic Withdrawal from the Western Hemisphere, 1904–1906." *Canadian Historical Review* 49:335–56.

Wells, Samuel F. 1990. *The Challenges of Power: American Diplomacy, 1900–1921*. New York: University Press of America.

Wendt, Bernd-Jürgen. 1983. "'Economic Appeasement'—A Crisis Strategy." In *The Fascist Challenge and the Policy of Appeasement*, ed. Wolfgang J. Mommsen and Lothar Kettenacker. London: George Allen and Unwin.

Westwood, J. N. 1981. *Endurance and Endeavour: Russian History, 1812–1980*. London: Oxford University Press.

Whetten, David A. 1980. "Organizational Decline: A Neglected Topic in Organizational Science." *Academy of Management Review* 5:577–88.

Whetten, David A. 1987. "Organizational Growth and Decline Processes." *Annual Review of Sociology* 13:335–58.

Williams, Beryl J. 1966. "The Strategic Background to the Anglo-Russian Entente of August 1907." *Historical Journal* 9:360–73.

Williams, Glyndwr. 1966. *The Expansion of Europe in the Eighteenth Century: Overseas Rivalry, Discovery, and Exploitation*. New York: Walker.

Williams, Rhodri. 1991. *Defending the Empire: The Conservative Party and British Defence Policy, 1899–1915*. New Haven: Yale University Press.

Williams, William A. 1972. *The Tragedy of American Diplomacy*. New York: W. W. Norton.

Williamson, Philip. 1984. "Financiers, The Gold Standard and British Politics, 1925–1931." In *Business and Politics: Studies of Business Activity in British Politics, 1900–1945*, ed. John Turner. London: Heinemann.

Williamson, Samuel R., Jr. 1969. *The Politics of Grand Strategy: Britain and France Prepare for War, 1904–1914*. London: Ashfield Press.

Wilmott, H. P. 1972. "Liberals at Sea." *Journal of the Royal United Services Institute for the Defence Studies* 117:61–63.

Wilson, Keith M. 1981. "British Power in the European Balance, 1906–14." In *Retreat From Power: Studies in Britain's Foreign Policy in the Twentieth Century*, ed. David Dilks. London: Macmillan Press.

Wilson, Keith M. 1985. *The Policy of Entente: Essays on the Determination of British Foreign Policy, 1904–1914*. Cambridge: Cambridge University Press.

Wilson, Keith M. 1987. *Empire and Continent: Studies in British Foreign Policy from the 1880s to the First World War*. New York: Mansell.

Wohlstetter, Albert. 1968. "Illusions of Distance." *Foreign Affairs* 46:242–55.

Wurn, Clemens A., ed. 1993. "The Great Depression, Tariff Reform and the Steel Industry, 1931–1932." In *Business, Politics, and International Relations: Steel, Cotton, and International Cartels in British Politics, 1924–1939*. Trans. Patrick Salmon. Cambridge: Cambridge University Press.

Yapp, Malcolm A. 1987. "British Perceptions of the Russian Threat to India." *Modern Asian Studies* 21:647–65.

Zakaria, Fareed. 1992. "Realism and Domestic Politics." *International Security* 17:177–98.

Zakaria, Fareed. 1998. *From Wealth to Power: The Unusual Origins of America's World Role*. Princeton: Princeton University Press.

Zammuto, Raymond F., and Kim S. Cameron. 1985. "Environmental Decline and Organizational Response." In *Research in Organizational Behavior*, ed. L. L. Cummings and Barry M. Staw. Vol. 7. Greenwich: JAI Press.

Zartman, William I. 1967. "Africa as a Subordinate State System in International Relations." *International Organization* 21:545–64.

Index

Abyssinia, Italian invasion of, 90, 166
Accommodationist strategy, 13, 40, 44, 136, 137. *See also* Cooperation
Admiralty, British, 62, 76, 77, 116, 118, 174; Franco-Russian threat and, 64, 65, 67; Japanese alliance and, 72; Mediterranean fleet and, 79–80; Singapore defense and, 103, 112
Africa, 47, 52
Agriculture, 24, 51, 59–60, 64, 96, 103, 162
Air force, British RAF, 113, 114–15, 116
Akita, Shigeru, 72–73
Almirantazgo (Seville Admiralty Board), 131–32, 146
Americas, 71, 74, 135, 144–45, 151, 196–97n. 37. *See also* Colonies
Amu statement, 91
Anglo-French Agreement of 1904, 51, 68–69
Anglo-French naval agreement, 79–80
Anglo-German agreements, 77–78; Coal Agreement (1939), 119–20; Naval Agreement (1935), 116, 165, 166, 189n. 64; Standstill Agreement (1931), 109, 110
Anglo-Japanese Alliance, 72–74
Anglo-Russian Entente (1907), 69
Aragon, 140, 149, 163
Aristocracy: British, 64, 81; Castilian, 137, 144
Arms limitation agreements, 12, 13, 98, 101; free traders and, 34, 45, 113. *See also* Naval arms limitations; *and specific agreements*
Arms race, 35, 38, 78; free-trader opposition to, 23, 54–55. *See also* Rearmament
Army, British continental, 55, 84, 113, 116–17
Asia, 9, 90; Central, 47, 53, 65, 69, 155. *See also* Far East; *and specific country*
Asian Monroe Doctrine, 91
Asquith, Herbert Henry, 76, 77
Atlantic Charter (1941), 95, 121
Austria, 52, 92, 93, 144
Autarky and self-sufficiency, 20, 25, 87, 94, 106; German, 92, 93. *See also* Economic self-sufficiency

Balance of payments, 54, 113–14
Baldwin, Stanley, 104
Balfour, Arthur, 55, 61, 188n. 44
Banker's Industrial Development Corporation (BIDC), 105
Bank of England, 56–57, 63, 68–69, 73, 105, 110; German cooperation and, 107–8, 109; gold standard and, 57, 60, 96, 98, 100, 106; rearmament and, 111, 113

Banks, 68, 76, 107; merchant, 63, 84, 106, 108. *See also* City of London
Belgium, 52. *See also* Flanders
Bismarck, Otto von, 52
Boulding, Kenneth E., 10
Brazil, sugar plantations in, 126, 130, 134, 142, 164, 196n. 28
Briand, Aristide, 94
Britain, France and. *See* France, Britain and
Britain (1889–1912), cooperation strategy in, 1, 12, 16, 43–84, 162, 177–78n. 14; China trade and, 47, 48–49, 50, 53; distributional consequences of, 80–81; economic stability and military in, 38, 167–68; Franco-Russian Alliance and, 64–65; Germany and, 75–79, 82, 83–84; imperial contenders and, 51–53; Japanese alliance with, 72–74; liberal contenders and, 48–51; naval power and, 6, 11, 43, 65–67, 186–87n. 36; regional contenders and, 46–48; Russian entente with, 69–70; United States and, 9, 31, 48–49, 70–71, 83. *See also* Economic nationalist coalition, British; England, Spain and; Free-trade coalition, British (1889–1912)
Britain (1932–39), restrained punishment strategy in, 85–121; coalition strength in, 157–58; commercial conciliation, 107–10; distributional consequences in, 119; economic nationalists and, 86–88, 96, 97, 101–7, 119–21; Japanese challenge to, 89, 90–91; military security and, 165–67; rearmament of, 15, 88, 101–3, 111–19, 192n. 40; regional challengers to, 9, 89–95; United States and, 85, 90, 94–95, 116, 121. *See also* Anglo-; Free-trade coalition, British (1932–39)
British Bankers' Association, 110
British navy, 43, 46, 47, 55, 62, 65–67; Estimates for, 44, 79; Fisher Reforms, 74–75, 167– 68; rearmament and, 103, 112–13, 115–16, 193n. 50. *See also* Admiralty, British
Brooks, Collin, 106–7
Brüning, Heinrich, 92
Bureaucrats (civil servants), 24, 30–31, 36

Cain, Peter J., 64, 111, 184n. 17
Calleo, David P., 51–52
Campbell-Bannerman, Sir Henry, 55, 76
Canal treaty, 70–71
Capitalism, gentlemanly, 88, 113, 119, 120
Caribbean area, 71, 130, 145
Carr, Edward Hallet, 39
Casa de la Contratación, 131
Castile, 38, 148–49, 150–51, 163. *See also* Cortes of Castile
Catalonia, 14, 39, 140, 148, 149, 164
Catholic League, 123, 144
Central Asia, 47, 53, 65, 69, 155
Central European Customs Union, 51–52, 92–93. See also *Mitteleuropa*
Chamberlain, Austin, 67, 74
Chamberlain, Joseph, 59–61, 67, 168, 185n. 22
Chamberlain, Neville, 89, 107, 108, 121, 166; rearmament and, 115, 117, 193n. 53
Chiang Kai-shek, 110
China, 47, 48–49, 50, 53, 108–10, 115; Japan and, 49, 90, 91–92, 110, 166
Churchill, Winston, 77, 78, 79, 95, 121, 167
City of London, 66, 69, 96, 98, 110, 186n. 34; economic cooperation and, 64, 107–8; free-trade coalition and, 55–56, 84, 120; Japan and, 72–73; ravaged service industries of, 105–6; restoration of, 100–101; stagnation in, 184n. 18

Clarke, Sir George, 74
Clayton-Bulwer Treaty (1850), 70
Coalitional power, 26–30, 153, 154, 156. *See also* Economic nationalist coalition; Free-trade coalition; Liberal coalition
Coinage debasement, 137, 146. See also *Vellón* (copper) coinage
Cold War, 21, 38, 180n. 6
Colonies: English, 107, 135; French, 50; Spanish, 131, 151. *See also specific colonies*
Commercial policy. *See* Foreign commercial policy; Mercantilism; Trade policy
Committee of Imperial Defence (CID), 71, 74, 82, 102
Compagnie des iles d'Amerique (French trading company), 132, 135
Competition, free-trader promotion of, 22–23
Compromise, coalitional, 28. *See also* Accommodationist strategy
Conference of Aix-la-Chapelle, 164
Conservative Party (Britain), 77, 87, 102, 104, 106; defeat of, 45–46; economic nationalists and, 61–62, 97
Contenders: power transition and, 4, 179n. 4; punishment of, 5; regional, 8–9. *See also* Imperial contenders; Liberal contenders
Continental-sized armies, 55, 84, 113, 116–17
Continental System (Napoleon), 21
Cooperation, 39, 120, 161; economic, 107–10; economic nationalist challenge to, 28, 33; liberal contenders and, 159–60; as self-reinforcing strategy, 13, 37, 88; strengthening of free traders and, 2, 27, 29–32, 157, 158
Cooperative grand strategy, 1, 13, 16, 53–54, 104; chain store paradox, 177n. 12; of free-trade coalition, 12, 86, 95–96, 154–55; in post–World War I Britain, 98; in Spain, 125. *See also* Britain (1889–1912), cooperation strategy in
Copeland, Dale C., 4
Cortes of Castile (Spanish parliament), 13–14, 124, 125, 147–48, 156; Crown war policy and, 146, 149, 150; opposition to taxation by, 137–38, 140
Council of Finance (Spain), 124, 139, 146, 148
Council of Portugal, 124, 139, 146
Council of State (Spain), 124, 139
Council of the Indies, 124, 146
Creditworthiness, 99–100, 138, 145, 150, 185n. 20
Cuba, 130, 146
Currency reform, 92, 97, 109–10. See also *Vellón* (copper) coinage
Curzon, George Nathaniel, Lord, 72
Czechoslovakia, 93, 166

Debt repayment, 58, 100, 185n. 20
Defence Requirements Committee (DRC), 112–13, 117, 118
Defense spending, 23, 117, 118, 139, 162. *See also* Military spending
De Guzmán, Gaspar. *See* Olivares, Count-Duke (Gaspar de Guzmán)
Deterrence theory, 6, 177n. 12
Devolution policy, 161–62, 167, 171
Disarmament, 87, 98, 101, 165. *See also* Arms limitation agreements
Disengagement, decline and, 162
Distributional consequences, 157; Britain, 80–81, 119; in Spain, 146–47
Domestic coalitions, 21–26. *See also* Economic nationalist coalition; Free-trade coalition; Liberal coalition
Domestic instability, 38–39
Domestic politics, 6–8; international politics and, 153–58
Domestic trade policy, 20
Dominions (British), 107, 110–11
Dual (Franco-Russian) Alliance, 64, 65, 66, 69

Dusseldorf Agreement, 120
Dutch East India Company (VOC), 129, 130, 133, 134, 135, 194n. 10
Dutch Republic, 127–28, 141–43, 162, 164; economic power of, 131, 132. *See also* United Provinces (Netherlands)
Dutch-Spanish truce. *See* Twelve Years' Truce

East Asia, 91
East India Company (English EIC), 130, 133, 134, 194n. 10, 195n.12
East Indies, 129–30
Economic cooperation, 107–10
Economic decline, British, 166–67
Economic growth, 23, 171; military spending and, 11, 37–39
Economic liberalization, 25–26, 35. *See also* Mercantilism; Open Door Policy
Economic nationalist coalition, 1, 34–39, 156–57, 158; defection from, 29; free-trade moderation of, 12–13; great power tenure and, 40–41; liberal contenders and, 37–39; managing decline and, 161; preferred program of, 24–26; punishment of contenders by, 2, 27–28, 33, 34–35, 155–56; in Spain (1621–40), 124, 125–26, 136, 138–40, 145, 150, 162
Economic nationalist coalition, British, 44, 59–64, 84, 119; Anglo-German alliance and, 78; Conservative Party and, 61–62, 97; empowerment of, 120, 121; military services and, 62–63, 83; opposition to entente with France by, 68; opposition to U.S. investment by, 70; preferred program of, 105–7, 154; punishment strategy of, 86–88, 140–45, 147; strategy, 96, 97, 101–4; tariff reform and, 59–61
Economic policy, 96–97, 101, 154; beggar-thy-neighbor, 32, 35, 96, 155. *See also* Fiscal (and monetary) policy; Foreign commercial policy
Economic sanctions, 23
Economic self-sufficiency, 51, 103, 105, 120, 131. *See also* Autarky and self-sufficiency
Economic strength, 46–47, 117, 162
Elizabeth I, queen of England, 134
Elliott, John H., 160
Empire organizations (Britain), 102, 103–4
Endicott, Stephen F., 110
England, Spain and, 13, 134–35, 151, 156; East Indies and, 126–27, 129–30. *See also* Britain
Entente Cordiale (1904), 51, 68–69
Europe, NATO and, 170. *See also specific country*
Expansionism, 52. *See also* Imperial contenders
Export trade, 113–14. *See also* Trade policy

Far East, 9, 50, 112, 167, 171; Russian power in, 64–65, 66. *See also specific country*
Federation of British Industry (FBI), 102, 105, 119
Fiscal (and monetary) policy, 22, 30–31, 98, 101, 116; expansionary, 26, 33; Gladstonian orthodoxy, 44, 54, 57, 99; Spanish, 137, 146. *See also* Economic policy; Sterling Area; Taxation
Fischer, Fritz, 52
Fisher, John, 43, 77, 115
Fisher Naval Reforms, 74–75, 167–68
Flanders, 140, 141, 145, 146, 163, 164
Foreign commercial policy, 8, 16, 36, 160–61, 169; in Britain, 45, 87, 89, 167; imperial vs. liberal, 1–3, 19–21, 153–54. *See also* Imperial preferences (Britain); Protectionism; Trade policy
Foreign Office (Britain), 67–68, 71
Four Power Treaty, 115
Four Year Plan (Nazi Germany), 93
Fox, Edward W., 21

France, Britain and, 6, 11, 84, 85, 97, 168, 185n. 20; alliances, 68–69, 79–80; as challenger, 12, 15, 47–48, 50–51, 64; China trade and, 49; Franco-Russian Alliance and, 64, 65, 66, 69; Napoleonic era, 16, 21, 160; naval power of, 75–76, 167; punishment of, 45; self-sufficiency of, 90; tax revolt in, 39; Thirty Years' War and, 123
France, Spain and (1621–40), 13, 126, 127, 141, 142, 151; Catalonia and, 149, 164; imperial ambitions and, 132, 135–36; War of Mantua and, 128–29, 143–44, 156, 163
Francis, Eric, 105–6
Free trade, in British empire, 60, 165. *See also* Imperial preferences (Britain); Mercantilism
Free-trade coalition, 157, 161; cooperative strategy of, 154–55, 168
Free-trade coalition, British (1889–1912), 14, 36, 54–59, 155, 169; accommodation by, 40, 44; Anglo-German alliance and, 75, 76–77, 78; cooperative strategy of, 2, 27, 33–34, 44–45, 53, 63–64, 82, 83, 158; defection from, 29, 34; economic nationalists and, 12–13, 16, 21; great power tenure and, 40, 41; imperial contenders and, 33–34, 39; policy preferences of, 21–24
Free-trade coalition, British (1932–39), 7, 80, 86, 91, 107; fiscal orthodoxy and, 110–11; reluctance to rearm by, 103, 113–18; strategy of, 88, 95–96, 98–101, 104, 120–21
French, David, 57, 83
Friedberg, Aaron, 6, 176n. 8, 177n. 14

Gasiorowski, Mark, 31
General Election of 1906 (Britain), 45
Gentlemanly capitalism, 88, 113, 119, 120
German Naval Laws (1907–13), 76, 79
Germany, 38, 39, 85, 166, 193n. 52; challenge to Britain from, 47–48; China trade and, 49, 50; as imperial contender, 51, 75–79, 82; punishment of, 45, 83–84, 144, 185n. 20; regional leadership of, 52, 169–70, 171
Germany, Britain and (1932–39), 113, 114–15, 119–20; economic health of, 107–8, 109; as imperial contender, 12, 13, 89, 90, 92–94; *Mitteleuropa* plan and, 90, 92, 183n. 12; naval agreements of, 116, 165, 166, 189n. 64. *See also* Anglo-German agreements
Giffen, Sir Robert, 81
Gilpin, Robert, 21, 37, 176n. 8
Gladstone, Herbert, 66
Gladstonian tradition, 44, 54, 57, 99. *See also* Fiscal (and monetary) policy
Gold reserves, 117
Gold standard, 54, 57, 60, 72, 95, 98; abandonment of, 12, 87, 106; restoration of, 96, 99, 100, 102
Goldstein, Joshua S., 8, 176n. 9
Goldstein, Judith, 30
Goschen, George, 66
Government: coalitional views of, 22, 25; economic policies and, 96–97. *See also* Bureaucrats
Gowing, M. M., 117
Grand strategies, 3–8, 26–40; domestic politics and, 8; international factors shaping, 26–35; long cycle theory and power transition in, 3–5; ratchets in coalitions, 26–29; reversals and rollbacks of, 36–37; self-reinforcing suboptimality in, 37–40. *See also* Cooperative grand strategy; Punishment as grand strategy
Great Britain. *See* Britain; British
Greater East Asia Co-prosperity Sphere, 91, 92
Great power tenure, 153–71; British, 165–68; devolution and, 161–62, 167,

Great power tenure (*continued*)
171; extension of, 160–62; free-trader strategy and, 40–41, 154–55; international politics and, 153–58; managing decline and, 158–60; punishment strategy and, 155–56; self-reinforcing strategies and, 156–58; Spain, 162–64; theoretical implications in, 168–69; United States, 14, 169–71
Grenville, J. A. S., 70
Gustavus Adolphus, king of Sweden, 126, 130

Haggard, Stephen, 25–26
Hague Conference (1899), 67–68
Hague Peace Conference (1907), 76, 78
Hamilton, E. W., 184nn. 17–18
Hamilton, George, 65, 66
Hancock, W. K., 117
Hankey, Maurice, 84, 112
Hay, John, 48–49
Hay-Pauncefote Treaty (1901), 70–71
Hegemonic decline, 176nn. 8–9; case selection method, 14–16; causes of, 16–17; dilemmas in managing, 158–60. *See also* Great power tenure
Hegemonic stability theory, 168–69
Hegemony, challengers to. *See* Imperial contenders; Liberal contenders
Hicks Beach, Sir Michael, 67, 73
Hindenburg Program (Germany), 38
Hitler, Adolph, 91, 93, 108, 166
Hogan, Michael J., 7
Hopkins, Anthony G., 64, 111, 184n. 17
Hostility spiral, 23, 32–33, 35, 71, 159, 169, 171. *See also* Arms race
Howard, Michael E., 77
Hull, Cordell, 95

Imperial Conference (1917), 97
Imperial contenders, 20–21, 30, 89, 90–94, 182n. 32; Britain and, 51–53, 83; economic nationalists and, 35–36, 40–41; free-traders' accommodation of, 22, 28, 33–34, 39; punishment of, 27–28, 39, 155, 157; Spain and, 15, 125, 132–36; strategies of, 16; vs. liberal contenders, 1–3. *See also specific country*
Imperial preferences (Britain), 45, 59, 60, 90, 101, 106–7, 121
Import duties, 60, 97, 107. *See also* Imperial preferences (Britain); Protectionism; Tariffs
Income tax, 81, 100, 185n. 20
India, 47, 65, 69, 73–74, 171; British in, 127, 130; independence of, 95
Industry, 22, 30, 33, 55, 59, 106; economic nationalists and, 24, 25–26, 102; growth of, 73, 89, 127, 182n. 27; inefficient, 32, 36–37, 98, 102; protective tariffs for, 36–37, 56, 60, 105; rearmament and, 88, 114, 118, 119, 121; regional competition with Britain, 43, 47; Spanish, 146–47, 151; subsidies for, 87
Inskip, Sir Thomas, 117–18, 194n. 53
International environment, 15, 23, 40, 82, 158–59
International politics, 7–12; domestic politics and, 6, 7–8; great power tenure and, 153–58; power differentiation and, 10–12
Isthmian canal treaty, 70–71
Italy, 12, 13, 89, 94, 164; expansion of, 90, 166; Spain and, 128–29, 143–44, 156

Japan, 12, 13, 107, 119, 168, 190n. 5; arms limitation and, 115, 116, 165–66; British alliance with, 72–74; as challenger to Britain, 50, 89, 90–92; China trade and, 49, 90, 91–92, 110; economic cooperation of, 108–9; Korea and, 50, 183n. 8; military-industrial capacity of, 47; regional leadership of, 9, 167, 169–70, 171; threat from, and rearmament,

112, 113, 193n. 50; war with Russia (1904–5), 10, 73

Kahler, Miles, 6
Kaufman, Robert, 25–26
Kennan, George, 176n. 11
Kennedy, Paul M., 37, 124, 166–67, 176n. 8
Kim, Woosang, 4
Korea, 50, 183n. 8
Kugler, Jacek, 4

Labor, 25, 55, 105, 121
Labor shortage, 103, 114, 118, 191n. 23
Labour Party (Britain), 55, 101, 103, 116; rearmament and, 113, 118
LaFeber, Walter, 21
Lambelet, John C., 75, 189n. 60
Land values and taxation, 81
Leadership: challenges to, 11, 15, 162, 169; cooperation and, 161; declining, 17, 179n. 4; devolving hegemony and, 41; transfer of, 4, 9. *See also* Great power tenure; Regional leadership
League of Nations, 13, 86, 93, 101, 109, 113
Lebensraum (Nazi expansion policy), 92, 93
Leith-Ross, Sir Frederick, 108
Lend-Lease Act (U.S.), 95, 121, 190n. 11
Levy, Jack S., 159
Liberal coalition, in Spain (1621–40), 13, 124–25, 136–38, 141, 150, 156
Liberal contenders, 1–3, 159–60, 161, 182n. 32; punishment of, 155, 169
Liberal contenders, to British hegemony, 20, 48–51, 83; economic nationalists and, 37–39; free traders and, 27, 29–30, 31, 41; punishment of, 32–33. *See also* France; Japan; United States
Liberal government (Britain), 66–67, 69, 75
Liberal Party (Britain), 46, 55, 58, 61, 81, 83
Liberal peace theory, 162
Lippmann, Walter, 3
Lloyd George, David, 77, 81, 97
Logrolling, coalitional, 86
London Naval Conference (1930), 103, 115, 116, 165
Long cycle theory, 3–5, 9
Louis VIII, king of France, 127
Louis XIV, king of France, 164
Louis XVI, king of France, 39
Lynch, John, 151

Manchuria (Manchukuo), 21, 50, 53, 65, 90, 109; Japanese invasion of, 89, 91, 92
Marder, Arthur J., 75
Marshall Plan for European reconstruction, 7
Maurer, John, 78
McKenna, Reginald, 77
McKinley, William, 48
Mediterranean Sea, 47, 68, 79–80, 90, 94
Méline Tariff of 1892, 50
Mercantilism, 52, 125, 131, 132, 141
Merchant banks, 63, 84, 106, 108
Merchants, 146
Metallurgy, 127, 151
Mexico, 145, 149, 151
Middle East, 97, 167
Military buildup, 32–33, 34, 88. *See also* Arms race; Rearmament
Military-industrial complex, 25, 26, 32, 37. *See also* Industry, rearmament and
Military power, 10, 31, 44, 170; British, 57, 165–68; cooperation and, 30; Dutch, 127; economic nationalist view of, 24–26; economic strength and, 46–47, 167–68; free-trader view of, 36; Spanish, 140

Military services, British, 62–63, 87, 99, 102–3, 112; army, 55, 84, 113, 116–17. *See also* British navy; RAF
Military spending, 5, 57–58, 111–12, 161; arms race and, 177–78n. 14; defense, 23, 117, 118, 139, 162; economic growth and, 11, 37–39, 171; hegemonic decline and, 4, 160; Spanish, 138, 139, 141–42
Millones (Spanish sales tax), 125, 138, 140, 143, 147, 150
Mitteleuropa (German expansionist plan), 51–52, 90, 92, 183n. 12
Modelski, George, 4
Monetary policy, 26, 57, 106. *See also* Fiscal (and monetary) policy; Gold standard; *Vellón* (copper) coinage
Monger, George W., 80
Monroe Doctrine, 91, 188n. 44
Morocco, 50–51, 68
Morrow, James D., 4
Munich Agreement (1938), 166
Mussolini, Benito, 94

Napoleonic France, 16, 21, 160
National Insurance and Unemployment Act (Britain, 1911), 80–81
National interest, decline and, 159
National Service League, 62
National Shipbuilders' Security, 105
National Union of Manufacturers, 105
NATO (North Atlantic Treaty Organization), 170
Naval alliances, 64, 65, 72–73
Naval arms limitations, 77–80, 103, 115, 163; Anglo-German, 77–78, 116, 165, 166, 189n. 64
Naval blockades, 11, 23, 84
Naval Defence Act of 1889 (Britain), 15, 65–66, 186–87n. 36
Naval expansion, 11, 118
Naval standard, two-powered, 62, 67, 71, 75–76, 80
Navy, British. *See* Admiralty, British; British navy
Navy, Dutch, 127
Navy, Spanish *armada*, 139, 142–43, 145, 146
Navy League (Britain), 62, 63, 67, 77
Neorealists, 5, 161–62
Netherlands, 15. *See also* Spanish Netherlands; United Provinces (Netherlands)
New Netherlands Company, 134, 135
New Standard (Britain), 112, 118
Nicholas II, czar of Russia, 11
Nine Power Treaty, 115
Nixon Doctrine, 31, 180n. 6
Norman, Montagu, 100
North China Development Company, 92

Old Age Pensions Act (Britain, 1909), 46, 80
Olivares, Count-Duke (Gaspar de Guzmán), 13, 124, 138, 139–40, 144, 145, 197n. 40; Union of Arms and, 148–50, 164
Open Door Policy, 20, 52, 90, 94, 153; China trade and, 48–49, 50, 53
Organski, A. F. K., 4, 176n. 8
Ottawa Conference (1932), 12, 90, 95, 107, 110–11
Ottoman Empire, 16, 17, 123, 128, 143, 182n. 27
Outside-in and inside-out argument, 1. *See also* Second image reversed plus a second image

Pan-European Union, 94
Paris Agreements (1916), 96
Parker, Geoffrey, 164
Parliament (British), 54
Parliament, Spanish. *See* Cortes of Castile
Parliament Act of 1911 (Britain), 81
Peace dividend, 31, 80, 171

Peace of Cherasco (1631), 143
Peace of Pyrenees (1659), 126
Pelletan, Camille, 68
Pentagon (U.S.), 160
People's Budget of 1909 (Britain), 81
Persian Gulf, 135, 170, 171
Peru, 145, 149, 151
Philip II, king of Spain, 123
Philip III, king of Spain, 138
Philip IV, king of Spain, 13, 39, 138, 139–40, 147–48; Union of Arms scheme and, 148, 163–64. *See also* Spanish Crown
Politics, domestic, 6–8, 153–58
Portugal, 14, 123, 164; Council of, 124, 139, 146; empire of, 127, 133, 135; tax revolt in, 39; Union of Arms and, 148, 149–50
Powell, Colin, 10
Power: coalitional, 26–29, 153, 154, 156; differentiation of, 10–12; distribution of, 35, 46; international political, 7–12, 153–58. *See also* Great power tenure; Military power
Power transition theory, 3–5, 9, 16
Preemptive war, 39–40
Primacy, 170
Protectionism, 53, 56, 96, 106, 191n. 25; economic nationalists and, 24, 59–61; free trader opposition to, 30, 35, 55; hegemonic stability theory and, 168–69; industry and, 36–37. *See also* Tariffs
Punishment as grand strategy, 16, 87, 155–56, 161, 171; contenders and, 5, 27–28, 32–33, 39; economic nationalist coalition and, 2, 27–28, 33, 34–35, 155–56; free-trader opposition to, 12, 34, 45, 155, 157. *See also* Britain (1932–39), restrained punishment strategy in; Spain, punishment strategy in (1621–40)

Radicals (Britain), 58, 70, 76–77, 78
RAF (Royal Air Force), 113, 114–15, 116
Railways, 53, 65, 69, 71, 73, 110
Raw materials, 93, 119. *See also* Resources
Realists, 5, 8, 161–62, 180n. 6
Rearmament, Britain and, 15, 88, 101–3, 111–19, 192n. 40; free traders and, 103, 113–18; navy and, 103, 112–13, 115–16, 193n. 50. *See also* Military buildup
Reciprocal Trade Agreements Act (U.S., 1934), 94
Regional hegemony, 31, 161, 167–68, 178n. 16; Britain and, 46; competitors for, 9–10; Spain and, 123, 126–30
Regional leadership, 31, 89–95, 160, 169–70; German challenge to, 52, 89, 90, 92–94, 169–70; Italy and, 90, 94; Japan, 89, 90–92, 169–70
Resources: allocation of, 40, 148; extraction of, 5, 38, 138, 160, 182n. 27
Richelieu, Cardinal, 127, 128, 135, 164
Rome, Visigoths and, 160, 182n. 27
Roosevelt, Franklin, 95
Roosevelt, Theodore, 48
Rosecrance, Richard, 31
Royal Absolutism, in Spain, 125, 140, 147. *See also* Philip IV; Spanish Crown
Royal air force (British RAF), 114–15, 116
Royal navies. *See* Admiralty, British; British navy; Spanish *armadas* (navy)
Russia, 15, 39, 85, 155, 168, 185n. 20; as challenger to Britain, 12, 21, 52–53, 64–65, 69–70; China trade and, 49, 50; French alliance with, 64, 65, 66; naval power of, 67; punishment of, 45; regional leadership of, 47–48; war with Japan (1904–5), 10, 73. *See also* Soviet Union
Russo-Japanese War (1904–5), 10, 73

Schacht, Hjalmar, 93
Schweller, Randall, 162
Second image reversed plus a second image, 1, 26, 153, 168–69
Security strategy, 158, 165–67. *See also* Defense spending; Military
Selborne, Lord (Roundell Palmer), 44, 67, 74
Selective engagement policy, 162, 170
Self-determination, 95
Self-reinforcing strategies, 13, 88, 104, 120–21; great power tenure and, 156–58; optimality in, 37–40
Self-sufficiency. *See* Autarky and self-sufficiency; Economic self-sufficiency
Seville Admiralty Board, 131–32, 146
Shanghai, 90, 110
Shipbuilding, 67, 105, 127, 151. *See also* Naval; Navy
Siberia, 10, 65
Singapore, 102, 103, 112, 166, 168
Sinking Fund (debt program), 58, 100, 184n. 18
Sino-Japanese War (1937), 110
Smoot-Hawley Tariff (1930), 94
Snyder, Jack, 7
Social reforms, in Britain, 80–81, 182n. 27
Solingen, Etel, 7
South Vietnam, 31
Soviet Union, 21, 38, 92, 160, 176n. 11. *See also* Russia
Spain, French challenge to. *See* France, Spain and (1621–40)
Spain, punishment strategy in (1621–40), 15, 16, 38, 123–51, 160; Cortes of Castile and, 14, 137–38, 147–48; distributional consequences of, 146–47; economic capacity and, 162–64; economic nationalists and, 124, 136, 138–40, 145, 162; English challenge to, 13, 126–27, 129–30, 134–35, 151, 156; imperial contenders and, 15–16, 125, 132–36; liberal coalition in, 13, 124–25, 136–38, 141, 150, 156; regional contenders and, 123, 126–30; strategy pervasiveness, 140–45; Union of Arms and, 126, 148–50
Spanish *armadas* (navy), 139, 142–43, 145, 146
Spanish civil war (1936), 85
Spanish Crown, 123, 125, 146, 162–63, 196n. 28, 197n. 40; Cortes of Castile and, 14, 147–48; taxation and, 137–38, 144; Union of Arms and, 140, 148, 150. *See also* Philip IV
Spanish Netherlands, 127–28, 141, 143, 144, 164. *See also* United Provinces (Netherlands)
Spencer, John, 66
Spencer Act of 1894 (Britain), 65–66, 67
Spice Islands, 126, 129
Spice trade, 129, 133–34, 194n. 11
Spínola, Ambrogio, 124, 136
Sprout, Harold, and Margaret Sprout, 6
State-owned enterprises, 26, 33, 36–37
States-General (Dutch parliament), 133
Sterling Area, 13, 88, 95, 103, 110–11, 121
Stradling, Robert, 143
Sugar plantations, in Brazil, 126, 130, 134, 142
Supplementary Law of 1908 (Germany), 77
Surat, 135
Sweden, 126, 130, 164

Tariff Reform League, 59–61
Tariffs, 24, 50, 94; protection and, 56, 59, 183n. 5, 185–86n. 26; reform of, 44, 46, 59–61, 81. *See also* Protectionism
Taw, Jennifer, 31
Taxation: in Britain, 38–39, 58, 59, 81,

100, 114, 185n. 20; in Spain, 125, 137, 138, 140, 142–44, 147, 150
Ten Year Rule, 87, 101, 102, 103; revocation of, 15, 111–12
Textile industry, 105, 107, 151
Third World, 14, 171, 176–77n. 11
Thirty Years' War, 123, 137
Thompson, William R., 4
Tomlinson, Jim, 101
Trade deficit, 113–14
Trade policy, 93; domestic, 20; economic cooperation and, 107–10. *See also* Foreign commercial policy; Protectionism
Trades Union Congress (TUC), 105
Trading companies, 131–32, 133, 141. *See also specific companies*
Trans-Caspian Railway, 65
Trans-Siberian Railway, 65, 66
Treasury Department (Britain), 13, 63, 96, 99–100, 110, 113; Anglo-Japanese cooperation and, 108–9; arms expenditures and, 116, 117, 189n. 64; Estimates of, 57, 173–74; free-trade coalition and, 56, 57–58, 59, 84, 98; gold standard and, 96, 106; naval funding and, 193n. 50; RAF strategy and, 115; rearmament resistance from, 88, 114, 118, 158; Sterling Area and, 111; trade deficit and, 114
Treaty of Munster (1648), 127, 164
Treaty of Pyrenees (1659), 164
Trotter, Ann, 91
Tweedmouth, Lord, 76
Twelve Years' Truce (1609–21), 124, 125, 127, 137, 139, 141; Dutch expansion and, 129, 130, 133, 134
Two-powered naval standard, 62, 67, 71, 75–76, 80

Union of Arms (Spain), 126, 140, 148–50, 163–64
United Provinces (Netherlands), Spain and, 13, 126–30, 145, 151, 156, 163; as Dutch Republic, 127–28, 131, 132, 141–43, 162, 164; imperial ambition and, 129–30, 133–34. *See also* Spanish Netherlands; Twelve Years' Truce
United States, 31, 82, 83, 85, 116, 168, 176–77n. 11; arms limitation agreements and, 165–66; Cold War and, 21; free-trade coalition in, 7; Hay-Pauncefote Treaty and, 70–71; Lend-Lease Act and, 95, 121, 190n. 11; as liberal challenger to Britain, 12, 13, 48–49, 90, 94–95; naval buildup of, 187–88n. 43; regional leadership of, 9, 47, 48, 160, 167, 188n. 44, 198n. 12; tenure as great power, 14, 169–71

Valencia, 140, 149, 163
Vellón (copper) coinage, 125, 137, 142, 146
Visigoths, Rome and, 160
VOC. *See* Dutch East India Company (VOC)
Von Caprivi, Leo, 52

War chest, 57–58, 99, 114, 117, 184n. 18; Spanish, 148. *See also* Military spending
War Office (Britain), 62, 69, 74, 79, 174, 188n. 52. *See also* Military
War of Mantua, 128–29, 143–44, 156, 163
Washington Naval Conference (1921–22), 103, 115, 116, 165
Weltpolitik (German world policy), 51
West India Company (Dutch WIC), 126, 128, 130, 134
West Indies, 71, 130, 134, 135
Williams, William Appleman, 7
Witte, Sergey, Count, 53
World War I, 83–84, 96